Lecture Notes in Computer

Edited by G. Goos, J. Hartmanis and J.

Advisory Board: W. Brauer   D. Gries   J. Stoer

Springer
Berlin
Heidelberg
New York
Barcelona
Budapest
Hong Kong
London
Milan
Paris
Santa Clara
Singapore
Tokyo

Dror G. Feitelson   Larry Rudolph   (Eds.)

Job Scheduling Strategies for Parallel Processing

IPPS '96 Workshop
Honolulu, Hawaii, April 16, 1996
Proceedings

Springer

Series Editors

Gerhard Goos, Karlsruhe University, Germany

Juris Hartmanis, Cornell University, NY, USA

Jan van Leeuwen, Utrecht University, The Netherlands

Volume Editors

Dror G. Feitelson
The Hebrew University, Institute of Computer Science
Givat Ram Campus, Ross Building, 91904 Jerusalem, Israel

Larry Rudolph
MIT, Lab. for Computer Science, NE43-228
545 Technology Square, Cambridge, MA 02139, USA
E-mail: {feit,rudolph}@cs.huji.ac.il

Cataloging-in-Publication data applied for

Die Deutsche Bibliothek - CIP-Einheitsaufnahme

Job scheduling strategies for parallel processing : proceedings
/ IPPS '96 workshop, Honolulu, Hawaii, April 1996. Dror G.
Feitelson ; Larry Rudolph (ed.). - Berlin ; Heidelberg ; New
York ; Barcelona ; Budapest ; Hong Kong ; London ; Milan ;
Paris ; Santa Clara ; Singapore ; Tokyo : Springer, 1996
  (Lecture notes in computer science ; Vol. 1162)
  ISBN 3-540-61864-3
NE: Feitelson, Dror G. [Hrsg.]; International Parallel Processing
  Symposium <10, 1996, Honolulu, Hawaii>; GT

CR Subject Classification (1991): D.4, D.1.3, F.2.2, C.1.2, B.2.1, B.6.1, F.1.2,
C.2

ISSN 0302-9743
ISBN 3-540-61864-3 Springer-Verlag Berlin Heidelberg New York

Typesetting: Camera-ready by author
SPIN 10549739   06/3142 – 5 4 3 2 1 0   Printed on acid-free paper

Preface

This volume contains the papers presented at the workshop on Job Scheduling Strategies for Parallel Processing held in Honolulu, Hawaii, as a prelude to the IPPS'96 conference. All the papers have gone through the usual refereeing process with the full version being read and evaluated by at least five members of the program committee. We would like to take this opportunity to thank the program committee, Nawaf Bitar, David Black, Jim Cownie, Allan Gottlieb, Scott Hahn, Mal Kalos, Phil Krueger, Richard Lagerstrom, Miron Livny, Virginia Lo, Reagan Moore, Ken Sevcik, Mark Squillante, Bernard Traversat, and John Zahorjan, for an excellent job. Thanks are also due to the authors for their submissions, presentations, and final revisions for this volume. We would like to thank the MIT Laboratory for Computer Science and the Computer Science Institute at Hebrew University for the use of their facilities in preparation of these proceedings.

As multi-user parallel supercomputers become more widespread, job scheduling takes on a crucial role. The number of users of parallel supercomputers is growing at an even faster pace and so there is an increasing number of users who must share a parallel computer's resources. Job scheduling strategies must address this need.

There is a spectrum of groups that are interested in job scheduling strategies for parallel processors. At one end are the vendors of parallel supercomputers who supply the scheduling software for managing jobs on their machines. In the middle are researchers in academia, National Labs, and industrial research labs who propose new scheduling strategies and methods for evaluating and comparing them. At the other end of the spectrum are the users and providers of parallel processing resources who have a set of demands and requirements.

This is the second occurrence of the workshop. The previous workshop was held a year earlier, as part of the IPPS'95 conference in Santa Barbara. The proceedings of that workshop have been published as Springer-Verlag Lecture Notes in Computer Science Vol. 949.

At the workshop there were many interesting discussions between people in the three groups (but we were too busy to be part of many of them). We were encouraged by this since we believe it is important to increase communication so that academics work on the right problems and vendors and computation centers make the best use of the novel solutions. We hope these proceedings help parallel supercomputing to achieve its fundamental goal of satisfying the needs of the user.

Jerusalem, August 1996   Dror Feitelson
Larry Rudolph

Contents

Toward Convergence in Job Schedulers for Parallel Supercomputers

Dror G. Feitelson and Larry Rudolph

Institute of Computer Science
The Hebrew University, 91904 Jerusalem, Israel
{feit,rudolph}@cs.huji.ac.il

Abstract. The space of job schedulers for parallel supercomputers is rather fragmented, because different researchers tend to make different assumptions about the goals of the scheduler, the information that is available about the workload, and the operations that the scheduler may perform. We argue that by identifying these assumptions explicitly, it is possible to reach a level of convergence. For example, it is possible to unite most of the different assumptions into a common framework by associating a suitable cost function with the execution of each job. The cost function reflects knowledge about the job and the degree to which it fits the goals of the system. Given such cost functions, scheduling is done to maximize the system's profit.

1 Introduction

Both theoreticians and practitioners have been investigating and implementing various types of schedulers, and analyzing their performance over a wide range of workloads, leading to a large and varied body of knowledge [13]. However, many of the assumptions as to the type of workload and the goals of the scheduler are incompatible. We argue that the best features can and should be combined.

The following principles are common features of all scheduling systems:

- The scheduler services all jobs that are submitted.
- Jobs that provide optional resource requirement specifications are rewarded.
- Jobs that are coded in a "schedulingly friendly" style are rewarded.
- Accounting and quality of service are the tools used to reward jobs.

The road to convergence starts with an explicit understanding of the differences that are to be bridged. The differences stem from different basic assumptions relating to performance metrics (Section 2), workload (Section 3), and scheduler actions (Section 4). This paper therefore begins by reviewing these assumptions. We can identify several common combinations of assumptions, which have led to the creation of isolated "clusters of assumptions" (Section 5). Then, we propose several ways to achieve convergence (Section 6).

Before continuing, the following plea for cooperation is issued. At the very minimum, we wish that all articles about job schedulers, either real or paper design, make clear their assumptions about the workload, the permissible actions allowed by the system, and the metric that is being optimized.

2 Assumptions About the Goals of a Job Scheduler

There are many scheduling systems for parallel computers and even more that are being proposed and analyzed. The systems are widely disparate both in what they hope to accomplish and in the ways they hope to accomplish it. This section reviews some the various, sometimes conflicting goals of schedulers.

2.1 Run Jobs

The primary goal of all schedulers is to enable the successful execution of a job, hopefully a parallel one, on a parallel machine. While obvious, this goal should never be forgotten. In particular, maximizing secondary goals should not starve certain class of jobs,

Secondary scheduling goals, described in the following subsections, vary and depend on satisfying the needs of the group versus the needs of the individual. These goals can be broadly classified as being system centric or user centric. Some are measurable well-defined metrics, while others are functional desiderata. They are summarized in Table 1.

	user centric	system centric
metric	response time	utilization throughput
function	run jobs	
	emulate dedi-cated machine	administrative preferences

Table 1. *Classification of scheduler goals.*

2.2 Maximize Utilization of the Machine

It might appear obvious that a scheduler should maximize the utilization of the machine. Utilization can be defined in either of two ways: either as the percentage of CPU cycles *actually used* for productive computation, or as the percentage of CPU cycles *allocated* to user jobs that pay for them. The difference is that the first definition integrates the efficiency of user code into the equation, while the latter makes a clear distinction between the allocation of resources by the operating system and their use by the user.

The problem with utilization as a metric is that it is largely dependent on system load (Fig 1). Consider a simple queuing model of an operating system scheduler: requests to run jobs arrive, and they are serviced by the system. When load is low and all jobs can be serviced, the utilization is equal to the load. When load is high and the system saturates, utilization is equal to the saturation point.

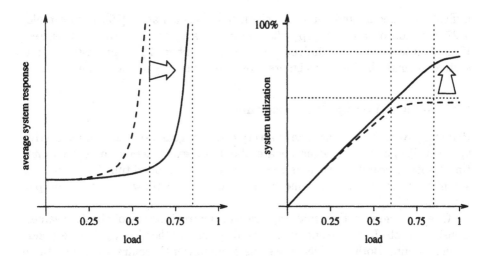

Fig. 1. *Utilization depends on the system load and on how efficiently the system handles it, i.e. at what point does it saturate. Arrows indicate improvement in system efficiency.*

Therefore the goal of a system designer is not to increase utilization *per se* but rather to delay the onset of saturation. In other words, A "good" system will be able to sustain a higher load before becoming saturated, which means that a higher utilization is possible if the load demands it.

Another problem with the utilization metric is that adopting it may lead to starvation of certain jobs. For example, if the job stream includes many jobs that require all the processors in the system, and only a handful of jobs that require fewer processors and cause significant fragmentation, it is best from a utilization point-of-view to only schedule the jobs that need all the processors.

2.3 Maximize Throughput

Throughput is the number of jobs completed per unit time. The throughput metric is similar to the utilization metric in the sense that it is affected by system load and efficiency. But, whereas utilization is maximized when there are mainly massively parallel jobs executing for long time periods, the throughput metric is maximized when there are many small (in parallelism and in CPU usage) jobs.

The rationale behind this metric is that the higher the throughput the more users are satisfied. In general, maximizing the average throughput also minimizes the average response time for a job. This is true only when there is no knowledge about the execution time of a job. If that is known, then scheduling the shortest jobs first will reduce the average response time without affecting the average throughput rate.

Throughput has the same problem as utilization: by focusing on the average values, the system may undermine the primary goal. A parallel job mix may be difficult to schedule and can cause significant fragmentation [16]. For example, a 27 node job on a 32 node parallel machine leaves an awkward 5 nodes free. If one is interested in maximizing the average number of jobs processed by the system, it might be better to ignore jobs that cause fragmentation altogether.

2.4 Reduce Average Response time

Reducing average response time is a very common goal, especially in interactive systems. While there is some debate about the exact definition of "response time", most researchers use it as a synonym for "turnaround time," i.e. from job submittal[1] to job completion time, rather than the time till when the first output is produced [41]).

One problem with the usual response time metric is its use of absolute values. Consider a job J_a that responds in one day and another job J_b that responds in one minuite. Both jobs have the same computational requirement, then there might be something wrong with the scheduler. On the other hand, if job J_a requires 24 hours of computation time, then the one day response time is pretty good whereas if job J_b only required 1 microsecond of computation time, then the one minute response time may be bad. Jobs can be perceived as having different weights, depending on their run time. A possible solution to this problem is to use the average *slowdown* as a metric instead, where slowdown is the ratio of the time it takes to run the job on a loaded system divided by the time it takes on a dedicated system (this is sometimes also called the "response ratio" [4]). This normalizes all jobs to the same scale.

Another problem with this metric is its linear regard to time. Actually response time should be measured as perceived by those who are interested, e.g. human users. For humans, the difference between a response of 1ms and 100ms is immeasurable, but the difference between 1s and 100s is very annoying [18].

Finally, it should be noted that not all jobs require the same level of service in terms of response time. Interactive jobs require interactive response times, preferably of not more than a couple of seconds. Time critical jobs require application-dependent response times (e.g. tomorrow's weather forecast should be ready in time to be useful). And some jobs do not have any specific time constraints. In fact, most parallel systems make a distinction between batch jobs and direct jobs, with batch jobs executed only at night or when the machine would otherwise be idle. However most efforts at modeling do not take this distinction into account.

2.5 Fairness vs. Administrative Preferences

Fairness is not often advocated as a requirement on its own accord, but it underlies the requirements for maximizing throughput and minimizing average re-

---

[1] We are following Steve Hortney's campaign to use the term *job submittal* in place of the masocistic term *job submission*; despite the fact that jobs are at the mercy of the scheduler.

sponse time. But should all jobs be treated the same? For example, we have already noted that batch jobs do not require short response times.

Since all jobs are not created equal, it is often desirable to give preference to certain classes of jobs. For example, is there any preference to schedule two 8 node jobs in place of a single 16 node job? There is no abstract answer to this question; it is dictated by the management personnel of the supercomputer. Due to the high cost of parallel supercomputers, and their resulting use as shared resources that are specifically targeted at large computational problems, some installations do indeed try to encourage highly parallel jobs at the expense of those with only moderate parallelism.

Encouraging highly parallel jobs can be viewed as "fairness to threads." A job with more threads, that exhibits a larger degree of parallelism, is assumed to require more computational resources, and is therefore given better service. That is, administrative preferences may cause the system to be unfair to to users or to jobs (that is, all jobs are not considered equal).

2.6 Give the Illusion of a Dedicated Parallel Machine

Multiuser workstations and other non-parallel computers attempt to provide the user with the illusion of a dedicated machine. This is especially true for interactive jobs. When a parallel computer supports multiple users via time slicing or space slicing, it is generally desirable to provide the illusion of a dedicated parallel machine. We define this to mean that if a job receives $1/k$ of the total CPU cycles, then the job should take about k times as long to complete as it would on a dedicated machine, without taking any special actions.

To understand the issue here, consider a job scheduler that allows the individual activities of each parallel job to be time sliced independently. An activity may then waste many CPU cycles waiting for a message to be sent by another activity that is currently not executing. Had the machine been dedicated to the job, this wasted time would not occur. Thus, a user might be charged more CPU time, just because the scheduler decided to execute several jobs in an uncoordinated fashion (a simple solution for this case is therefore to use gang scheduling [17]).

2.7 Issues That Are Often Ignored

An important observation is that most simple metrics have simple failure modes in which they cause starvation for a class of jobs that do not promote the pre-defined metric. For example,

- Maximizing utilization may not schedule jobs that cause fragmentation
- Maximizing throughput may not schedule large jobs
- Minimizing response time ignores the fact that batch jobs do not need it nor want to pay for it

A more subtle observation is that a scheduling-centric metric cannot account for interactions with other resources that may become depleted first. For example, memory is a critical resource and if it is not managed correctly, an application may suffer from thrashing. Consider for a moment a job that consists of two processes, a consumer and a producer. The producer sends messages to the consumer process. If the rate of production is equal to the rate of consumption, and the two processes execute simultaneously in parallel, memory can be used efficiently. On the other hand, if they do not execute simultaneously, each message may need to be buffered. Buffering consumes system resources and could cause other jobs to frequently page fault. Unchecked scheduling of parallel jobs may quickly deplete "swap" disk space. Many large installations provide massive storage systems with latency times measured in the minutes. Such time frames must be handled differently from the times involved with a simple page fault.

In the area of functional requirements, the need to support whatever users may want to do is often overlooked. There are a number of examples of over-sophisticated schedulers that may end up limiting their users:

- Users sometimes want full control over the number of processors used to run their jobs, e.g. in order to generate speedup curves. A scheduler that sets the number automatically and does not provide an override mechanism makes this impossible to achieve.
- Different applications are easier to write in different programming styles, and users also have their personal preferences. Schedulers that limit the styles that are supported may thus alienate users that would rather use another style. This applies, for example, to schedulers that require all jobs to be able to adapt to changes in resource allocation at runtime, something that is difficult to achieve in certain cases.

Finally, in modern complex systems it is often the case that the scheduler must interact with external agents, e.g. as part of a system for heterogeneous computing [20, 30]. As part of such interactions, the scheduler might need to make reservations for future use. This functionality is often missing, and the performance implications (e.g. loss of resources due to reservations) are usually not included in models and analysis.

3   Assumptions About the Workload

Although the basic object that is to be scheduled is a job, there is a major division on the characteristics of jobs and what the scheduler knows about them. We restrict our attention to *parallel jobs*. That is, jobs that are composed of independent communicating activities. There is an underlying assumption that communication time is fast, e.g. the time to communicate a word of information is only about an order of magnitude longer than the time required for a CPU to fetch a word from its memory. We exclude client-server type jobs and other distributed computing jobs.

The definition of a parallel job from the point of view of a scheduler, unfortunately, is not so clear cut. There are many styles of parallel programs, and many structures that are imposed by some runtime systems and compilers. We identify four types of jobs based on the number of processors to be used by the job. This number may be specified by the user, either within the program itself or as part of job submittal specification, or it may be dictated by the scheduler. In addition, the number of processors may be fixed at the start of program execution or may change during the course of the computation. There are thus four classes (Table 2). Although one of the problems with the field is that there are too many conflicting terms, we risk adding to the complexity by proposing yet another set of terms. We feel that these terms may help highlight the differences.

who decides number	when is it decided	
	at submittal	during execution
user	Rigid	Evolving
system	Moldable	Malleable

Table 2. *Classification of job types based on specifying number of processors used.*

3.1 Rigid Jobs

A *rigid* job requires a certain number of processors in order to execute, as specified by the user at job submittal time; there may be other resource requirements as well, such as CPU time and memory, but we'll focus on the requirement for processors. A rigid job will not execute with fewer processors and will not make use of any additional processors. The scheduler does not know anything about the job besides the number of processors it needs.

From the programmer's perspective, the reasons for using a rigid formulation vary. In some cases it is simply what the system interface supports, so even jobs that are written as moldable jobs must be submitted as rigid ones. Applications written in High Performance Fortran are usually inflexible and there are often optimal decompositions based on the problem size. For example, it might be very inefficient to decompose a job with an array of size 100 into 17 processors.

3.2 Evolving Jobs

An *evolving job* is one that may change its resource requirements during execution. Note that it is the application itself that initiates the changes. The system must satisfy the requests or the job will not be able to continue its execution. Again, the scheduler knows nothing about the job except for its current requirement for processors.

Although such jobs are not common, there is much activity in the community to define a standard for dynamic processor requests. Such facilities already exist in the PVM interface [21], and they are also in the process of being incorporated into the MPI-2 standard.

The reason for the interest in this feature is that many parallel jobs are composed of multiple phases, and each phase has different characteristics. In particular, different phases may contain different degrees of parallelism. By telling the scheduler about these changes, it is possible for jobs to obtain additional resources when needed, and relinquish them when they can be used more profitably elsewhere (thereby reducing the cost of running the job). Also, this type of jobs is commonly modeled by task graphs with changing widths [55].

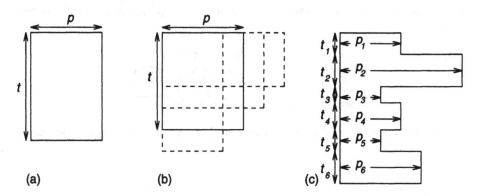

Fig. 2. (a) Rigid jobs define a rectangle in processor-time space. (b) Moldable jobs use one out of a choice of such rectangles. (c) Evolving and malleable jobs both have a profile with a changing number of processors. The difference is that in evolving jobs the changes are initiated by the job, while in malleable ones they are initiated by the system.

3.3 Moldable Jobs

A job may be flexible in the number of processors that it requires and may allow the system to dictate the allocated number of processors. There are two types of such flexible jobs, which we call *moldable* and *malleable*. With moldable jobs, the number of processors is set at the beginning of execution, and the job initially configures itself to adapt to this number. After it begins execution, the job cannot be reconfigured. It has already conformed to the mold.

If the number of processors is selected by the user and presented to the scheduler as a requirement, the job is actually rigid from the scheduler's point of view. But, given a range of choices, the scheduler can set the number of processors based on knowledge about the system load and competing jobs, knowledge that is typically not available to the user. This has been called "adaptive partitioning" in the literature [44].

A moldable job can be made to execute over a wide range of processors. There is often a minimum number of processors on which it can execute, and above that number, additional processors can be used to improve performance, up to some saturation point. The resource requirement of a minimal number of processors is usually due to memory and response time constraints. From a local efficiency point of view, there is a best number of processors for the job, at the knee of the speedup curve. But since the scheduler cares about maximizing some overall system performance properties, it might be best if the job is executed at another point. In any case, knowledge about application characteristics is typically required [46].

Programs written using the SPMD style, e.g. with the MPI library package, are often moldable. Moreover, workload traces from real parallel systems show that indeed the same application may run several times using different partition sizes [14].

3.4 Malleable Jobs

The most flexible type of jobs are *malleable* ones that can adapt to changes in the number of processors during execution. The main programming styles that permits this flexibility consists of many short independent tasks that access shared data in a very stylized way. For example, if all the tasks have no side effects, then to reduce the number of processors, some tasks are terminated and restarted later on the remaining processors [43].

It is fairly well accepted to call changing the number of processors at runtime "dynamic partitioning". We prefer to call the jobs "malleable" rather than "dynamic" because the term "dynamic" does not indicate who is doing the dynamic allocation. On the other hand, the shape of a malleable object can be changed by an outside entity, while an evolving object is one that changes of its own accord. However, note that evolving and malleable should usually come together, because one job's evolution will cause others to have to reconfigure.

Analyzing the benefits of dynamic partitioning and malleable jobs has been the subject of much recent research [36, 7, 28, 39, 34, 23]. This research typically compares the cost of reconfiguration with the resulting improvement in overall performance. But such comparisons do not give a full picture. In many cases, changing the number of processors allocated to a job requires complex interactions between the operating system and the application's runtime system [2]. For example, if the thread running on a certain processor holds a lock and then the processor is taken away, there may be no way to free the lock. Implementing the required interfaces to solve such problems naturally complicates the system, and makes it harder to implement, which is one reason why malleable jobs are currently not supported on any commercial parallel machines.

An interesting benefit of malleable jobs is that the option for changes can be used to allow the system to collect information about the job at runtime, by trying several configurations and checking the resulting performance. This information can later be used to guide allocation decisions [37]. This approach has obvious advantages over requiring the information to be available in advance, as is needed for moldable jobs.

4 Assumptions About Permissible Actions

A scheduler must execute in the environment of an existing operating system and machine architecture. This environment restricts the operations it is allowed to perform. In some machines, the operating system provides a *single system image*. That is, it does not matter from which processor an action is executed, they are all identical. Shared Memory Parallel Processors (SMPs) often have this feature and it is also being explored in some distributed systems [29]. When there is no single system image, it is difficult to migrate tasks. The machine architecture may impose restrictions on the types of processor partitions available and the ability to share access to the communication substrate.

The most limited system has partition sizes of a fixed number of processors, and allows only one job to execute from start to finish in a partition at any time. The scheduler simply needs to keep track of empty partitions and map incoming jobs to the appropriate partition. At the extreme, there would be only one partition and so only one job can execute at a time. But most systems allow many more powerful options.

4.1 Flexible Partitioning

Nowadays, most systems allow the processors to be partitioned on a job by job basis. This is sometimes referred to as *space slicing*. The exact number of processors may be forced to match the topology of the machine, as in hypercube topologies in which partitions must also be hypercubes but of a smaller dimension. But in many cases, especially when the network topology is hidden from the programmer, there are no such restrictions and partitioned may be formed using arbitrary subsets of processors.

A rigid job is submitted for execution along with a specification of the number of processors that it requires. The scheduler then creates a partition of that size and schedules the job to execute within that partition [53, 32, 20, 1, 9, 31, 33]. With moldable jobs, it is the scheduler that selects the partition size [44].

Evolving and malleable jobs require partitions that are not only flexible but can also change dynamically at runtime. This places an added burden both on the programmer, who must write application code that requests and adapts to such changes, and on the scheduler, that must handle the re-allocation decisions and coordinate them with the applications.

One common heuristic for dynamic partitioning is to strive for equal sized partitions (usually called "equipartitioning") [35]. The problem with this approach is that it might require all jobs to be interrupted whenever something changes. An alternative is to use *folding* [35]. With folding, the number of processors allocated to a job can only grow or shrink by factors of 2. That is, the partition size may be halved or doubled. When a partition is halved, the runtime system may choose to simply "fold over" the application, and time-slice two tasks on each processor. Thus an application that has a balanced workload over a particular partition size is likely to remain balanced after a folding operation. Many speedup curves resemble step functions, with poor speedup values for non powers of two number of processors. However, there is some debate over the benefits of folding [28, 39].

4.2 Preemption and Time Slicing

Dynamic partitioning, discussed above, requires certain processors to be preempted and re-allocated in order to accommodate load changes. Another type of preemption is that used in order to time-slice multiple applications, as is commonly done on uniprocessors. We identify this feature for special attention since many systems cannot support such preemption due to limitations on the message-passing architecture. For example, some machines require that the interface to the network be set up before a job begins execution. There may be no easy way to switch jobs without compromising the integrity of the messages. On some systems, switching message space protection from one job to another is permitted but is a very time consuming operation.

An extension of preemption is the ability to preempt all the members of a parallel job at the same time, as well as restarting all the members of another job. This is called "gang scheduling". It is generally agreed that if time slicing is used, then it should be implemented via gang scheduling, rather than letting each processor do its own uncoordinated time slicing. The reason is that with gang scheduling all the processes of a given job execute simultaneously on different processors, thus supporting the use of fine-grain interactions [17]. An interesting observation is that it is desirable to also preempt the network, i.e. to flush any traffic that belongs to the job that is being de-scheduled, so as to present a clean slate to the new job [26].

Gang scheduling suffers the overhead of context switching and corrupts cache state, but for a large enough time quantum these overheads can be made insignificant [23]. On the other hand, time slicing in general reduces the average response time provided the distribution of execution times has a large variance [40], which in fact it typically occurs [14].

4.3 Migration

Migration refers to the ability of a scheduler to move an executing job or some of its components to other processors. As such it is an extension of preemption: a task stops running on a certain processor, and it restarts on another processor. Reasons for migration include packing in order to reduce fragmentation [6, 12], and the need to withdraw from a workstation when its owner returns [42].

Migration is simple on shared memory machines, because threads do not have any state that is local to the processor except for their cache and TLB footprints. The challenge is to ensure that interacting threads map to distinct processors.

Migration is significantly more problematic in distributed memory machines as it requires migrating the local memory which can be a very expensive operation. The ability to migrate a task is often hindered by systems whose message passing libraries specify physical processor numbers as source or destination fields for messages. Note that the elimination of virtual to physical processor mapping increases the speed of a communication. Many systems map the network FIFO queues into user space; disconnecting and reconnecting may also require significant overhead.

4.4   Change Job Execution Order

A scheduler may be able to process jobs in an order different from the job submittal order. Many batch systems have some such flexibility [32, 24, 53]. Of course, this flexibility is only useful if there is some information as to the resource requirements of the waiting jobs as well as any deadlines or response time requirements.

We mention this option since it easily leads to violation of the primary goal of a scheduler – the execution of every job. Some aging mechanism is required to ensure that jobs are not passed over for arbitrarily long time periods.

5   Research Clusters

The spectrum of job schedulers for parallel machines may be expected to span a large part of all the different options for assumptions about goals, metrics, and workloads. In fact this is not so. Several "clusters" have formed, each with its own set of assumptions, and often oblivious of the others. This section identifies and characterizes these "clusters of assumptions," as a prelude to suggestions for some degree of convergence in the next section. The clusters are summarized in Table 3. The most controversial part is probably our classification of the goals. Mostly, if the scheduling system ensured that jobs run with all their required resources in a timely fashion, response time was considered as a goal. We evaluated the goals of utilization and throughput by considering how the scheduler treats large batch jobs and small interactive jobs.

5.1   Rigid Jobs and Variable Partitioning

Maybe the simplest scheduling scheme is to reduce the role of the operating system to that of a processor rental agency. Jobs request a certain number of processors, and the system provides them for exclusive use if they are available. The only goal is to (eventually) run the jobs. No knowledge about job behavior is assumed, and no special actions need be supported, except some measure of partitioning the machine. This scheme has been called "variable partitioning" or "pure space sharing" in the literature.

Despite its simplicity and the resulting drawbacks in terms of responsiveness, fragmentation, and reliability, this scheme is widely used. It is especially common on large distributed memory machines [53, 27, 20, 9, 31]. The reason is that it gets the job done, albeit not optimally, but with relatively little investment in system development. In an industry where time-to-market is a crucial element

	variable partitioning	gang scheduling	shared queue	adaptive partitioning	dynamic partitioning
goals					
run jobs	yes	yes	yes	yes	yes
utilization	no			yes	yes
throughput	no		yes	yes	yes
response	no	yes		no	
admin					
dedicated	yes	yes	yes		no
workloads					
rigid	yes	yes	yes	yes	no
evolving	no	no	yes	no	yes
moldable	yes	yes	yes	yes	no
malleable	no	no	no	no	yes
actions					
partitioning	yes	yes	no	yes	yes
preemption	no	yes	yes	no	yes
synchronized	n/a	yes	no	n/a	no
migration	no	no	yes	no	
ordering	yes	n/a	n/a		

Table 3. *"Clusters" of common combinations of assumptions.*

of success, this is a true virtue [1]. As a result, users sometimes have to revert to signup sheets as the actual processor allocation mechanism.

Because variable partitioning cannot run jobs immediately if the requested number of processors is not available, jobs often have to be queued. As a result this scheme implies a batch mode of operation. With sufficient backlog, it is then possible to select an execution order that improves system utilization and throughput [32, 48]. Thus even this simple scheme has bred some interesting research. In addition, it has prompted research into improvements such as adaptive and dynamic partitioning (see below).

5.2 Rigid Jobs and Gang Scheduling

Gang scheduling has been re-invented many times over because it is an intuitive extension of timesharing on uniprocessors. It also supports interactive use and gives the illusion of using a dedicated machine, without placing restrictions on the programming model and without assuming knowledge about the workload. It has therefore enjoyed considerable popularity among vendors, at least in the form of "hype" (all vendors claim to support some form of gang scheduling) but good implementations also exist. There have been a number of experimental implementations [38, 15, 12, 54, 22, 25] that demonstrate its usefulness.

Academically speaking, gang scheduling has repeatedly been shown to be inferior to dynamic partitioning (see below), but only by a small margin [23, 8]. The main drawbacks cited are interference with cache state, and possible loss of resources to fragmentation. As the first can be lessened by using long time quanta [23], and recent research suggests that the second is not so severe [12], it seems that the advantages of gang scheduling generally outweigh its drawbacks.

However, there are still some unresolved issues. The main one concerns the possible interaction between gang scheduling and over-committing memory resources. Time slicing between two active jobs requires more memory that executing these jobs sequentially. The direct solution is to provide adequate swapping to disks, but so far little research has been done on this issue, and parallel systems are notoriously underpowered in terms of I/O. Another criticism of gang scheduling is the lack of fault tolerance — if a processor fails, many jobs may have to be aborted. While important, this problem is not unique to gang scheduling: it is also present in other scheduling schemes and in other components of parallel operating systems, e.g. message passing facilities.

In summary, the finer the granularity of interaction between members of a parallel job, the more gang scheduling is required.

5.3   Evolving Jobs and a Shared Queue

Another simple extension of timesharing on uniprocessors is to use a shared queue. Each processor chooses a process from the head of the centralized ready queue, executes it for a time quantum, and then returns it to the tail of the queue. As processors are not allocated permanently to jobs, the number of processes in a job may change during runtime without causing any problems. This scheme is especially suitable for shared memory multiprocessors, and indeed it is used on many bus-based systems [50, 3].

Using a shared queue as described above may suffer from three drawbacks: contention for the queue, frequent migration of processes, and lack of coordinated scheduling. The issue of possible contention has lead to the design of wait-free queues, where different processes can access the queue simultaneously by using suitable hardware primitives, such as fetch-and-add. Indeed, this was one of the driving forces in the design of the NYU Ultracomputer, and its support for fetch-and-add via a combining multistage network [11]. However, the idea of combining network has not caught on because of their added complexity and design costs.

Migration occurs in this scheme because processes are typically executed on a different processor each time they arrive at the head of the queue. As a result, any state that may be left in a processor's cache is lost. It has been suggested that this effect can be reduced by using affinity scheduling, where an effort is made to re-schedule the process on the same processor as used last time [49, 10]. However, it is not clear to what degree data indeed remains in the cache, and in any case, affinity scheduling is largely equivalent to just using longer time quanta [51].

The third issue, lack of coordinated scheduling, may cause problems for applications where the processes interact with each other frequently. The only solution is to use gang scheduling. While gang scheduling and a shared queue seem to be in conflict with each other, a scheme that integrates both has been designed in the context of the IRIX operating system for SGI multiprocessor workstations [3].

Finally, it should be noted that this scheme benefits from similarity with runtime systems and thread packages that run within the confines of a single job.

5.4 Moldable Jobs and Adaptive Partitioning

As noted above, variable partitioning is a simple but somewhat inefficient scheduling scheme. The inefficiencies result both from fragmentation, where the remaining processors are insufficient for any queued job, and from the fact that jobs may request more processors than they can use efficiently. It is therefore an interesting question to assess the degree to which efficiency can be improved by adding flexibility and information about the characteristics of different jobs.

The model adopted for this line of research is that jobs can be molded to run on different numbers of processors, and some information about their average parallelism or execution profile is provided. This allows the system to judiciously choose partition sizes, without significantly affecting the programming model. Thus when the system is lightly loaded, jobs are allowed to use larger numbers of processors, even if they do not utilize them efficiently, but when system load increases, jobs are cut down to size [44, 47, 46]. It has also been suggested that the system keep some processors idle on the side in anticipation of additional arrivals [45].

In summary, this approach has generated a rather large body of research, but it has yet to lead to any implementations in real systems.

5.5 Malleable Jobs and Dynamic Partitioning

A more extreme approach to system optimization calls for sacrificing common programming models along with the illusion of a dedicated machine in order to promote efficiency. In some sense, this approach demonstrates the best performance that can be achieved, given full system flexibility in the allocation of resources, and jobs that are willing to cooperate with the system (and through it, with each other).

The programming model requires each job to accurately inform the system their resource requirements, and be able to adapt to changes in resource allocation that result from fluctuations in system load. The system uses information about the characteristics of the jobs to decide on the optimal allocation: jobs are only given additional processors if there is nothing better to do with them. When a new job arrives, some processors are taken from existing jobs and given to the new job, so that it will not have to wait. When a job terminates, its processors are distributed among the other jobs, so as not to waste them [52, 34, 35].

A good implementation requires co-design of the operating system, the runtime system, and the programming environment [2]. Indeed, no production implementation for parallel machines have been reported so far, despite much research that shows the benefits of this approach in terms of efficiency. On the other hand, this approach has the unique advantage that jobs may be able to tolerate system faults: a faulty processor is similar to one that is taken away and given to another job. Likewise, jobs running on a network of workstations will be able to tolerate workstations that drop out of the processor pool when they are reclaimed by their owners. Therefore this approach has lately become prominent in the context of network computing [5, 43].

6 Steps Towards Convergence

The field of job scheduling for parallel processing is in flux. It is being driven by the needs of growing numbers of installations. Sadly, there seems to be a growing divergence between the practical approaches adopted by actual users and the more sophisticated approaches advocated by theoreticians. Our goal here is to point out ways in which this gap can be bridged, and show how the different communities can benefit from the work of each other.

6.1 Step One: Be Explicit About the Differences

One of the problems in the field is the difficulty in relating the various research results to each other. In some cases such comparisons are actually comparing apples with oranges as if they were equivalent, in some the comparison is dismissed because it mistakenly seems to be irrelevant, and in some cases it is just hard to see whether or not the comparison makes sense.

The root of the problem is with the significant implicit assumptions and imprecise, confusing terminology. For example, dynamic partitioning research papers usually do not make explicit the assumption that jobs are coded in a style that tolerates changes in resource allocation at runtime, and that jobs are willing to cooperate in order to achieve greater overall (system) efficiency. Dynamic partitioning also assumes that the speedup functions for the jobs are not trivial step functions in which no speedup is achieved until a critical number of processors is made available and that additional processors do not affect job performance; such speedup functions describe rigid jobs. Likewise, work on gang scheduling usually does not make explicit the assumption that all programming styles must be supported with no changes. Gang scheduling research assumes that most jobs are not "embarrassingly parallel jobs" that require infrequent interaction. When these assumptions are clarified, it is evident that the two schemes operate in different frameworks. It is true that both strive for greater system efficiency, but each does so in a different framework based on different assumptions about the workload, so a comparison between them is debatable at best.

The other problem is one of terminology. For example *gang scheduling* means the same thing as *coscheduling* except that coscheduling will also schedule only some threads of a parallel job instead of leaving idle processor. Other researchers use the terms *hard* and *soft* gang scheduling to denote these differences. Such practices make it harder for readers to figure out what the results are about, and increase the cognitive load. While it is true that existing terminology is not always optimal and may suffer from historical artifacts, it is still usually better to stick with the established terms.

To summarize, we recommend that each paper should state the assumptions use consistent terminology, and resist the urge to define new terms or give new meaning to old ones.

6.2 Step Two: Acknowledge Deficiencies and Search for Solutions

Each scheme, by way of being dependent on a set of assumptions, has weaknesses when the assumptions are violated. Rather than assuming them away, one should try to overcome them by incorporating the ideas of other schemes. This may make the difference between a theoretical proposal and a real system.

For example, major weaknesses of variable partitioning are the loss of resources to fragmentation and the lack of responsiveness. Different schemes have been proposed to overcome one or the other of these problems: gang scheduling improves responsiveness, while adaptive and dynamic partitioning reduce fragmentation and improve throughput, provided the assumptions regarding the workload are met. But each scheme still has weaknesses when its assumptions are not met in full.

While gang scheduling improves system responsiveness through the use of time slicing, and also alleviates the ill-effects of fragmentation to some degree, it does not allow for optimizations based on global knowledge of the system load. Thus each job runs on a predefined number of processors, and this number cannot be changed. Efficiency may be improved if support for malleable jobs is included. Then, jobs are indeed malleable can be re-shaped to improve efficiency based on knowledge of the speedup curve. If the workload does not include sufficient small jobs, malleable jobs can also be re-shaped to fill in holes and reduce fragmentation.

Dynamic partitioning improves efficiency by eliminating fragmentation and reducing the processor allocation towards the optimal operation point for each job when load is high. However, it must still deal with unfavorable conditions, such as non-malleable jobs, jobs that do not provide the required information about their operation characteristics, and situations in which too many jobs have been submitted to run all of them at once. These problems can be addressed using mechanisms of adaptive partitioning and gang scheduling.

The bottom line is that combining ideas from different scheduling schemes can lead to important benefits for real systems. This does not mean that research on the individual schemes is not important — on the contrary, it is definitely necessary to focus on a narrow scheme and reduce the number of variables in order to perform a detailed analysis. But when it comes to building real systems, it is necessary to take a broader view.

6.3   Step Three: Broaden the Scope

Since expensive supercomputers should address a broad spectrum of application programs, a job scheduler should be able to handle a workload consisting of all sorts of jobs, be they rigid, evolving, moldable, or malleable, and all levels of resource specifications. Moreover, a scheduler should implement the constantly evolving policies and goals of the computer installation. Although we do not propose a scheduler that achieves these goals, it is important to state take steps in this direction.

Consider, for a moment, an 8 processor system and two parallel jobs. Suppose the jobs are malleable and the system is extremely flexible in that the two jobs can be executed in a gang scheduled, time-sliced manner with 8 nodes allocated to each job, or it can use space slicing and dedicate 4 nodes to each job. Suppose further that each job achieves linear speedup. Should the scheduler use space or time slicing? If the jobs require the same execution time, then there should be little difference, and system overheads should dictate the choice. Now suppose one job was submitted first and is allocated 8 nodes exclusively. When the second job arrives, is it more expensive to repartition the first job or to gang schedule them? The answer now depends on the computational times of the jobs – the number of context switches times their cost versus the repartitioning cost.

As the load on the system changes, the fraction of system resources allocated to each job changes. In time sharing system, it is easy to see this change. In space sharing systems, dynamic repartitioning attempts to share the resource of the processor. However, it is important to keep in mind that there are other resources such as physical memory and disk swap space.

So, one point is to understand the tradeoffs between the various modes of sharing.

Specifically, we propose the use of *cost functions* that reflect the policies and goals of the computer installation. For a given workload and cost function, the aim of a scheduler is to maximize the revenues of the system. There may be many different schedulers, some better suited to specific workloads and cost functions.

The cost function is defined on the execution of a job. It may be totally fictional; that is users do not pay money to have their job executed, but there is almost always some accounting when there is a scarce resource. Different job types can have different cost functions. The abstract notion of money that the system receives by executing a particular job at a particular time allows a scheduler to handle all types of jobs. Instead of ill defined notions such as "gets better service" there is a precise accounting for service. Policy decisions can be reflected through the cost function and not through the scheduler allocation algorithms.

Incentives   The more flexible and fully specified a job, the easier it is to schedule. It may be difficult to write a malleable or even a moldable job, and the user may not wish to take the time to uncover a job's resource requirements and speedup curves. So, there should be an incentive to the user to write a malleable program and to provide the system with lots of information about the program execution requirements. There are many types of incentives, but the two most popular choices are reduced cost and improved service; the adage "time is money" may equate the two.

Since the biggest drawback of scheduling of rigid jobs is fragmentation, it should be possible to use malleable jobs to fill in the leftover space. In addition, some fraction of the processors should be reserved for malleable jobs. The exact fractional value is clearly a system specific policy decision.

It seems natural to schedule jobs in the order that they arrive (or by some priority measure). But what resources should be given to flexible jobs? The system might have a different opinion than the user. For example, the user may want fast response time, therefore desire the maximum number of processors, while the system may want to satisfy the maximum number of users and thus allocate the minimal size to a malleable job. Given a 32 processor machine and two jobs, one rigid job requiring 24 processors and the other completely malleable, the system may allocate only 8 processors to the malleable one, thereby giving preferential treatment to the rigid job.

In other words, a reasonable scheduling strategy is to first take care of rigid jobs. Then, any remaining, unassigned processors due to fragmentation can be evenly distributed among the flexible ones. When new jobs arrive, the existing malleable jobs can be squeezed to their minimal size, and the new job allocated processors according to an equipartitioning strategy.

But should malleable jobs always be squeezed to their minimal size? Is it fair to slow down malleable jobs for the sake of executing another rigid job? Will users learn to choose the resource requirements that make their job complete sooner independently of the job's real requirements? For example, malleable jobs may be declared as rigid ones to prevent their interruptions. There is no universally correct answer to these concerns. The tradeoff can only be solved given the goals of the computer installation. A possible approach is to reserve a fraction of the system resources for each type of job. Particular classes can be encouraged and given preferential treatment by varying the fraction of resources. Such a strategy, however, restricts the ability of the scheduler and the policy maker. What happens when there are no rigid jobs? Are the resources wasted?

Using Cost Functions By defining a cost function, there is then something to maximize. For a given workload and cost function, some schedulers will maximize revenues better than others. But no matter the quality of the scheduler, changing the cost function will affect how the users view the machine. This provides flexibility to the system manager and allows exploration of the cost function space.

As a by-product, there is a common goal for theoreticians and practitioners: maximize revenues. Of course the theoretician may assume that there is much that is specified with the job, while the practitioner may have to approximate, infer, or guess at this information.

Note that there are actually two types of cost functions. The one just addressed concerns the when, where, and how a job is scheduled. It reflects the value to the scheduler of executing a job at a particular time. This indirectly affects the quality of service received by individual jobs.

It makes sense also to speak of a potentially different cost function that defines how much the user will have to pay. One can encourage certain types of jobs by charging users differently. It may be necessary to have two different functions since the scheduler gives preference to higher valued jobs whereas users give preference to lower valued jobs.

We assume that changes in the value of a job to the scheduler do not directly affect the offered workload. Of course once users figure out which jobs execute early, they may change the jobs submitted for execution. On the other hand, changes in the cost of a job to the user will quickly change the contents of the offered workload.

We shall ignore the cost to a user and concentrate on the cost function that defines the value of a job to the scheduler.

In what follows, we consider various components of a cost function. Real cost functions are expected to be developed in close collaboration with management personnel of the supercomputer center in order to address policy. The development follows the ideas found elsewhere [19].

The Importance of a Job It may be decided that the amount of parallelism of a job is important. Suppose a job is executed on p processors. When computing the *importance* of a job, a modified value of p may be used, such as $p' = k_0 p$. If $k_0 < 1$ then parallelism is discouraged; if $k_0 > 1$ then it is encouraged. Similarly, the total amount of CPU time used by a job, t, might be deemed important. So another constant is required to scale the time: $t' = k_1 t$.

The policy might be to encourage the use of medium sized parallelism, say 32 processors. The knee of the cost function should therefore be at this preferred number.

Other resource requirements can be similarly scaled in a way to reflect the importance of a job at the given installation. The final importance of a job is then some function of the scaled components. A simple function is addition, e.g. $t' + p'$, or multiplication, e.g. $t' \cdot p'$, but with multiplication, elapsed time or time per processor may make more sense since total time already incorporates the amount of parallelism. The scaled time per processor is simply t'/p.

If a job has a dynamic parallelism profile, then these values can be defined piecewise over periods when the number of processors is fixed, and then added up, as in

$$\text{Importance}(J) = \sum_i \frac{t'_i}{p_i} p'_i$$

The Global Affect of a Job Executing one job may preclude the scheduler from executing another, less valuable job, but it may also leave idle resources. Thus there is a second component to a job that must take account for what else is happening in the machine. Let us call this the *affect* of executing a job.

Suppose there are several jobs executing at any one time in a space slicing manner. During this snapshot in time, there are L idle processors. Then one could assign a value of $-\frac{p_j}{P} L$ as the affect of the job during this time slice (i.e. the cost is this factor multiplied by the time).

The affect of a job as defined is bad. The more wasted processors, the more negative the value. This function gives proportional blame for the idle resources based on the size of a job.

Deadlines and Response Time No matter how important is a job, without some accounting of deadlines or response time, there is no reason for a job to be scheduled at a particular time. The scheduler simply waits until it has enough jobs that it can pack together without waste. When there is a deadline associated with a job, then the cost function can reflect some policy. For example, the value of a job may decrease the longer it misses its deadline. A function that has the value continue to decrease (below zero) ensures that each job will eventually be executed[2].

	Job	Type	CPU	Min PEs	Max PEs	Arrival	Deadline
	J_0	Rigid	6	6	6	0	1
(a)	J_1	Rigid	6	6	6	0	1
	J_2	Malleable	10	1	8	0	2
	J_3	Malleable	10	1	8	0	2

(b)

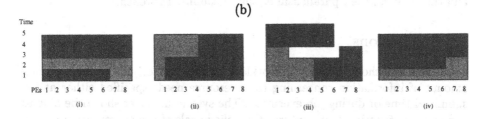

Fig. 3. *Example of scheduling rigid and malleable jobs under different cost functions. (a) characteristics of the jobs in the workload. (b) possible schedules.*

One suggested function [19] is:

$$(\text{deadline} - \text{response time})/\text{Importance}$$

---

[2] Note that this differs from the strategy of airlines that want to maximize their on-time performance, so that once a flight is delayed by more than 15 min, there is little pressure to minimize the delay. A better analogy is with the construction industry where fines are levied for each month delay in completing a building.

This makes sense once one recalls that our definition of importance is based on the total use of resources. The suggested function therefore scales the delay according to the resources used. The idea is that if a one month job misses its deadline by a day, it is not as bad as a 5 minute job missing its deadline by a day.

Consider the example of four jobs in a machine with 8 processors shown in Fig. 3. They all arrive at time 0 and want immediate service. There are several ways to schedule these four jobs; four examples are shown in the figure, although there are others. Which is the right schedule? The answer is that there is no right or wrong schedule; there is only those that maximize the cost function. Consider a simple cost function, like the one defined above, and assume that importance is taken to be CPU time. The cost is then

$$\text{Cost}(J) = \frac{\text{deadline} - \text{response time}}{\text{CPU}}$$

With this function, schedule (i) gives the best score since shorter jobs have a some what worse penalty for missing their deadlines. Increasing the importance of the smallness of a job, say by using an importance function that squares the computation requirements: i.e. $1/\text{CPU}^2$, configuration (ii) is the best. If bigger jobs are more important, then schedule (iii) would be chosen, assuming that fragmentation or low system utilization is less critical than missing deadlines. Finally, we note that schedule (iv) would not be chosen since the malleable jobs complete at the same time as in schedule (i) and the rigid jobs finish later. Extending the deadlines of the rigid jobs would make the two schedules equivalent.

We note that the types of simple cost and importance functions just discussed, often results in malleable jobs that start execution with few processors and then expand their parallelism as their deadlines approach.

7 Conclusions

Job schedulers should support a workload of all types of jobs, with a varying amount of information concerning their resource needs specified either at job submittal time or during job execution. The system manager should be able to define a cost function that captures the policy goals of the computation center. The question is how to get there from where we are today.

First, it is important to continue the investigation into current workloads to get a better understanding of the resource requirements of parallel applications as well as how resources affect their performance. Some of this can be gotten from runtime monitoring and gathered from job statistics at the supercomputer centers. Another important input is from the designers of parallel programming languages and programming environments, who may come up with new requirements and desiderata.

Second, many on-line schedulers use amortized cost analysis to make decisions that are within a constant factor of the optimal, off-line algorithm. But, without an explicit statement of what it is that the scheduler is trying to maximize, there can be no way to evaluate the success of an on-line algorithm.

Finally, it is important to keep the assumptions made by different researchers in mind. In particular, it is necessary to always check to what degree the results depend upon these assumptions, and to keep a lookout for ideas that may be applicable to a wider class of jobs and systems than envisioned initially.

References

1. T. Agerwala, J. L. Martin, J. H. Mirza, D. C. Sadler, D. M. Dias, and M. Snir, "SP2 system architecture". IBM Syst. J. **34(2)**, pp. 152–184, 1995.
2. T. E. Anderson, B. N. Bershad, E. D. Lazowska, and H. M. Levy, "Scheduler activations: effective kernel support for the user-level management of parallelism". ACM Trans. Comput. Syst. **10(1)**, pp. 53–79, Feb 1992.
3. J. M. Barton and N. Bitar, "A scalable multi-discipline, multiple-processor scheduling framework for IRIX". In Job Scheduling Strategies for Parallel Processing, D. G. Feitelson and L. Rudolph (eds.), pp. 45–69, Springer-Verlag, 1995. Lecture Notes in Computer Science Vol. 949.
4. P. Brinch Hansen, "An analysis of response ratio scheduling". In IFIP Congress, Ljubljana, pp. TA-3 150–154, Aug 1971.
5. N. Carriero, E. Freedman, D. Gelernter, and D. Kaminsky, "Adaptive parallelism and Piranha". Computer **28(1)**, pp. 40–49, Jan 1995.
6. M-S. Chen and K. G. Shin, "Subcube allocation and task migration in hypercube multiprocessors". IEEE Trans. Comput. **39(9)**, pp. 1146–1155, Sep 1990.
7. S-H. Chiang and M. Vernon, "Dynamic vs. static quantum-based parallel processor allocation". In Job Scheduling Strategies for Parallel Processing II, D. G. Feitelson and L. Rudolph (eds.), Springer-Verlag, 1996. Lecture Notes in Computer Science.
8. M. Crovella, P. Das, C. Dubnicki, T. LeBlanc, and E. Markatos, "Multiprogramming on multiprocessors". In 3rd IEEE Symp. Parallel & Distributed Processing, pp. 590–597, 1991.
9. D. Das Sharma and D. K. Pradhan, "A fast and efficient strategy for submesh allocation in mesh-connected parallel computers". In IEEE Symp. Parallel & Distributed Processing, pp. 682–689, Dec 1993.
10. M. Devarakonda and A. Mukherjee, "Issues in implementation of cache-affinity scheduling". In Proc. Winter USENIX Technical Conf., pp. 345–357, Jan 1992.
11. J. Edler, A. Gottlieb, C. P. Kruskal, K. P. McAuliffe, L. Rudolph, M. Snir, P. J. Teller, and J. Wilson, "Issues related to MIMD shared-memory computers: the NYU Ultracomputer approach". In 12th Ann. Intl. Symp. Computer Architecture Conf. Proc., pp. 126–135, 1985.
12. D. G. Feitelson, "Packing schemes for gang scheduling". In Job Scheduling Strategies for Parallel Processing II, D. G. Feitelson and L. Rudolph (eds.), Springer-Verlag, 1996. Lecture Notes in Computer Science.
13. D. G. Feitelson, A Survey of Scheduling in Multiprogrammed Parallel Systems. Research Report RC 19790 (87657), IBM T. J. Watson Research Center, Oct 1994.
14. D. G. Feitelson and B. Nitzberg, "Job characteristics of a production parallel scientific workload on the NASA Ames iPSC/860". In Job Scheduling Strategies for Parallel Processing, D. G. Feitelson and L. Rudolph (eds.), pp. 337–360, Springer-Verlag, 1995. Lecture Notes in Computer Science Vol. 949.
15. D. G. Feitelson and L. Rudolph, "Distributed hierarchical control for parallel processing". Computer **23(5)**, pp. 65–77, May 1990.

16. D. G. Feitelson and L. Rudolph, "Evaluation of design choices for gang scheduling using distributed hierarchical control". *J. Parallel & Distributed Comput.*, 1996. to appear.

17. D. G. Feitelson and L. Rudolph, "Gang scheduling performance benefits for fine-grain synchronization". *J. Parallel & Distributed Comput.* 16(4), pp. 306–318, Dec 1992.

18. D. G. Feitelson and L. Rudolph, "Parallel job scheduling: issues and approaches". In *Job Scheduling Strategies for Parallel Processing*, D. G. Feitelson and L. Rudolph (eds.), pp. 1–18, Springer-Verlag, 1995. Lecture Notes in Computer Science Vol. 949.

19. M. Frank, V. Lee, W. Lee, K. Mackenzie, and L. Rudolph, "An online scheduler respecting job cost functions for parallel processors". Manuscript in preperation, M.I.T. Cambridge, MA, 1996.

20. J. Gehring and F. Ramme, "Architecture-independent request-scheduling with tight waiting-time estimations". In *Job Scheduling Strategies for Parallel Processing II*, D. G. Feitelson and L. Rudolph (eds.), Springer-Verlag, 1996. Lecture Notes in Computer Science.

21. A. Geist, A. Beguelin, J. Dongarra, W. Jiang, R. Manchek, and V. Sunderam, *PVM 3 User's Guide and Reference Manual.* Technical Report ORNL/TM-12187, Oak Ridge National Laboratory, May 1994.

22. B. Gorda and R. Wolski, "Time sharing massively parallel machines". In *Intl. Conf. Parallel Processing*, Aug 1995.

23. A. Gupta, A. Tucker, and S. Urushibara, "The impact of operating system scheduling policies and synchronization methods on the performance of parallel applications". In *SIGMETRICS Conf. Measurement & Modeling of Comput. Syst.*, pp. 120–132, May 1991.

24. R. L. Henderson, "Job scheduling under the portable batch system". In *Job Scheduling Strategies for Parallel Processing*, D. G. Feitelson and L. Rudolph (eds.), pp. 279–294, Springer-Verlag, 1995. Lecture Notes in Computer Science Vol. 949.

25. A. Hori et al., "Time space sharing scheduling and architectural support". In *Job Scheduling Strategies for Parallel Processing*, D. G. Feitelson and L. Rudolph (eds.), pp. 92–105, Springer-Verlag, 1995. Lecture Notes in Computer Science Vol. 949.

26. A. Hori, H. Tezuka, Y. Ishikawa, N. Soda, H. Konaka, and M. Maeda, "Implementation of gang-scheduling on workstation cluster". In *Job Scheduling Strategies for Parallel Processing II*, D. G. Feitelson and L. Rudolph (eds.), Springer-Verlag, 1996. Lecture Notes in Computer Science.

27. S. Hotovy, "Workload evolution on the Cornell Theory Center IBM SP2". In *Job Scheduling Strategies for Parallel Processing II*, D. G. Feitelson and L. Rudolph (eds.), Springer-Verlag, 1996. Lecture Notes in Computer Science.

28. N. Islam, A. Prodromidis, and M. Squillante, "Dynamic partitioning in different distributed-memory environments". In *Job Scheduling Strategies for Parallel Processing II*, D. G. Feitelson and L. Rudolph (eds.), Springer-Verlag, 1996. Lecture Notes in Computer Science.

29. Y. A. Khalidi, J. Bernabeu, V. Matena, K. Shirriff, and M. Thadani, "Solaris MC: a Multi Computer OS". In *Proc. USENIX Conf.*, Jan 1996.

30. A. A. Khokhar, V. K. Prasanna, M. E. Shaaban, and C-L. Wang, "Heterogeneous computing: challenges and opportunities". *Computer* 26(6), pp. 18–27, Jun 1993.

31. P. Krueger, T-H. Lai, and V. A. Dixit-Radiya, *"Job scheduling is more important than processor allocation for hypercube computers"*. *IEEE Trans. Parallel & Distributed Syst.* **5(5)**, pp. 488–497, May 1994.

32. D. Lifka, *"The ANL/IBM SP scheduling system"*. In *Job Scheduling Strategies for Parallel Processing*, D. G. Feitelson and L. Rudolph (eds.), pp. 295–303, Springer-Verlag, 1995. Lecture Notes in Computer Science Vol. 949.

33. W. Liu, V. Lo, K. Windisch, and B. Nitzberg, *"Non-contiguous processor allocation algorithms for distributed memory multicomputers"*. In *Supercomputing '94*, pp. 227–236, Nov 1994.

34. C. McCann, R. Vaswani, and J. Zahorjan, *"A dynamic processor allocation policy for multiprogrammed shared-memory multiprocessors"*. *ACM Trans. Comput. Syst.* **11(2)**, pp. 146–178, May 1993.

35. C. McCann and J. Zahorjan, *"Processor allocation policies for message passing parallel computers"*. In *SIGMETRICS Conf. Measurement & Modeling of Comput. Syst.*, pp. 19–32, May 1994.

36. T. D. Nguyen, R. Vaswani, and J. Zahorjan, *"Parallel application characterization for multiprocessor scheduling policy design"*. In *Job Scheduling Strategies for Parallel Processing II*, D. G. Feitelson and L. Rudolph (eds.), Springer-Verlag, 1996. Lecture Notes in Computer Science.

37. T. D. Nguyen, R. Vaswani, and J. Zahorjan, *"Using runtime measured workload characteristics in parallel processor scheduling"*. In *Job Scheduling Strategies for Parallel Processing II*, D. G. Feitelson and L. Rudolph (eds.), Springer-Verlag, 1996. Lecture Notes in Computer Science.

38. J. K. Ousterhout, *"Scheduling techniques for concurrent systems"*. In *3rd Intl. Conf. Distributed Comput. Syst.*, pp. 22–30, Oct 1982.

39. J. D. Padhye and L. W. Dowdy, *"Preemptive versus non-preemptive processor allocation policies for message passing parallel computers: an empirical comparison"*. In *Job Scheduling Strategies for Parallel Processing II*, D. G. Feitelson and L. Rudolph (eds.), Springer-Verlag, 1996. Lecture Notes in Computer Science.

40. E. W. Parsons and K. C. Sevcik, *"Multiprocessor scheduling for high-variability service time distributions"*. In *Job Scheduling Strategies for Parallel Processing*, D. G. Feitelson and L. Rudolph (eds.), pp. 127–145, Springer-Verlag, 1995. Lecture Notes in Computer Science Vol. 949.

41. J. Peterson and A. Silberschatz, *Operating System Concepts*. Addison-Wesley, 1983.

42. J. Pruyne and M. Livny, *"Managing checkpoints for parallel programs"*. In *Job Scheduling Strategies for Parallel Processing II*, D. G. Feitelson and L. Rudolph (eds.), Springer-Verlag, 1996. Lecture Notes in Computer Science.

43. J. Pruyne and M. Livny, *"Parallel processing on dynamic resources with CARMI"*. In *Job Scheduling Strategies for Parallel Processing*, D. G. Feitelson and L. Rudolph (eds.), pp. 259–278, Springer-Verlag, 1995. Lecture Notes in Computer Science Vol. 949.

44. E. Rosti, E. Smirni, L. W. Dowdy, G. Serazzi, and B. M. Carlson, *"Robust partitioning schemes of multiprocessor systems"*. *Performance Evaluation* **19(2-3)**, pp. 141–165, Mar 1994.

45. E. Rosti, E. Smirni, G. Serazzi, and L. W. Dowdy, *"Analysis of non-work-conserving processor partitioning policies"*. In *Job Scheduling Strategies for Parallel Processing*, D. G. Feitelson and L. Rudolph (eds.), pp. 165–181, Springer-Verlag, 1995. Lecture Notes in Computer Science Vol. 949.

46. K. C. Sevcik, "Application scheduling and processor allocation in multiprogrammed parallel processing systems". *Performance Evaluation* **19(2-3)**, pp. 107–140, Mar 1994.

47. K. C. Sevcik, "Characterization of parallelism in applications and their use in scheduling". In *SIGMETRICS Conf. Measurement & Modeling of Comput. Syst.*, pp. 171–180, May 1989.

48. J. Skovira, W. Chan, H. Zhou, and D. Lifka, "The EASY - LoadLeveler API project". In *Job Scheduling Strategies for Parallel Processing II*, D. G. Feitelson and L. Rudolph (eds.), Springer-Verlag, 1996. Lecture Notes in Computer Science.

49. M. S. Squillante and E. D. Lazowska, "Using processor-cache affinity information in shared-memory multiprocessor scheduling". *IEEE Trans. Parallel & Distributed Syst.* **4(2)**, pp. 131–143, Feb 1993.

50. S. Thakkar, P. Gifford, and G. Fielland, "Balance: a shared memory multiprocessor system". In *2nd Intl. Conf. Supercomputing*, vol. I, pp. 93–101, 1987.

51. J. Torrellas, A. Tucker, and A. Gupta, "Evaluating the performance of cache-affinity scheduling in shared-memory multiprocessors". *J. Parallel & Distributed Comput.* **24(2)**, pp. 139–151, Feb 1995.

52. A. Tucker and A. Gupta, "Process control and scheduling issues for multiprogrammed shared-memory multiprocessors". In *12th Symp. Operating Systems Principles*, pp. 159–166, Dec 1989.

53. M. Wan, R. Moore, G. Kremenek, and K. Steube, "A batch scheduler for the Intel Paragon MPP system with a non-contiguous node allocation algorithm". In *Job Scheduling Strategies for Parallel Processing II*, D. G. Feitelson and L. Rudolph (eds.), Springer-Verlag, 1996. Lecture Notes in Computer Science.

54. F. Wang, M. Papaefthymiou, M. Squillante, L. Rudolph, P. Pattnaik, and H. Franke, "A gang scheduling design for multiprogrammed parallel computing environments". In *Job Scheduling Strategies for Parallel Processing II*, D. G. Feitelson and L. Rudolph (eds.), Springer-Verlag, 1996. Lecture Notes in Computer Science.

55. J. Zahorjan and C. McCann, "Processor scheduling in shared memory multiprocessors". In *SIGMETRICS Conf. Measurement & Modeling of Comput. Syst.*, pp. 214–225, May 1990.

Workload Evolution on the Cornell Theory Center IBM SP2

Steven Hotovy
Cornell Theory Center
Ithaca, NY 14853
shotovy@tc.cornell.edu

Abstract. *The Cornell Theory Center (CTC) put a 512-node IBM SP2 system into production in early 1995, and extended traces of batch jobs began to be collected in June of that year. An analysis of the workload shows that it has not only grown, but that its characteristics have changed over time. In particular, job duration increased with time, indicative of an expanding production workload. In addition, there was increasing use of parallelism.*

As the load has increased and larger jobs have become more frequent, the batch management software (IBM's LoadLeveler) has had difficulty in scheduling the requested resources. New policies were established to improve the situation.

This paper will profile how the workload has changed over time and give an in-depth look at the maturing workload. It will examine how frequently certain resources are requested and analyze user submittal patterns. It will also describe the policies that were implemented to improve the scheduling situation and their effect on the workload.

1 Introduction

1.1 Background

There is a great deal of interest in workload characterization for parallel systems. Developers of job scheduling policies have a keen interest in the profiles of real parallel workloads as opposed to the synthetic data with which they often work. Managers of parallel systems wish to understand the workload so that they can make informed decisions about policy and procedures.

Parallel workloads are more challenging to characterize than their serial counterparts, if for no other reason than the multiplicity of processors. Some parallel systems, like the IBM SP2 at the Cornell Theory Center, contain a wide variety of different resources – memory per node, special software on fixed nodes, nodes devoted to I/O, etc. Such systems offer particular challenges for workload characterization.

Another complicating factor for parallel systems is that they are typically difficult to program, which means that program development and debugging activities will play a larger role than for serial systems. A mature workload, dominated by large production jobs, will take more time to develop on parallel systems. And even a mature workload may continue changing as users, after gaining confidence in system reliability and stability, attempt more ambitious simulations involving more processors running for longer periods of time.

To date, however, there has been very little published on actual parallel workloads. One obvious reason is that, until recently, parallel computers were used principally for research and development, not production. Nonetheless, some interesting research in workload characterization has been done. Cypher and co-workers [2] studied the memory, communication, computing and I/O resource requirements and utilization patterns of a number of scientific codes on distributed memory machines. In the Joint NSF-NASA Initiative on Evaluation (JNNIE) project [6], five NASA centers and the four NSF Supercomputer Centers identified 22 key applications and ran parallel versions of these programs on a diverse set of parallel machines. These applications involve key disciplines supported by these agencies, but are not meant to represent a typical workload. The most complete study of a production parallel workload was that done by Feitelson and Nitzberg [3]. They analyzed NQS trace records over the fourth quarter of 1993 for the 128-processor iPSC/860 at NASA Ames. In an earlier paper [7], the Cornell Theory Center (CTC) identified six classes of future key applications, and estimated the amount of resources these types of jobs would likely consume. These data represented an anticipated load, not the current workload, however. In a subsequent paper [4], the CTC analyzed the early workload on the SP2. As the SP2 has matured, this early workload has grown and changed considerably, so a more complete analysis of the maturing workload is called for.

This study highlights the evolution of the batch workload on the CTC IBM SP2 over an 8-month period. It expands on previous studies in that the workload is not viewed as a static entity, but one with several phases, each of which should be treated separately. The later, production-oriented phase is analyzed in more detail, providing information that will be useful to developers of job scheduling and resource management strategies.

This paper also examines the effect of policies on workload behavior, a subject which has received scant attention. Changes to policy were motivated by the fact that resource utilization for the later workload was being limited by inefficiencies in the resource management software. This paper discusses the motivation behind these policy decisions, and the effect they had on workload characteristics.

1.2 The SP2 System

The Cornell Theory Center IBM SP2 system [1] contains 512 nodes with an aggregate peak speed of 137 Gflops and a combined physical memory of 79 GBytes. The system, which was made available for production use in early 1995, is heterogeneous in that it contains a mixture of *wide* nodes and *thin* nodes. On the CTC SP2, *wide* nodes have been configured with 4 times the data cache and 4 times the data bandwidth between cache and memory compared to *thin* nodes. The nodes also vary in the amount of physical memory attached, from 128 MB up to 2048 MB.

The 512 processors themselves are segregated by the services they provide. The bulk of the processors, 430 in number, are devoted to running batch jobs. The remainder are used for interactive use, I/O gateways, special projects, and system testing.

The pool of batch nodes consist of both wide and thin nodes, and come in a variety of memory sizes. Table 1 details the node type/memory combinations.

The SP2 is also equipped with a High-Performance Switch, which directs data communication among the nodes. This switch runs under two protocols: the standard IP protocol (HPS-IP), and a more efficient one which resides in user space (HPS-USER).

Each node has 2GB of disk capacity. None of this storage is used for permanent files, however. Rather, this storage is used for swap space, caching of permanent files,

Node Type	128	256	512	1024	2048
Thin	352	30	0	0	0
Wide	0	22	21	4	1
Total	352	52	21	4	1
Percent	81.9	12.1	4.9	0.9	0.2

Table 1. Configuration of Batch Partition by Physical Memory (in MB) and Node Type

and temporary space for users. Permanent data are stored on external AFS file servers or on the NSL Unitree mass storage system.

Management of the batch system was provided by LoadLeveler [8], IBM's job management software. A fuller discussion of the LoadLeveler environment follows.

1.3 LoadLeveler Considerations

LoadLeveler provides a number of keywords to assist in the scheduling and execution of jobs. The most important ones from the standpoint of workload characterization are:

- Batch queue name
- The minimum number of processors required
- The maximum number of processors that can be used
- The switch protocol (USER or IP) to be used for parallel jobs
- The amount of memory requested
- The node type (THIN or WIDE)
- Mass storage (Yes or No)
- Node-locked software (ABAQUS or FIDAP)

LoadLeveler allows for dynamic definition of batch queues. Our initial definition of queues, all based on a maximum execution (wall-clock) time for a job, were:

- 15-minute
- 3-hour
- 6-hour
- 12-hour
- 18-hour

Within a given queue, there are no inherent limits to other resources, such as the number of processors, which the user may request. LoadLeveler will automatically cancel jobs that exceed the wall-clock limit for the queue, however. The LoadLeveler job scheduler is given control of assigning nodes from the entire pool of 430 processors. All queues draw from this same pool.

LoadLeveler employs space-sharing in the allocation of parallel jobs, i.e., once a node is assigned to a particular job, it is not available for further work until the job is completed. The scheduler uses a least heavily loaded algorithm to select candidate nodes. LoadLeveler imposes no limit on the number of jobs that may be queued in a given queue. LoadLeveler also employs an aging algorithm that increases the priority of jobs which have been waiting longer to receive service.

1.4 Initial Policies

The CTC established several initial policies which had an effect on batch performance. To equalize access to the SP2, the Center originally established a maximum of 2 jobs per user that could be executing simultaneously (although there was no limit per user for the number of jobs waiting in the batch queues). This limit was subsequently modified several times in response to a changing workload, as will be discussed below.

Another policy was that all batch queues, except for the 15-minute one, will be given the same initial priority. The 15-minute queue was assigned a higher initial priority because it is intended for program development and debugging where turnaround time is more critical.

2 An Overview of the Changing Workload

At the most general level, the workload can be characterized both by the number of jobs and by the amount of wall-clock time accumulated by those jobs. To quantify the latter, it is convenient to define the term **User Node Time**, which is the sum of the wall-clock times used by the job on each participating processor.

Daily LoadLeveler logs from June 18, 1995 through March 2, 1996 (except for the weeks of September 3, September 10 and December 3) were used in the analyses of this section. There was no data for the 2 weeks in September because of a problem with the data collection mechanism; data for the week of December 3 is not meaningful because much of the SP2 was dedicated to I-WAY work for Supercomputer '95.

2.1 Weekly Workload Averages

Figure 1 depicts the developing workload at this general level on a week-by-week basis. One clear trend is the consistently increasing use of the machine as measured by User Node Time through the beginning of October. Through October and November, however, the User Node Time oscillates between 40,000 and 50,000 node-hours per week despite that fact that maximum capacity is about 70,000 node-hours. The peak of 50,000 corresponds to 70 percent of capacity and the average of about 42,000 node-hours over these 2 months is only 60 percent. One can also observe a slow decline in User Node Time in 1996. This is caused by the fact that some of the nodes previously assigned to servicing batch jobs were taken away for special projects.

The number of jobs exhibits a different behavior, though. It varies between 2,000 and 3,000 jobs through mid-October, but then begins to decline, despite the fact that the User Node Time remains at its peak. At the end of 1995, the number of jobs settles down to about 1,000 per week, a factor of 3 decrease from the high in late August. 1996 shows a slight increase to about 1500 jobs weekly.

Figure 1 leads one to suspect that:

- The workload profile began to change in September and continues to change;
- The consistent, relatively low average utilization of about 60 percent may be due less to the the workload itself than to shortcomings in the system's ability to service the workload.

31

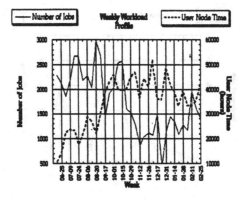

Fig. 1. Weekly Workload.

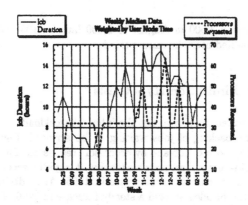

Fig. 2. Median Job Duration and Processors Requested.

2.2 The Changing Workload Hypothesis

Figure 2 lends credence to the first hypothesis. The solid line represents the median
job duration weighted by User Node Time. A median value of 11 hours for the week
of June 25th means that half the User Node Time comes from jobs which run in 11
hours or more. This value dropped throughout the summer months to a low of 6 hours
in mid-August, at which point it began a steady increase to about 15 hours late in
1995. This is an increase of 250 percent over a 3 month period and reflects a rapid
maturation in the workload from a code development/modest production environment
to one dominated by large production jobs.

Figure 2 also shows the median number of processors requested weighted by User
Node Time. In most cases, the median value is 32 processors, primarily because 32-way
jobs account for about 30 percent of the total User Node Time in a given week. Yet
on several occasions, the median value reached 50 and then 60 processors. This shows
that not only are jobs running longer, they tend to be using more processors on the
average. Taken with the average job duration data, this explains why the number of

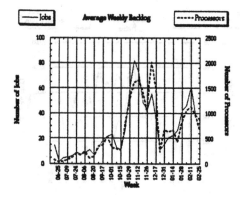

Fig. 3. Average Weekly Backlog.

jobs dropped from nearly 3,000 in August to 1,000 later in 1995 while the aggregate node-hours nearly doubled over the same period.

2.3 The System Limitation Hypothesis

One indication that system response, not the inherent workload, is the limiting factor would be a consistent backlog of jobs waiting to be serviced. Figure 3 displays the weekly average backlog, both by job and by processors requested. The backlog gradually increased through mid-September, at which point it rapidly accelerated, reaching a peak of 80 jobs and over 2000 processors late in 1995. After declining in December during the holidays, the backlog started a steady increase in 1996. While this was only a weekly average, it does suggest that instances where there were no jobs queued to run occurred very infrequently.

Figure 4, which shows wait time information, adds more support for the hypothesis. Through the middle of September, the average wait times for both the 15-minute queue and the production queues (all the rest) were relatively low. For both, the median wait times were significantly lower than the mean, typically less than 1 minute. During this period, one could characterize the wait time distribution as one highly skewed toward very short wait times, with a few exceptions which lasted a very long time (at times, more than a day).

For the next month, wait times fluctuated, never going beyond 200 minutes. From mid-October to mid-November, however, the wait times grew enormously to over 800 minutes. Wait times for the 15-minute queue settled down through the rest of the reporting period, while for the production queues it maintained a level of around 400 minutes.

There is one other notable change in the wait time data. From late October on, the median wait times for the production queues can be as much as 50 percent of the mean. This suggests a wait time distribution very different from the earlier one – a much larger percentage of people are faced with long wait times. This is further evidence that the system is unable to deliver more than 50,000 node-hours per week for the existing workload.

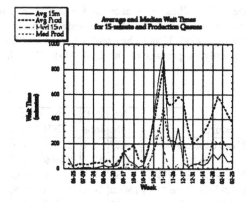

Fig. 4. Average and Median Wait Times.

2.4 Notes on Further Wait Time Analysis

The wait time data should be viewed with some care. Scarce resources – large numbers of processors, the single mass storage node, etc. – will have an effect on wait times. The CTC policies regarding the maximum number of simultaneously executing jobs and initial job priorities also influence wait times. LoadLeveler itself can cause certain jobs to wait a very long time – hence the disparity between median and mean wait times in the first half of the reporting period. In addition, user behavior can be a factor. For example, during periods of long turnaround times, a few users would submit LoadLeveler jobs and then immediately place them in Hold status. While the jobs were in Hold status (and increasing in priority because of aging), users would prepare their input files. When the files were ready, they would release the job, which would then get quick service because of its high priority. This action will create an artificially high wait time for the job.

3 Characterization of the Maturing Workload

As was mentioned above, the workload began to change in September from a code development/modest production environment to one featuring more substantial production jobs. In this section, we will analyze the workload for the time period from September 17th through December 2 in more detail, highlighting its heterogeneous nature.

3.1 Requests for General Resources

Table 2 describes the demand for the varying resources. Only 2.4 percent of the jobs requested the single mass storage node, but these jobs constitute 7 percent of the user-node hours. Thus larger jobs, which tend to generate larger amounts of I/O, make use of the mass storage feature. Wide nodes are requested by roughly 1 of every 8 jobs. This is a surprisingly high number, and probably reflects those applications for which CPU performance is enhanced by the larger data cache and greater cache-memory bandwidth of the wide nodes. These jobs account for less than 5 percent of the user node time, however. Since there are fewer than 50 wide nodes, such jobs by necessity will be serial or modestly parallel. Hence they will generate less User Node Time than the typical job. In fact, only 35 percent of the User Node Time for wide nodes come from parallel jobs.

Resource	No. Jobs	Pct. Jobs	No. UNH	Pct. UNH
Mass Storage	427	2.4	32284	7.0
Wide Nodes	2303	12.8	24409	4.7
Node-locked S/W	80	0.5	4	0.0
0-128MB Mem	15099	84.1	441175	95.8
129-256MB Mem	1987	11.1	16220	3.5
257-512MB Mem	652	3.6	2296	0.5
513-1024MB Mem	100	0.6	314	0.07
1025-2048MB Mem	109	0.6	654	0.14

Table 2. Requests for Resources for Maturing Workload

3.2 Requests for Memory

The breakdown of memory requested is very illuminating. About 85 percent of the jobs, consuming over 95 percent of the user-node hours, requested 128MB of memory or less. There is corresponding less demand for nodes with larger amounts of main memory. It should be noted that memory requested reflects demand for resources, not necessarily what type of nodes were actually used for a particular job. LoadLeveler will try to use nodes with 128MB of memory to service a smaller job, but should there an insufficient number of 128MB nodes available, it will engage nodes with more memory.

One of our concerns is whether the varying resources of the SP2 are adequate to the demands of the workload. In this light, it is helpful to compare the usage of nodes by memory in Table 2 with the configuration in Table 1. One can see that the 128MB nodes are relatively over-requested since they account for about 82 percent of the nodes available but nearly 96 percent of the user-node hours. The single 2GB node is requested proportionally to its contribution of user-node hours. The remaining nodes, however, are definitely under-requested. One reason for this is the relatively small number of large nodes, which discourages significant parallel use of them. In fact, parallel jobs requesting more than 128MB of memory account for a miniscule 0.3 percent of all parallel User Node Time.

3.3 Requests for Processors

Another critical resource is sufficient nodes for parallelism. Figures 5 and 6 display the demand for particular numbers of processors. Several items stand out. One is that serial jobs constitute a non-negligible portion of the workload. In fact, over half the submitted jobs are serial, although they account for only 8.6 percent of the user-node hours. These serial jobs are, for the most part, legacy applications from the IBM

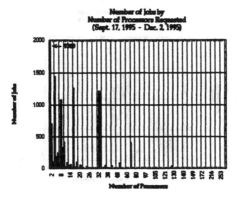

Fig. 5. Number of Jobs by Number of Processors Requested.

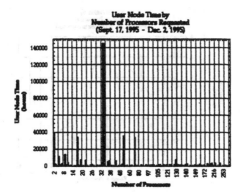

Fig. 6. User Node Time by Number of Processors Requested.

ES/9000 which was taken out of operation last year. Third-party applications, notably computational chemistry, also contribute to the serial load.

Another striking feature is the amount of work done by jobs requesting a number of nodes that are a power of 2, especially 32-way jobs. Power-of-2 jobs constitute about 55 percent of the User Node Time, 31 percent of which is due to 32-way jobs alone. It is not clear why power-of-2 jobs should be so prevalent – the SP2 does not place any restrictions on the number of nodes that can be requested, and its flat topology does not cause degraded performance for certain node combinations that other topologies (hypercube, 2-D mesh, etc.) do. It may be that the users want portability with other parallel systems which do have limitations; it may also be that powers of 2 naturally fit with the phenomenon being modeled.

3.4 Job Duration Profiles

The correlation of job duration with the number of processors requested is a matter of some interest to job schedulers. Figure 7 plots the average job duration as a function

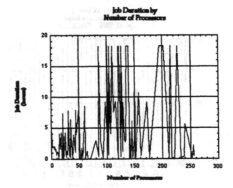

Fig. 7. Job Duration by Number of Processors Requested.

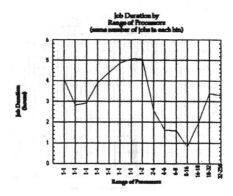

Fig. 8. Job Duration (binned) by Number of Processors Requested.

of number of processors requested. The shape is very erratic and correlations, if any, are difficult to perceive.

One problem with this presentation of data is that it is not weighted by the number of jobs requesting a given number of processors. As was mentioned above, over half the jobs for the CTC maturing workload are serial. One can compensate for this by creating bins with equal numbers of jobs, in order of increasing numbers of processors. The results for 15 bins is shown in Figure 8.

The first 7 bins are for serial jobs only. The data was processed in chronological order, so these bins reflect temporal changes in the average jobs duration of serial jobs from mid-September through early December. It is clear that after a brief drop-off in late Septmber to a low value of about 3 hours, the mean job duration increased steadily to its high of over 5 hours at the end of the period.

The next set of bins, from 2-4 processors through 8-16 processors, shows a steady decline in job durations. One suspects that jobs in this range are indicative of program development and debugging, with correspondingly lower run times. The last set of bins shows an increase in job durations with a leveling off for the very largest jobs. Jobs in

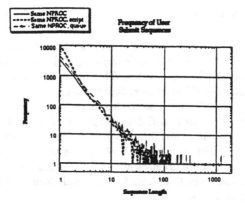

Fig. 9. Frequency of User Submit Sequence Lengths.

this range represent production use of the machine and account for the vast majority of cycles.

3.5 User Job Submittal Sequences

Another important measure of the workload is the degree to which users submit sequences of similar jobs. In our case, we define 3 different classes of "similar" jobs for a given user:

1. Same number of processors requested
2. Same number of processors requested and same batch script
3. Same number of processors requested and same LoadLeveler queue

The results appear in Figure 9. As one would expect, the least restrictive definition of similar jobs (definition 1) exhibits the fewest short sequences and the most long sequences. Definition 3 shows only a slight difference from the least restrictive, while the requirement that there be the same batch script generates far more sequences of length 1 and consistently fewer for sequences 5 or greater.

The most striking aspect of the data, however, is the virtually linear decrease up to sequences of about 50 in length, regardless of definition. Since the plots are log-log, it suggests a Zipf's distribution. Based on linear regression for the first 50 datapoints, the coefficient for the Zipf's distributions for each of the three user sequence definitions was -1.85, -2.1 and -2.0 respectively.

4 Policy and Procedures

Throughout most of the reporting period, CTC policies remained as they were in the beginning. One modification was made early – to encourage use of the machine while the load was still relatively modest, the limitation of 2 simultaneously running jobs per user was raised to 4 in August.

4.1 New Batch Class

As the wait times started their dramatic increase in early November, the CTC considered several policy changes. Two were implemented. On November 20, a new batch class for short-running jobs was created. This queue imposed a limit of a 15-minute run-time and a maximum of 8 processors that could be requested, and 8 thin nodes were reserved for this queue. The purpose of this queue was to provide faster turn-around for small program development and debugging jobs. The effect was pronounced. The mean wait time dropped from 965 minutes for the single 15-minute queue the previous week to an average of 280 minutes for both queues the following week. The median wait time dropped even more dramatically, from 147 minutes the previous week to 16 minutes the next. And from that time forward, wait times for the 15-minute queues have remained relatively low.

This decrease in wait time is due in large part to the new batch class. During the 2 weeks immediately following the activation of the new batch class, there were 367 jobs in the standard 15-minute queue with an average wait time of 309.4 minutes. As for the new class, there were 262 jobs submitted with an average wait time of 17.9 minutes, a factor of 17 less than for the standard queue. Thus these smaller jobs received much better service than if they had to contend with larger jobs in the standard queue.

4.2 Reduction in Number of Simultaneously Running Jobs

With the increase in demand for the SP2 and resulting contention for resources, there was a concern about equitable access to the machine. Thus it was decided to review the policy of a maximum of 4 simultaneously running jobs. An analysis of the data for the two weeks of maximum backlog (November 5 through November 18) showed that over 10,000 node-hours, or 12.4 percent of the total volume, came from jobs whose users already had at least 2 other jobs running at the same time . This number was deemed excessive, so on November 26 the number of simultaneously running jobs for a given user was reduced from 4 back down to 2.

4.3 Future Directions

Inefficiencies in the current LoadLeveler job scheduler are a major cause for the long wait times and relatively low ceiling of 50,000 node-hours. To improve this situation, the CTC is planning to incorporate the EASY scheduler [5] into its environment. This scheduler offers several advantages:

- It requires much less overhead to acquire nodes
- It is deterministic and can thus inform users when their job will run
- As the workload progresses, it will update the time when jobs will run, shortening the time to execution if possible
- It has the ability to backfill with smaller jobs

Work is underway to interface EASY with the LoadLeveler API, thus minimizing the impact on our users. At first, EASY will be given a portion of the nodes to manage jobs which require no special resources. However, as EASY is enhanced to provide full resource management, it will replace the LoadLeveler job scheduler completely.

5 Conclusions

During the period of time when batch trace records have been analyzed, the workload on the CTC IBM SP2 has undergone a significant change. Through mid-September, it can be characterized as one featuring program development and debugging with a certain amount of modest production work. From that time onward, however, production computing has become more prominent. The median job duration, weighted by node-hours generated, increased from 6 hours in July to a peak of 15 hours in November. The median number of processors used also increased.

The workload data shows an upper bound of about 50,000 user-node hours consumed per week, despite the theoretical maximum of over 70,000. An examination of average weekly backlog data shows an increase from 250 nodes in early October to over 2000 in early December. During that same period, average wait times for the 15-minute queue rose from less than 50 minutes to about 900 minutes. All this is evidence that the upper bound is driven by system limitations in servicing the workload, not in the workload itself.

During the period of maturing workload (mid-September through early December), we observed that the 128MB nodes are most heavily requested in proportion to their numbers. The single 2GB node is also well used, but the remaining nodes are relatively under-requested. We also observed a sizable serial workload, primarily a legacy from a prior IBM mainframe.

A look at job duration profiles showed that jobs requesting 2-16 processors had relatively shorter run times than those requesting more processors. This is likely due to the fact that these smaller jobs reflect program development, whereas jobs with more processors are doing production work. User submittal patterns were examined, and it was found that the frequency of similar job submittals followed a Zipf's distribution.

The paper detailed several policy changes made in response to the changing workload and backlog of work to be done. Adding a new 15-minute queue for small parallel jobs had a dramatic, positive effect on the wait times. There was also a discussion of plans to incorporate the Argonne EASY scheduler into the CTC environment, with the hopes that this will increase the throughput of the machine.

References

1. T. Agerwala, J.L. Martin, J.H. Mirza, D.C. Sadler, D.M. Dias and M. Snir, "SP2 System Architecture". *IBM Systems Journal*, Vol. 34, No. 2, 1995.
2. R. Cypher, A. Ho, S. Konstantinidou and P. Messina. "Architectural Requirements of Parallel Scientific Applications with Explicit Communication". In *Proceedings of the 20th Annual International Symposium on Computer Architecture*, May, 1993. p. 2-13.
3. D.G. Feitelson and B. Nitzberg. "Job Characteristics of a Production Parallel Scientific Workload on the NASA Ames iPSC/860". *IPPS'95 Workshop on Job Scheduling Strategies for Parallel Processing*, April, 1995.
4. S.G. Hotovy, D.J. Schneider and T. O'Donnell. "Analysis of the Early Workload on the Cornell Theory Center IBM SP2". In *Proceedings of ACM SIGMETRICS Conference*, 1996 (to appear).
5. D.A. Lifka. "The ANL/IBM SP Scheduling System". *IPPS'95 Workshop on Job Scheduling Strategies for Parallel Processing*, April, 1995.

6. W. Pfeiffer, S. Hotovy, N.A. Nystrom, D. Rudy, T. Sterling and M. Straka. *JNNIE: The Joint NSF-NASA Initiative on Evaluation.* San Diego Supercomputer Center Technical Report GA-A22123, July, 1995.

7. M.E. Rosenkrantz, D.J. Schneider, R. Leibensberger, M. Shore and J. Zollweg. "Requirements of the Cornell Theory Center for Resource Management and Process Scheduling". *IPPS'95 Workshop on Job Scheduling Strategies for Parallel Processing,* April, 1995.

8. *IBM LoadLeveler Administration Guide,* IBM Document Number SH26-7220-02, October, 1994.

The EASY - LoadLeveler API Project

Joseph Skovira, Waiman Chan, Honbo Zhou
International Business Machines
David Lifka
Cornell Theory Center

Abstract. *With the increasing use of distributed memory massively parallel machines (MPPs) such as the IBM SP, the need for improved parallel job scheduling tools has sparked many recent developments. IBM's LoadLeveler is being used at the Cornell Theory Center, but problems exist with the current scheduling algorithm applied to the job mix on the 512-node SP. In order to address Cornell's difficulties, Joseph Skovira began to consider enhancements to LoadLeveler. At about the same time, David Lifka, developer of the EASY parallel job scheduler, began working at CTC. With Waiman Chan and Honbo Zhou of IBM LoadLeveler development, we have developed a LoadLeveler API that allows external schedulers like EASY to control the starting and stopping of jobs through LoadLeveler.*

1 Introduction

The EASY-LoadLeveler collaboration is interesting for several reasons. First, both EASY and LoadLeveler benefit. By interfacing to LoadLeveler, the EASY algorithm can more readily be expanded to heterogeneous MPPs using information already maintained by LoadLeveler. LoadLeveler benefits because parallel job scheduling can be externalized where it can then be easily customized for requirements at different sites. Second, both LoadLeveler and EASY have been proven on MPPs – both codes scale and have a measure of stability because of their maturity. Finally, this work introduces a new model for job scheduling. In effect, the task is segmented into administration and scheduling. In our case, LoadLeveler handles the administration (e.g., the job queue) information regarding node resources of the machine, status of jobs running throughout the machine, and information about the machine node status. EASY takes care of the job scheduling, that is, when a particular job should run and on which nodes it should run. Since the interface is externalized to a small number of calls, and since EASY is written in Perl, changes to the scheduling algorithm or policy can be quickly made at different sites without affecting the compiled code of LoadLeveler.

2 Background of EASY and LoadLeveler

EASY was originally developed at Argonne National Laboratory for use on Argonne's 128-node SP system. As required by many sites, Argonne had parallel job scheduling requirements not met by any commercial or research project then available (including LoadLeveler). The EASY algorithm was developed with several fundamental principles in mind. First, the job queue would be ordered by submission time – jobs would be considered for execution in the order they were submitted. If the first job in the queue could be scheduled to run on available nodes, it would be executed. If the next job in the queue could not run because enough nodes were not available, it would wait until enough nodes became free in order to run. This leads to the second principle: the scheduling algorithm is deterministic. Jobs in the queue are never delayed from running by jobs submitted to the queue after them. Finally, while a job is waiting for resources to free, smaller jobs further down the queue can be run as long as they complete before the waiting job is scheduled to run. In this way, jobs can be backfilled onto available nodes in order to make better use of machine resources. EASY is currently used by many MPP sites throughout the world and is known for its efficient scheduling, simplicity, and robustness. One note is that EASY schedules homogeneous nodes of an MPP. A mechanism in the algorithm to deterministically schedule special resources is currently under development.

Referring to the definition in [1], Loadleveler is a distributed, network-based, job scheduling program. LoadLeveler is a modified version of Condor that is sold by IBM. Condor was originally designed to schedule clusters of workstations. LoadLeveler was built on this base as a scheduler for MPP's, in particular, the IBM SP. LoadLeveler will locate, allocate, and deliver resources from across a network while attempting to maintain a balanced load, fair scheduling, and an optimal use of resources. The goal of LoadLeveler is to make better use of existing resources by using idle compute nodes and to optimize batch throughput. LoadLeveler is also used by many SP sites worldwide and is a product fully supported by IBM. However, the code is written in C and changes to its function (including parallel job scheduling) require redesign and re-release of the product by IBM.

3 Combining EASY and LoadLeveler

Although EASY is a standalone scheduling system that is proven to work on existing MPP systems, there are several reasons to integrate EASY with LoadLeveler instead of just enhancing EASY. First, LoadLeveler contains much more configuration information regarding the machine than EASY records, especially regarding differences between the nodes of a machine. The machine information is updated using the SP resource manager so that system changes are quickly reflected in the LoadLeveler data. Because these records and distribution mechanisms have proven reliable in LoadLeveler, we decided to take advantage of them in order to enhance EASY. Future versions of EASY will make use of this information to perform exact resource matching.

Another advantage occurs because LoadLeveler maintains daemons at every SP node. These Startd daemons are used to start user tasks at a particular node of the machine. Because these daemons are in place, starting and stopping jobs by the EASY scheduler occurs much faster than with standalone EASY, which uses rsh. This eliminates some amount of startup and shutdown overhead.

Using the new system, it becomes much simpler to switch between LoadLeveler and EASY scheduling. In fact, future modifications might include the capability to partition a single machine into pools of nodes which are scheduled using 2 (or more) different algorithms. This might prove useful as a way to take advantage of different algorithms strengths depending on the parallel job mix.

At the start of this effort, we considered which scheduling algorithm to interface with LoadLeveler, and the choice of EASY was a clear one. EASY is currently one of the most popular schedulers available for parallel jobs that provides deterministic queuing combined with straightforward interface features and simple administration. Also, being written in Perl, the algorithm is simple to understand and modify (both in terms of scheduling and policy). Both EASY and LoadLeveler are supported; LoadLeveler as an IBM product and EASY as a public domain code maintained by David Lifka. To cap the decision, the LoadLeveler group realizes the worth of the EASY algorithm, and David Lifka understands the information from LoadLeveler that can be used to enhance the EASY algorithm for resource scheduling.

A final choice to make was whether to include the EASY algorithm within LoadLeveler or to provide an interface for use with a modified version of the EASY code. The choice of an API was clear for several reasons. Including the EASY algorithm within LoadLeveler would require a rewrite from Perl to C, which would add time to the projected deployment of this solution. In fact, inclusion as C code proves more damaging due to the more static nature of the result. In order to change the scheduling algorithm, there would have to be a release of the LoadLeveler product. Even then, the scheduling algorithm would be static for all sites. By using an API, changes can be both prototyped and deployed quickly. In addition, different sites can implement different scheduling solutions tailored to their individual job mixes – a very powerful aspect of this solution. In fact, the API allows the EASY code to be totally replaced by an algorithm entirely designed by another SP administrator. As long as the API calling formats are followed, any scheduling algorithm can be implemented. The API may also be used to develop system administration tools an example of which is the service policy currently implemented by EASY. Using an external tool, nodes could be taken out of service quickly without restarting and reconfiguring LoadLeveler. Because the schedule API provides information about the nodes and the jobs, any reconfiguration of these data structures is possible by an external tool.

4 The Application Programming Interface between LoadLeveler and EASY

From the outset, we intended the API to be as straightforward as possible. Our first version was intended to provide the minimum functionality necessary to interface the EASY scheduler. As we learn more about the functioning of external scheduling algorithms, the interface will be appropriately expanded. The current interface consists of 4 calls. These calls are illustrated in figure 1, which also includes an illustration of job division between LoadLeveler and EASY. In figure 1, note that there were 3 tasks required to interface LoadLeveler with EASY. The first was to enhance LoadLeveler to provide the appropriate calls to be used by EASY. Next, the standalone EASY code was modified to interface with the new API functions. Finally, an interface layer was developed to convert the information returned in the LoadLeveler C structures into data as required by the EASY code, written in Perl. The following functions are provided by LoadLeveler to support external scheduling using the EASY scheduler:

ll_get_job: Retrieve the job queue - This call returns the contents of the LoadLeveler job queue. All jobs currently in the queue, including those running and waiting to run, are returned by this call.

ll_get_node: Retrieve the node status - The status of all SP2 nodes in the system is returned by this call.

ll_start_job: Start a job - EASY uses this call to begin the execution of a previously queued parallel job. Once EASY has determined that a job is to be started, it issues this call to LoadLeveler, along with a specific set of nodes on which to start the parallel job.

ll_cancel_job: Cancel a job - EASY issues this command to cancel a job when the execution time has exceeded a limit which the user has set.

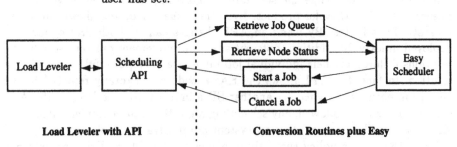

Figure 1 - Job partitioning and interface calls

Figure 2 shows how EASY would make use of the provided calls to examine the current job queue and machine status, decide which job to schedule, then start a job. At Cornell, this new version is being tested, maintaining the existing LoadLeveler interfaces for the users (which include job submission and job command files). In addition, this new version will provide a wall-clock run-time variable in LoadLeveler, which EASY requires, and EASY commands for examining the operation of the job scheduling system. EASY tools like spq, spusage, and xspusage will become available for the Cornell users.

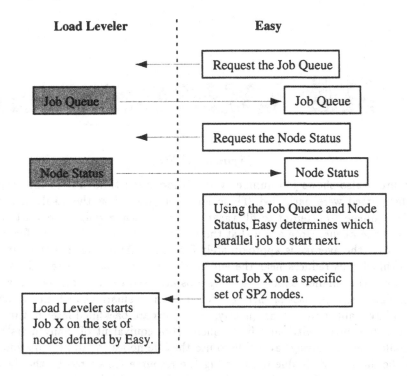

Figure 2 - Starting a job across the Interface

5 Performance and Scalability

During our initial testing, we have started to collect performance statistics for the LL-EASY code. Figures 3 and 4 shows the results obtained from submitting 1000 jobs to an 8 node SP2 system using LL-EASY. Figure 3 shows the time it takes to start jobs from the FIFO queue. These jobs were not backfilled into available resources but, rather, started once they arrived at the top of the queue. The startup time axis represents the total startup time beginning with the scheduler requesting job information from LoadLeveler, deciding which job to start, calling LoadLeveler to start the job, and completing with the job actually being dispatched by LoadLeveler to the appropriate nodes. The longest time recorded was 13 seconds for job 31, the average was approximately 5 seconds. Note that the time decreases as the job queue is consumed (as expected). The discontinuities in the graph are caused by a lock on a resource file maintained by EASY which is asynchronously accessed by multiple daemons. We are developing a fix to solve this issue, but, even with this effect, jobs start very quickly. There is very little overhead in transferring even a large job queue from LL to EASY. Note also that rapid startup of the jobs is further enabled by the existence of the LL daemons at each of the nodes.

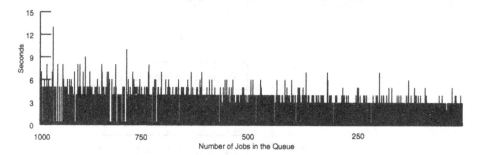

Figure 3 - FIFO Jobs

Figure 4 also shows job number versus submission time, but in this case, the jobs started were backfilled. These jobs were started as the result of a search of the queue to attempt to fill vacant resources while waiting to start the top job in the queue. Note again that the worst case time is 12 seconds for job 220 and that the average is approximately 5 seconds. Also note that the number of backfilled jobs reduces near the end of the test, also as expected. This occurs because the smaller, shorter running jobs are used early to fill the holes in the schedule. As time passes, there are fewer of these small jobs which can be used to fill available nodes, consequently, fewer jobs are backfilled later in time. This effect disappears with an infinite queue (the equivalent of many users!) since smaller jobs are always available to use the idle nodes. Again, the discontinuity of the data is partly due to accessing the resource file shared by the daemons. However, some of the spike amplitude in the backfill data is due to searching deep into the queue to find a job to backfill (note the spike for job 730). Although the search is quickly performed, it is not done for the FIFO jobs of figure 3, so later spikes in the backfill data of figure 4 tend to be larger than those of figure 3. Nonetheless, the time to start backfill jobs is also very short.

Figure 4 - Backfilled Jobs

So far, performance data for the algorithm is excellent. The short startup times indicate that the combined LL and EASY algorithms operate efficiently and can dispatch jobs even for a large queue in under 13 seconds per job, worst case, and under 5 seconds per job, on average. With this low overhead, utilization of the machine is not hindered by the scheduling algorithm.

6 Future Plans

We plan to incorporate deterministic scheduling of heterogeneous resources in the EASY scheduling algorithm by Spring 1996. This will include enhancements to the LoadLeveler API so that resource information can be passed to the scheduler. We also plan to incorporate dynamic process allocation in such a way that does not break the determinism of the EASY algorithm. EASY keeps track of the number of nodes that are available and that will not be required for the jobs waiting in the queue. If a parallel job needs additional resources during a run, a mechanism will be provided for the job to ask EASY for access to these nodes. We plan to build this capability in by late 1996.

References

1 Kaplan, J., Nelson, M., *A Comparison of Queueing, Cluster and Distributed Computing Systems*. NASA TM 109025 (Revision 1) - 1, NASA Langly Research Center, (1994)

2 Lifka, D., Henderson, M.,and Rayl, K.,ANL/MCS-TM-201, *Users Guide to the Argonne SP Scheduling System*, Mathematics and Computer Science Division, Argonne National Laboratory, Argonne, IL (1995)

3 Lifka, D., *The ANL/IBM SP Scheduling System*, Mathematics and Computer Science Division, Argonne National Laboratory, Argonne, IL (1995)

4 Rosenkrantz, M., Schneider, D., Leibensperger, R., Shore, M., Zollweg, J., *Requirements of the Cornell Theory Center for Resource Management and Process Scheduling*, Cornell Theory Center, Ithaca NY (1995)

A Batch Scheduler for the Intel Paragon with a Non-contiguous Node Allocation Algorithm

Michael Wan, Reagan Moore, George Kremenek and Ken Steube
San Diego Supercomputer Center
P.O.Box 85608, San Diego, Ca 92186-9784
E-mail: mwan, moore, kremenek, steube @ sdsc.edu

Abstract

As the system usage model for scalable parallel processors evolves from the single-user, dedicated access model to a multi-user production environment, a versatile batch scheduler is needed to match user requirements to system resources. This paper describes the design and performance of a batch scheduler for the Intel Paragon system that addresses the issues associated with a multi-user production environment, including scheduling for heterogeneous nodes, scheduling for long-running jobs, scheduling for large jobs, prime/non-prime time modes, and node allocation schemes. The Modified 2-D Buddy system (M2DB) for non-contiguous node allocation is introduced and studied in this paper.

1.0 Introduction

As large parallel processor systems become heavily used, there is a need for the system usage model to evolve from single-user, dedicated access to a much more versatile multi-user production environment. A key component for satisfying this need is a job scheduler capable of handling the scheduling of both interactive and batch jobs submitted by multiple users.

This paper describes the design and performance of a batch scheduler for a 416-node Intel Paragon system in production use at the San Diego Supercomputer Center (SDSC).

The usage requirements for interactive and batch jobs can be quite different. Typically, interactive usage is for debugging and short production jobs that use a small number of nodes, while batch usage is mostly for long production jobs using a large number of nodes. To handle the disparate node size and execution time scales, space sharing is used. The nodes of the Paragon may be divided into groups called partitions. In our usage model, two non-overlapping partitions -- the Interactive and Batch partitions, -- are used. Interactive jobs are processed in the Interactive partition, and long-running production jobs are executed in the Batch partition. A concern with this type of space sharing is that the Interactive partition may be idle a large fraction of the time, and typically is idle at night. This concern is mitigated when the number of nodes devoted to the Interactive partition is relatively small when compared to the total number of nodes in the computer.

The scheduling of jobs in the Interactive partition is supported by a sequential node assignment mechanism provided by the Paragon operating system. Jobs are scheduled on a first-come-first-serve basis. An interactive job is rejected if there are not enough free nodes to satisfy the request.

The scheduling of jobs in the Batch partition is handled by the SDSC batch scheduler which is the subject of this paper. The batch scheduler is based on the Network Queuing System (NQS) [1]. NQS is a client/server queuing system originally designed for vector supercomputers running the traditional UNIX operating system. The SDSC batch scheduler uses the job queuing framework provided by NQS to which we have added a scheduling layer for assigning node partitions on the Paragon parallel computer.

This project was funded by the SSD (Supercomputer Systems Division) of Intel Corporation. This software has been adopted by Intel and became a part of the software release for the Paragon supercomputer.

1.1 Design Requirements

The design requirements for the parallel batch scheduler are based on the need at SDSC to handle multiple classes of batch jobs, a heterogeneous hardware configuration, and time varying usage patterns. The related issues are:

• Node allocation - Allocating nodes to an application involves the selection of a set of nodes from a pool of free nodes in the 2-D mesh. The Paragon architecture allows non-contiguous node allocation; the nodes of a given parallel job do not have to be physically adjacent. This flexibility has the potential of greatly improving the node utilization of the system. This is particularly true after the system has been up for some time at which point the free nodes in the system tend to be fragmented. Non-contiguous allocation , however, may have the problem of message contention because of the potential for longer message paths (and more hops) and interference with messages from other jobs. Fortunately, with the wormhole routing [2] technology used in the Paragon communication backplane, the number of hops between nodes is no longer the dominant factor affecting message latency as shown in a communication contention study by Lo, et. al. [3]. Hence, the primary performance objective of the SDSC scheduling scheme is maximizing node utilization through non-contiguous allocation. The scheduling scheme does the following:

1) Allocates a job if there are enough free nodes available even if the set of nodes to be allocated is fragmented.

2) Allocates exactly the number of nodes requested. Jobs are scheduled on a space sharing basis. No time sharing is assumed.

3) Tries to minimize fragmentation to reduce communication contention.

• Prime/Non-prime times - The batch scheduler needs to support the notion of Prime (daytime) and Non-prime (night/weekend) times. The scheduler provides the flexibility of configuring the batch and interactive partitions differently during day and night. For example, during prime time, we may want to allocate a large number of nodes to the interactive partition while during non-prime time, most of the nodes should be allocated to the batch partition.

• Heterogeneous nodes - Paragon systems can contain nodes with various physical attributes. For example, nodes may have different memory sizes (16-MBytes or 32-MBytes), or may have a different number of CPUs (GP - single CPU or MP - two CPUs). The batch scheduler must be capable of scheduling nodes by hardware request type. In addition, an option is needed for jobs that can use multiple types of nodes. For example, a given job may be able to use either the 16 MB or the 32 MB GP nodes. The ability to schedule jobs that can utilize multiple node types as compared to restricting jobs to only a single node type can increase node utilization.

• Short running jobs - Since node allocation is based on space sharing only, long running batch jobs can block the execution of short jobs waiting in a batch queue. During prime time, we may need to reserve some nodes for the exclusive use of short running batch jobs.

• Large batch jobs - For a job mix consisting of both small and large jobs, the smaller jobs tend to get scheduled first because it is easier to fit the smaller jobs into the available nodes. Once we have several smaller jobs running in the system, it will become even more difficult for a large job to be scheduled because a large job may need the nodes used by the smaller jobs. Therefore, a mechanism is needed to enhance the chance of large jobs getting scheduled.

Section 2.0 gives a summary of the Paragon parallel batch scheduler design. Section 3.0 gives a summary of the workload characteristics, and Section 4.0 gives the performance analysis of the scheduler for the 416-node Paragon at SDSC.

2.0 The Paragon Parallel Batch Scheduler

The Paragon parallel batch scheduler is based on version 2 of the NQS queuing system. A scheduling layer was added to NQS to schedule jobs for the Paragon system. The following gives a summary of the enhancements:

2.1 Enhancement for NQS Commands

A new option "-lP" has been added to the "qsub" command which is used for submitting batch jobs. This new option allows users to request a specific number of nodes on which to run the batch job.

In addition, a new subcommand has been added to the "qmgr" command. The"qmgr" command is an interactive program used by the NQS administrator tocontrol and configure the local NQS system. The new subcommand

```
set per_request ncpus = N  QUEUE
```

allows an NQS administrator to specify the default number of nodes (N) for a specific batch queue (QUEUE). That is, if a job is submitted to a given batch queue without specifying the number of nodes for the job, it will default to the ncpus value of the specified queue.

2.2 Grouping of Nodes into "node sets" and "node groups"

In order to provide scheduling support for heterogeneous nodes and node reservation for short running jobs during prime time, it is necessary to provide a framework for partitioning the nodes in the system. The framework also provides a way to associate scheduling policies with physical node sets.

Nodes are first partitioned into non-overlapping "node sets". The physical attributes of nodes in a given "node set" should be identical because they are treated as such by the scheduler.

"Node groups" are then constructed by combining one or more "node sets".
Overlapping "node groups" are allowed. i.e., a given "node set" can be assigned to more than one "node group". Each NQS queue is associated with a single "node group". Scheduling policies are enforced by linking each NQS queue to a particular usage requirement. Queues may be set up for short-running jobs or for jobs needing large memory nodes, or nodes with multiple CPUs.

The two level grouping provides a mechanism for scheduling heterogeneous node sets as well as the flexibility for implementing scheduling policies. The "node set" provides a low level grouping of all nodes to be scheduled by the scheduler. These "node sets" are then assigned to various "node groups" to support specific scheduling policies. The following simple example illustrates the use of this framework for the scheduling of different types of nodes.

Consider a system with two different types of nodes - 8 nodes with 16 MB of memory and 16 nodes with 32 MB of memory. They are partitioned into two "node sets":

    node_set 1: 16 nodes with 32 MB of memory
    node_set 2: 8 nodes with 16 MB of memory

We create three "node groups" with the following "node set" assignment:

"node group"	"node sets" assigned to the "node group"
1	1
2	2
3	1, 2

"Node groups" 1 and 2 are for jobs that only want to run on the 32 MB and 16 MB memory nodes, respectively. "Node group" 3 is for jobs that can use nodes with either memory size.

The "node sets" associated with a given "node group" can be switched as a function of the time period (prime, non-prime or both) during which the nodes will be used. For example :

"node group"	"node sets" to use during prime time	"node sets" to use during non-prime time
4	1	1
5	–	1

"Node group" 4 uses "node set" 1 during both prime and non-prime times, but "node group" 5 can only use "node set" 1 during non-prime time. If we assign "node group" 4 to short running jobs and "node group" 5 to long running jobs, we in effect allow only short running jobs to use "node set" 1 during prime time. This configuration will give good throughput for short running jobs during the day.

Once a job has been selected for allocation, the scheduler selects free nodes by scanning the "node sets" associated with the "node group". It may take up to two passes to accomplish the task. During the first pass, the scheduler tries to find the "node set" with the minimum number of free nodes that can satisfy the entire request. If such a "node set" cannot be found, the scheduler will allocate free nodes from "the node sets" in the order specified in the definition of the "node group" that is associated with the NQS queue to which the job was originally submitted.

Within a "node set", nodes are allocated using the modified 2-D buddy strategy described in section 2.4.

2.3 Job Priority and Scheduling of Large Jobs

The original NQS system scheduled jobs according to the "queue priority" assigned to each NQS queue. Jobs were queued up at each NQS queue in the order of submission time. When NQS scheduled jobs to run, it looked through each queue, one queue at a time, starting with the queue with the highest "queue_priority". This simple scheme does not allow a job queued in a low priority queue to be scheduled ahead of jobs in the high priority queue, no matter how long it has been waiting in the queue.

To enhance scheduling flexibility, we introduced the concept of aging. With this scheme, the job priority is calculated as follows:

$$job\_priority = queue\_priority + age\_factor * time$$

where
　　queue_priority = priority associated with the queue to which the job is submitted;
　　age_factor = A constant factor to be defined by the NQS administrator;
　　time = time in hours the job has been waiting in the queue.

For scheduling purposes, all jobs are sorted in the order of job_priority and the scheduler picks jobs to run starting with the highest priority job. If there are not sufficient free nodes to schedule the highest priority job, the next highest priority job will be considered and so on.

For example, the queue_priorities of our LONG (12 hr limit) and SHORT (1 hr limit) queues are 10.0 and 12.0, respectively. With an age_factor of 0.1, it will take a LONG job 20 hours waiting in queue to make up the 2.0 difference in queue_priority for a short job.

As noted earlier, large jobs have a more difficult time getting scheduled to run then smaller jobs. To ensure that large jobs do get scheduled, we introduced the concept of blocking controlled by a constant "block_priority" that is set by the NQS administrator. Under blocking, nodes are deliberately kept idle until enough free nodes are available to schedule the large-node job. If blocking is enabled (by setting the "block_priority" to greater than zero), the scheduler will check whether the "job_priority" of the highest priority job is greater than the "block_priority". If it is and if there are not enough free nodes to schedule this job, scheduling of new jobs will be blocked until there are sufficient free nodes for this job. The idea is that if a large job is an important job (high queue_priority) or if it has been waiting in queue for a while (aging), idle nodes will be accrued through the blocking mechanism until the job is able to run.

For example, if

queue_priority = 10.0
age_factor = 0.1
block_priority = 15.0

a job will wait in this queue for 50 hours (to increase priority from 10.0 to 15.0 through aging) before blocking will begin.

2.4 The Modified 2-D Buddy System (M2DB)

The two-dimensional buddy system proposed by Li and Cheng [4] is an allocation strategy for a square mesh-connected system. The strategy is only applicable to situations where all incoming jobs are square submeshes of dimension (n x n) and the mesh is a square mesh of size (N x N), where both n and N are power of 2 integers. This geometric limitation could have an adverse
effect on the node utilization of the system if user jobs use other node sizes. The allocation and deallocation overheads of the strategy are both O(log n).

The Paragon architecture is typically a non-square mesh. The Paragon OS can allocate non-square and non-contiguous nodes to a job. The nodes of a given parallel job do not have to be physically adjacent. We introduce an allocation strategy - Modified 2-D Buddy System (M2DB), which is an extension of the 2-D buddy strategy. It uses the basic tree data structure of the 2-D Buddy System, but can take advantage of the geometric flexibility provided by the Paragon architecture. Basically, this strategy attempts to schedule a job by allocating one or more rectangular blocks. The blocks allocated to a job can be non-contiguous.

As described in section 2.2, the Paragon mesh is configured into disjoint "node sets"; "node groups" are then constructed as groups of these "node sets". Each node set is a rectangular submesh of nodes with the same physical attributes. The M2DB system is used to allocate nodes within each "node set". This strategy is similar to the Multiple Buddy Strategy (MBS) proposed by Lo et. al. [3]. The primary difference between the two strategies is in the Buddy generation scheme described in 2.4.2..

2.4.1 The Modified 2-D Buddy System (M2DB) allocation algorithm

Similar to the 2-D buddy system, M2DB attempts to satisfy a request by repeatedly breaking down the rectangular submesh of a "node set" into smaller blocks. The search algorithm is governed by the following steps:

1) The first step involves allocating an "anchor block" which is the first block to be allocated. First, the free block list is searched for a single free block that is the same size as the requested size. If such a block can be found, we are done.

2) If there are sufficient free blocks each smaller than the requested size but with the aggregate size greater than or equal to the requested size, go to step 4).

3) Search for the smallest free block that is larger than the requested size. Break the block into smaller blocks (buddies) and go to step 1). The algorithm for breaking down a block is described in 2.4.2.

4) There is now a pool of free blocks each smaller than the requested size but with the aggregate size greater than or equal to the requested size. Pick the largest block from this pool as the "anchor block" and the requested size is decremented by the size of the "anchor block".

5) After an "anchor block" has been selected, subsequent blocks are chosen that are as close as possible to the "anchor block", where closeness is defined as the sum of the distance between the four corners of the anchor block and the corresponding corners of the new candidate block. The distance between two points (x, y) and (X, Y) is defined as:

$$\text{distance} = (x-X)*(x-X)+(y-Y)*(y-Y)$$

where x, y define the number of nodes in the horizontal and vertical directions from the upper left corner of the mesh.

The objective is to minimize the communication path between each node in the anchor block and each node in the candidate block. That is, minimize the sum of the path length between each node in the anchor black and each node in the candidate block. We found from various hypothetical cases that using our four-corner equation generally gave the same answer as the more time consuming path length sum calculation.

6) If the size of the closest free block is greater then the remaining requested size, the block will be broken down into small blocks (buddies). Then step 5) is repeated.

7) Steps 5) and 6) are repeated until the remaining requested size is zero.

2.4.2 Buddy Generation Algorithm

In the M2DB system, each block is a rectangular submesh and is represented by <x, y, h, w> where <x, y> is the location of the upper left most node, and h and w represent the height and width, respectively of the rectangle.

In the normal 2D buddy system, a square block is split into four square buddies with identical size by splitting h and w in half. In the case of M2DB, since a block can be a rectangle of arbitrary w and h, we can split w and h in an arbitrary way and create buddies of arbitrary size. However, although it is no longer required that a job request size must be of power of 2 integer as in the case of the hypercube architecture, it is our experience that an overwhelming majority of the job request sizes are powers of 2. Therefore, a goal of the buddy generation algorithm should be to make the scheduling of jobs requesting a number of nodes that is a power of two as easy as possible.

Our M2DB algorithm breaks down a block into two or four smaller blocks (buddies), depending on the dimension (h and w) of the block. The dimensions of the buddies do not necessarily have to be identical. The M2DB Buddy generation algorithm is described in the following:

Determine the largest power of 2 integers, one for the width (W2) and one for the height (H2) that are less than or equal to the width (w) and the height (h), respectively, of the block to be split.

$$H2 <= h$$
$$W2 <= w$$

Depending on the values of h and w, the following situations arise :

1) h == w == H2 == W2, a power of 2 square mesh. The block will be broken down into four identical square buddies in the same manner as the normal 2D Buddy system. If the original block is represented by <x, y, w, h>, the four buddies are :

<x,	y,	W2/2,	H2/2>
<x+W2/2,	y,	W2/2,	H2/2>
<x+W2/2,	y+H2/2,	W2/2,	H2/2>
<x,	y+H2/2,	W2/2,	H2/2>

2) h == H2, w == W2, h > w, a power of 2 rectangular mesh. The block will be broken down into two identical buddies:

<x,   y,   2,   H2/2>
<x,   y+H2/2,   W2,   H2/2>

Two identical buddies are created by splitting h (the longer side) in half.

```
   W2
 ┌──────┐
 │      │
 │ H2/2 │
 │      │
 ├──────┤
 │      │
 │ H2/2 │
 │      │
 └──────┘
```

3) h == H2, w == W2, h < w, a power of 2 rectangular mesh. The block will be broken down into two identical buddies:

<x,   y,   W2/2,   H2>
<x+W2/2,   y,   W2/2,   H2>

Two identical buddies are created by splitting w (the longer side) in half.

```
    W2/2        W2/2
 ┌────────┬────────┐
 │        │        │
 │ H2     │        │
 │        │        │
 └────────┴────────┘
```

4) h == H2, w != W2, a rectangular mesh with a power of 2 only on one side. The block will be broken down into two unequal buddies:

<x,   y,   W2,   H2>
<x + W2,   y,   w-W2,   H2>

The non-power-of-2 side w is split into W2 and (w - W2) creating one large power-of-2 rectangular/square mesh and one smaller rectangular mesh.

```
     W2       w-W2
 ┌────────┬─────┐
 │        │     │
 │ H2     │     │
 │        │     │
 └────────┴─────┘
```

5) h != H2, w == W2, a rectangular mesh with a power of 2 only on one side. The block will be broken down into two unequal buddies:

<x,   y,   W2,   H2>
<x,   y + H2,   W2,   h - H2>

The non-power-of-2 side h is split into H2 and (h - H2) creating one large power-of-2 rectangular/square mesh and one smaller rectangular mesh.

```
      W2
 ┌──────────┐
 │          │
H2│          │
 │          │
 ├──────────┤
 │          │
h-H2│          │
 └──────────┘
```

6) h != w, h != H2, w != W2, a non-power-of-2 rectangular mesh. The block will be broken down into four unequal buddies:

<x,   y,   W2,   H2>
<x + W2,   y,   w - W2,   H2>
<x + W2,   y + H2,   w - W2,   h - H2>
<x,   y + H2,   W2,   h - H2>

The non-power-of-2 side h is split into H2 and (h - H2), and w is split into W2 and (w - W2) creating one large power-of-2 rectangular/ square mesh and three smaller rectangular meshes.

```
      W2       w-W2
 ┌─────────┬─────────┐
 │         │         │
H2│         │         │
 │         │         │
 ├─────────┼─────────┤
 │         │         │
h-H2│        │         │
 └─────────┴─────────┘
```

The deallocation procedure returns all blocks owned by a job to the free pool and combines the buddies to restore the parent block.

Similar to the Multiple Buddy Strategy (MBS), the overhead associated with M2DB for both allocation and deallocation is O(n) for a system with n nodes since a maximum of n blocks will be allocated or deallocated.

3.0 Workload characteristics and Performance

At SDSC, the 416 nodes are partitioned as follows:

For normal UNIX interactive login and uses.	6 nodes in the service partition
Nodes where the I/O servers reside. Unreachable by users.	10 I/O nodes
For use by parallel jobs.	400 nodes in the compute partition

The compute partition is further divided into a 32-node Interactive partition and a

368-node Batch partition. Of the 368 nodes in the Batch partition,

256 nodes have 32-MB of memory and 112 have 16-MB of memory. In the batch scheduler, these nodes are partitioned into three "node sets" :

node set 1	112 nodes with 16 MB of memory
node set 2	224 nodes with 32 MB of memory
node set 3	32 nodes with 32 MB of memory for short jobs

During prime time (which runs from 9:00 AM to 5:00 PM), "node set" 3 is reserved for the exclusive use of short jobs (1 hr. time limit) but is added back into the 32 MB node pool during non-prime time.

Multiple "node groups" were constructed with various combinations of these "node sets" to support NQS queues with different size and time limits. The allowed node sizes ranged from 1 to 256 nodes and the default time limit varied from 1 to 12 hours.

3.1 Workload Characteristics

The Workload characteristics and performance analyses were carried out over a six month period from 04/01/95 to 09/30/95.

Table 1 gives a summary of the overall system performance and node utilization during the six month period. As can be seen in the table, most of the usage (97.8%) occurred in the Batch partition even though more Interactive jobs were processed. This is because most Interactive jobs are small, short running jobs. At any given time, there were on average 7.7 jobs running in the system.

As expected, the node utilization in the Interactive partition is low (20.5%). This is particularly true during non-prime time. However, the utilization of the Batch partition is reasonably high (78.2 %), especially considering the fact that 32 nodes have been reserved for the exclusive use of short jobs (1 hr. limit) during prime time. These nodes tended to be under-utilized during this time period. The overall utilization (Interactive and Batch) is 73.6 %.

Table 2 gives the overall utilization on a monthly basis from April through September, 1995. June and August usage is low because of summer vacation during the school year.

Table 1 - Overall system performance and node utilization (04/01/95-09/30/95)

System down time as percent of wall clock time (*)	3.8 %
System up time as percent of wall clock time	96.2 %
Total number of Interactive jobs	22536
Total number of Batch jobs	13224
Average number of jobs running at any given time	7.7
Interactive partition Usage as percent of total usage (**)	2.2 %
Batch partition Usage as percent of total usage	97.8 %
Interactive partition Utilization while the system was up (***)	20.5 %
Batch partition Utilization while the system was up	78.2 %
Overall Utilization (Interactive and Batch)	73.6 %

* - System down time includes both scheduled hardware and software maintenance, and unscheduled interrupts.
** - Usage is computed in terms of node hours. i.e., the product of node_used and execution_time summed over jobs.
*** - Utilization is the ratio of the node hours actually in use as compared with the available node hours (total number of nodes times the wall clock time) expressed as a percentage.

Table 2 - Monthly node utilization

Month	Utilization
April	76.3
May	77.8
June	65.7
July	77.9
August	68.2
September	74.9
Average	73.7

Table 3 gives the usage distribution as a function of request size. The request size with the highest usage is 64 nodes, followed by 128 nodes and 32 nodes. Also given in the table are the number of jobs processed as a function of request size. In the

Batch partition, excluding system backup jobs that ran on a single node, the request size with the largest number of jobs processed is 64, followed by 32 and 16. For the Interactive partition, a request size of 4 nodes is most popular, followed by 16 and 8. Jobs which requested non power of 2 nodes are included in nearest power of two value.

Table 3 - Usage distribution by request size

Request size	Usage Distribution (% of total)	Number of Batch jobs	Number of Interactive jobs
1	0.15	4987	3364
2	0.05	65	3391
4	0.27	785	6683
8	4.88	1267	3543
16	7.74	1642	3676
32	16.22	2095	1845
64	39.69	3477	12
128	25.09	629	18
256	5.86	122	4

Table 4 gives the number of jobs processed as a function of execution time. An execution time of one hour or less was most popular. For longer running jobs, the 12 hour execution time was quite common reflecting the maximum run time limit of 12 hours for batch jobs. Interactive jobs have a soft time limit of 30 minutes i.e., an interactive job will not be terminated automatically when it exceeds the time limit until another job requires the nodes it is using. On the other hand, if batch jobs exceed their limit, they will be terminated automatically.

Table 4 - Execution time distribution

Execution Time (hr)	Number of Batch jobs	Number of Interactive jobs
1.0	8555	22308
2.0	560	88
3.0	352	29
4.0	511	22
5.0	514	19
6.0	293	6
7.0	282	3
8.0	394	2
9.0	730	5
10.0	151	4
11.0	144	3
12.0	738	47

4.0 Performance of the Batch Scheduler

The Batch scheduler performed reasonably well in terms of utilizing the Batch partition. As shown in Table 1, the average utilization in the Batch partition over the six month period was 78.2 %. This is similar to the 77 % utilization with the Multiple Buddy Strategy (MBS) and significantly better than the 34-46 % for contiguous schemes (2DB, first fit, best fit) described in Ref. [3]. The 21.8 % idle time was caused by the following factors :

1) Not enough jobs to keep all nodes busy.

2) Partition fragmentation - There may be free nodes in the system, but too few to hold the smallest job in the batch queue.

3) Scheduling policy - For example, reserving 32 nodes for the exclusive use of short running jobs, blocking for large job scheduling, etc.

Table 5 gives a summary of scheduling throughput measured in terms of expansion factor and the average wait time for each NQS queue. The average wait time is the average time the jobs have been waiting in a queue before they are scheduled for execution. The Expansion factor is calculated from the following equation :

$$\text{Expansion factor} = (\text{execution\_time} + \text{wait\_time}) / \text{execution\_time}$$

It is a ratio of the total wall clock time (from job submission time to the end of execution time) to the actual execution time. It is a measure of how quickly a job gets done in competition with the submitted job load compared to immediate execution of the job on a dedicated system.

The characteristics of each queue are encoded in the queue names as follows:

Each queue name starts with the character "q", followed by an optional character "f", followed by an integer, and then followed by one of the characters - "s", "m" or "l". "f" means fat nodes with 32 MB of memory. If "f" is not specified, the 16 MB node is assumed. The integer describes the maximum number of nodes that can be requested for each job.

"s" means short jobs with a time limit of 1 hour.
"m" means medium jobs with a time limit of 4 hours.
"l" means long jobs with a time limit of 12 hours.

In addition, there are two low priority queues called fstandby (for 32 MB nodes) and standby (for 16 MB nodes), with a time limit of 12 hours.

For example, the queue name "qf128m" means it is a 32 MB node queue with a maximum of 128 nodes and a time limit of 12 hours for each job.

Table 5 - Scheduling throughput and Expansion factor

Queue	Number of jobs	Usage % of total	av. wait time (hrs) *	av. exec. time (hrs)	expa-n-sion factor **
q4t	1635	0.0	0.1	0.0	71.9
q4s	684	0.0	6.3	0.1	51.0
q8s	107	0.0	0.0	0.2	1.2
q16s	366	0.0	7.0	0.1	93.6
q32s	267	1.2	1.1	1.0	2.1
q64s	226	0.3	1.0	0.3	4.9
q32m	299	1.2	2.6	1.6	2.7
q64m	110	0.5	2.0	1.1	2.8
q128m	165	0.9	7.3	0.5	15.4
q256m	177	0.4	9.1	1.6	6.8
qll	3080	0.1	2.3	0.3	8.6
q32l	1178	8.4	2.6	5.2	1.5
q64l	724	19.5	5.7	5.0	2.1
q128l	173	8.8	16.8	4.6	4.6
qf8s	155	0.0	0.7	0.1	7.2
qf16s	254	0.0	1.4	0.1	15.7
qf32s	348	0.6	1.3	0.5	3.4
qf32m	659	1.5	1.0	1.2	1.8
qf64m	182	0.5	2.7	0.7	4.6
qf128m	75	0.1	5.3	0.2	24.7
qf256m	14	0.1	32.5	0.6	59.3
qf32l	500	8.9	4.5	6.9	1.7
qf64l	259	9.1	8.6	6.7	2.3
qf128l	109	6.6	14.4	5.6	3.6
qf256l	74	7.4	23.7	5.6	5.2
standby	1132	10.3	6.5	6.5	2.0
fstandby	271	13.4	72.3	7.2	11.1

* Ave wait time - Average time the jobs have been waiting in queue before they were scheduled for execution.
** Expansion factor = (execution_time + wait_time) / execution_time

As can be seen, the expansion factor varies from 1.2 to 93.6. The queue with the largest expansion factor had poor turnaround primarily because the execution time was very short compared to the wait time. In this situation, the absolute value of the wait time is more meaningful.

In general, the following conclusions can be made :

1) The wait time increases with increasing number of nodes requested.

2) The wait time is larger for jobs requesting 32-MB memory nodes than for jobs requesting 16-MB nodes.

3) The wait time increases for jobs requesting larger amounts of time. Large long-running jobs block other large long-running jobs from executing, limiting the overall throughput of the queue.

Overall, the throughput of all job classes was reasonably good. For jobs requesting 64 nodes or less, the average wait time for most of the job classes was significantly less than 10 hours.

Raw scheduling data for the SDSC Paragon during 1995 can be found in Ref. [5].

5.0 Summary and Conclusions

This paper describes the design and performance of a batch scheduler for the Intel Paragon system that addresses the various issues associated with a multi-user production environment. Issues addressed include scheduling for heterogeneous nodes, scheduling for long jobs, scheduling for large jobs, prime/non-prime time modes and node allocation schemes. A Modified 2-D Buddy system (M2DB) for non-contiguous node allocation was implemented and its performance studied in this paper.

The use of non-contiguous allocation scheme resulted in reasonably good node utilization in the Batch partition. The utilization for the six months studied was 78.2 %. This is quite similar to the 77 % utilization achieved with the Multiple Buddy Strategy (MBS) described in Ref. [3] which is also a non-contiguous allocation strategy.

Overall, the scheduler performed as expected. The throughput of all job classes was reasonably good. The average wait time for short-running jobs was reasonably short. Large jobs had to wait longer to be scheduled with the average wait time generally less than 24 hours.

The 78.2 % utilization achieved is probably near optimum after taking into consideration the effects of scheduling policies (e.g., reserving nodes for short-running jobs and blocking for large jobs) and fragmentation. The system utilization is expected to improve if time sharing (more than one job can be scheduled to run in a node at a time) becomes practical on the Paragon system. The current scheduling scheme assumes only space sharing. i.e., a node can be used by only one job at a time.

With time sharing, blocking for large jobs is no longer necessary. Large jobs can be scheduled immediately to time share with other jobs if not enough free nodes are available. The need to reserve nodes for short running jobs also diminishes because these jobs can also be scheduled to run immediately to time share with other jobs. The effect of fragmentation may diminish if the scheduler over-subscribes the nodes through time sharing. Our current batch scheduler is capable of scheduling jobs on a time share basis through tiling of jobs and gang-scheduling of overlapping jobs. The scheme allows up to three overlapping layers of tiling. Time sharing among these layers is achieved through the gang-scheduling mechanism of the Paragon OS. By manipulating the job priorities and the "rolling quantum" (time slices) assigned to each job, a great deal of job control capability can be provided. For example, the scheme can be used to "expand" the batch partition during non-prime time and "contract" during prime time to make room for interactive jobs. However, time sharing of jobs places a heavy burden on the paging system and is not practical at this time due to I/O bandwidth performance and disk space limitations.

6.0 Acknowledgments

This project was funded by the SSD (Supercomputer Systems Division) of Intel Corporation. We would like to thank Joe Carter, Jerry Kearns, Roy Larson, and Don Ochoa of Intel Corporation for their support and guidance.

References

[1] B. Kingsbury, H. Walter, M. Bridge and T. Carver. "NQS, Network Queuing System, Version 2.0", Cosmic Program # ARC-13179.

[2] L. M. Ni and P. K. McKinley. "A survey of wormhole routing techniques in direct networks". IEEE Trans. Computers, 1993.

[3] V. Lo, K. Windisch, W. Liu and B. Nitzberg. "Non-contiguous Processor Allocation Algorithm for Mesh-connected Multicomputers", paper to be published.

[4] K. Li and K. Cheng. "A two-dimensional buddy system for dynamic resource allocation in a partitionable mesh connected system". Journal of Parallel and Distributed Computing, 12:79-83, 1991.

[5] FTP://ftp.sdsc.edu//pub/sdsc/parallel/
paragon/paragon95.txt.Z

Architecture-Independent Request-Scheduling with Tight Waiting-Time Estimations*

Jörn Gehring, Friedhelm Ramme

Paderborn Center for Parallel Computing
University of Paderborn
Fürstenallee 11
33102 Paderborn, Germany

[joern | ram]@uni-paderborn.de

Abstract. In the course of the last few years, the user's interaction with parallel computer-systems has changed. A continuous growth in the number of interactive HPC-applications can be observed. When considering partitionable MPP-systems with exclusive usage of the physically separated regions, issues like the average waiting-time become more dominant for the users than the total system-throughput.

In this paper, we focus on the problem of scheduling an arbitrary mixture of resource-requests for batch and interactive applications in an architecture-independent manner. To help users plan their daily work tight waiting-time estimations are indispensable. However, the resulting scheduling problem interferes with the problem of mapping requests onto certain MPP-architectures to reduce their internal fragmentations.

We will show that this conflict can be alleviated by a distributed prover-verifier methodology. At first, we will introduce the distributed resource-management software CCS with its architecture-independent scheduling method. The message-based approach presented is used to verify the pre-calculated schedules with help of the system-dependent mapping instances. Simulations with the accounting data of our center have shown that tight waiting-time estimations can be made while the architecture-independent scheduling approach is still preserved. We will show that by using this methodology the mean error-value of the predicted waiting-time can be reduced by 76 %. Finally, we will discuss the impact of such a distributed resource-management system on the metacomputing challenge.

Keywords: Distributed Resource Management, Request-Scheduling, Metacomputing

---

* This work was partly supported by the German "Ministerium für Wissenschaft und Forschung" and the research cooperation NRW-Metacomputing. Further grants were provided by the "Stifterverband für die Deutsche Wissenschaft."

1 Introduction

As parallel systems become more commonly used, there is a growing awareness for the need of a resource management software. Such software is indispensable for MPP-systems where jobs can be isolated from each other, giving each the fiction of a dedicated (virtual) machine, and where accounting functions should be carried out. When talking about problems related to the resource management task one should bear in mind some important observations:

- Reliable parallel computer systems exist and various industrial codes have been ported [4].
- In parallel high-performance computing, interactive applications with 'an engineer in the loop' demand reasonable computing performance, short response-times, and a seamless runtime-environment. Traditional batch programs will be replaced more and more by this type of interactive applications.
- Significant progress was made in the Wide-Area Network technology. Bandwidth and latency were improved by some orders of magnitude that make advanced metacomputer applications possible [18].

One should also notice that currently more than a dozen operating-systems, runtime-kernels, or message-passing libraries are in use. The user's requirements are of an extremely wide range [7]. While analyzing the accounting data of our center, we found that the requested resources range from a single MPP-node to complete systems that were occupied for some minutes or up to some days. In the profile, no significant pattern could be identified.

Having made this observation, we concluded that any approach to the resource management problem should be highly independent of the system architectures to be managed, and at the same time it should be independent of the programming-environments currently preferred by MPP-users. Both conditions are indispensable to turn the idea of a virtual machine-room into practice [1, 14, 18].

In order to solve the request-scheduling problem for such an environment (see 3.1), one has to think about new methodologies that meet the demands of service providers as well as those of interactively working users. Not only the resources of an MPP-system demand an adequate scheduling mechanism, each MPP-user has to schedule his own time-constraints. During the past, this topic was frequently underestimated [7]. Indeed, the inability to run a program when desired sometimes causes significant user frustration, especially during the development-stage.

A possible solution would be to tell a user the estimated waiting-time after a resource-request is submitted. If this estimation is tight, a user can plan his work much more efficiently. On the other hand, if the estimation is too weak, it may occur that a user goes to lunch while his request is fulfilled. When he returns, the time is expired, the resources are released, and the bill has been made. The frustration will be even greater and the MPP-systems become labeled as being not usable in daily work.

The best estimation of the waiting-time can be made when the request-scheduler considers the constraints of all other users as well as all properties of the MPP-architecture in question and all details adopted from the system-configuration and its surrounding environment. The effort to develop such a scheduler will be tremendous. The resulting software-module will be very complex and highly dependent on architecture and installation. The expected life-time of such a software will be comparably short.

In this paper we will present an architecture-independent request-scheduling method and study the resulting waiting-time estimation problem. We will start with a short description of the management model (Sec. 2.1) and its realization by the Computing Center Software CCS (Sec. 2.2). The basic algorithms used for the request-scheduling task are introduced in Section (3). In Section (4.1), we study the waiting-time estimations when using autonomous scheduling algorithms. A verification protocol is presented in Section (4.2). In Section (4.3) it is shown that the interference between the request-scheduling problem and mapping problem can be exploited to get tight waiting-time estimations while keeping the request-scheduler independent of the system architecture. The simulation runs were performed with the accounting data gathered at our center. The paper will finish with a prospect for the upcomming metacomputer challenge.

2 A Comprehensive Approach

The Paderborn Center for Parallel Computing, PC^2, is equipped with a number of partitionable and freely configurable MPP-systems. The largest machine is a partitionable GCel from Parsytec with 1024 T 805 nodes. The most powerful machine currently is a partitionable GCPP with 128 MPC 601 processors. The systems of the PC^2 are used by more than 250 people in about 80 different projects. More than 50% of the users are working outside Paderborn. Users from all over Germany have access to the PC^2 by the research-net (WIN) at 34 Mbps. Especially for small and medium sized enterprises, fast modem- and ISDN-connections are provided.

Being one of the Europort benchmark sites, several industrial codes have been ported to these machines [4], with users from seven European nations have been working remotely at the PC^2.

This user-community, combined with unsuited system-software, has been the background for the large Computing Center Software project[2] at the PC^2. Right from the beginning, CCS was not directed to a single machine. The aim was to make various types of MPP-systems transparently, and thus more efficiently usable than before. A comprehensive management model was developed which was implemented as a distributed software system. The subject of the CCS framework is the resource management task-force. On the one hand, CCS is a research package to study different optimization topics, on the other it is a production environment serving our whole machinery.

---

[2] The URL of the CCS home-page is: http://www.uni-paderborn.de/pcpc/ccs

2.1 The Model

There is more to building up a virtual machine-room than just linking the HPC-systems by a fast interconnection network. It is a seamless environment that provides transparent access to various system architectures, it supports different runtime environments, uncountable user demands and also all the necessary administrative requirements. Taking this comprehensive view, four research do-

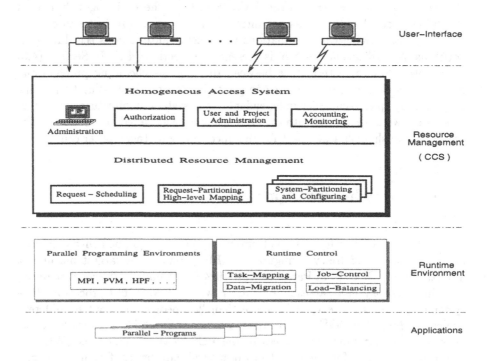

Fig. 1. A comprehensive metacomputer management model

mains can be identified which can be treated more or less independently (Fig. 1). While the CCS focus is on the resource management, a complementary project is initiated to improve the runtime environment [9].

In this paper we will study the interference between the architecture-independent request-scheduling task and the impact resulting from partitioning configurable MPP-systems.

The request-scheduling problem: When dealing with this problem, the utmost abstraction level can be assumed. Only the number of requested processors and an estimation of the occupation-time is taken into account. When the time is expired the resources are released. No assumptions are made about the facilities of the operating-system or the runtime-environment. Furthermore, we abstract from all constraints added by the architectures. Thus, the task is to determine a well-suited order of the hardware-requests to

- improve the overall utilization,
- reduce the average waiting-time,
- support interactive and batch applications simultaneously,
- support a priority mechanism while fairness has to be guaranteed,
- provide a high-level mechanism to decide if a resource-request can currently not be configured due to system internal fragmentations or whether this request can never be fulfilled by any machine under control. This decision should be made without knowledge of the architecture nor of the detailed system-configuration.

Another user-demand, not considered yet, is to support guaranteed reservations.

The architecture dependent mapping problem: This problem reflects the fact that most MPP-systems in public operation are variable- (or at least fixed-) partitionable. Thus, before a parallel program can be activated, a suited partition must be determined and the system must be configured accordingly. The shape of the partition might be subject of further optimizations. The goal of the mapping process is to reduce the internal fragmentation while fulfilling all of the architecture dependent constraints, (e.g.: each partition must have at least one I/O-link for host-access). An Intel iPSC, for example, must be partitioned into hypercubes of smaller dimensions, a Cray T3D into 3D-subcubes, a Parsytec GCel (GCPP) into rectangular subgrids. Such a subgrid must consist of so called atomic units. Due to hardware-internal restrictions, an atomic unit of a GCel is a 4x4 grid while an atomic unit of a GCPP is a 2x2 grid. While a GCel has some I/O-links into the inner area of its 2D-architecture, a GCPP can only be accessed from its outer border. Links and processor-nodes are dedicated to exclusive usage. With freely configurable MPP-architectures, completely different criteria come into question [8]. As there is (generally) no knowledge about the resource-requests of the future, further burdens are placed to the mapping decision.

2.2 The CCS Framework

The approach developed by PC^2 to tackle the resource management problem led to a distributed management-software running in the Unix environment in front of the HPC-systems. Its underlying multi-agent model was implemented as a system of communicating Unix daemons.

On the one hand, this gives the user the view of a virtual machine-room while on the other it offers various possibilities to optimize the selection of best suited machines, to improve the architecture dependent request mapping, and to optimize some of the conflicting scheduling goals. As a basic understanding of the distributed management model is necessary for this paper, a short description of CCS is given in the following. A detailed discussion of the software-package is presented in [16].

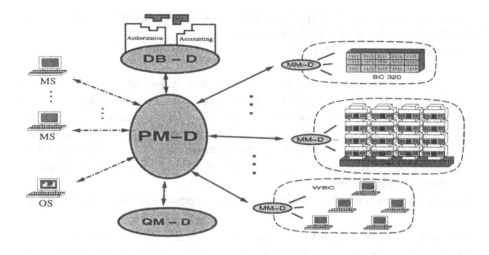

Fig. 2. The essential CCS daemons

The essential daemons of CCS are depicted in Fig. 2. The common user interface to CCS is the so called *Mastershell*. It offers a limited environment for creating Virtual Hardware Environments and running applications in interactive or batch mode. When a Mastershell comes up, a connection to the *Port-Manager Daemon* (PM-D) is established and data identifying the user (e.g. uid, hostname) are transferred. The PM-D uses this information to initiate a first authorization by asking the *Database Daemon* (DB-D). If the authorization failed, the user session is aborted immediately. Otherwise, the user has the whole command language of the Mastershell at his disposal. Currently, a replacement for the Mastershell is under construction. This new interface will turn the user's view into that of a client-server model. The multi-agent model of CCS, however, remains untouched. There are also discussions to develop a user-interface based on Java [2] to exploit the new internet facilities.

As an example, let us assume that a user requests a virtual hardware environment consisting of a number of processors in a certain configuration and exclusive usage for one hour. When such a request is ordered from the Mastershell the PM-D checks the user's limitations first, i.e. the number and kind of resources maximally allowed for the requesting user or project. If the request validation is successful, it is sent to the *Queue-Manager Daemon* (QM-D). The QM-D consists of a waiting-room and a request-scheduling module (Fig. 3). If the scheduler of the QM-D decides that a certain request should be fulfilled, this request is sent to the PM-D to be configured. In cooperation with the selected *Machine-Manager Daemons* (MM-Ds) the PM-D creates the requested hardware environment and supervises the corresponding time limits.

For authorization and accounting purposes the PM-D consults the DB-D. This daemon can be linked with two public interfaces, one for user management and the other for request accounting. In this way it is possible to connect commercial database systems or to adapt home-made software packages. When the requested resources are available, the user will be allowed to start an arbitrary application using nearly any type of runtime-environments.

Additionally, the PM-D provides logging facilities and preserves an operator interface for administering the virtual machine-room. Furthermore, the PM-D performs the request synchronization task and is responsible for the high-level request mapping. The MM-Ds perform the architecture dependent request mapping and the online system-configuration. If the MPP-architecture is flexible enough, various heuristics can be applied to reduce the internal fragmentation. An MM-D is the only architecture dependent part of the CCS-software. Thus, integrating a new system family can simply be done by re-implementing the corresponding MM-D. The QM-D is responsible for solving the request-scheduling problem in an architecture independent manner. A possible solution of this problem is outlined in Section (3).

This functional distribution of services gives CCS the power and flexibility to support a wide range of MPP-architectures [14].

The main features of CCS are the following:
- Uncoupled user- and system-views.
- Transparent access to MPP-systems with different architectures.
- Arbitrary mixture of interactive and batch applications within the virtual machine-room.
- Optimized request-scheduling.
- Dynamic partitioning of MPP-systems in order to reduce their internal fragmentations.
- Central authorization, accounting and charging facilities.
- Highly independent of the runtime-environment and the HPC architectures.
- Support for unstable WAN-connections. (Even if a dial-up line breaks down, a parallel application (batch or interactive) will continue running. A user can reconnect his 'old' application by logging in again and typing only two commands.)

The distributed method described turned out to be very flexible. However, doing request-scheduling without knowledge of the later mapping-decision leads to weak waiting-time estimations and thus unpleasant user-reactions. How this problem can be alleviated without sacrificing the architecture-independent approach is shown in (4.2).

3   Architecture-Independent Request-Scheduling

As all MPP-systems of the PC^2 are at least variably partitionable, there is no doubt that in the whole context request-scheduling plays a major role. Similar to Intel's iPSC and Paragon, or Cray's T3D, the Parsytec GC-systems are partitioned into disjoint sets of processors. Afterwards, a parallel job is executed in the physically separated regions of the systems. Thus, each parallel program comes along with an (explicit) request for hardware resources. Furthermore, the maximum duration for which an application is allowed to occupy its resources is given.

These requests are equal for batch and interactive applications. In addition, the interactive one needs a (virtual) terminal for keyboard input and screen output. Both types of applications are strongly competitive. While for batch applications the overall throughput is the first priority, users working interactively count the minutes until their hardware-requests are fulfilled. As a user is already satisfied when he can start working, issues like the total system throughput or the average response-time are less valuable. As the completion-time is subject to change, especially in interactive user-sessions, the average waiting-time seems to be much more important.

3.1 The Scheduling Model

Hundreds of papers have been written about job scheduling in parallel systems (see [6]). However, there is a large discrepancy between what is studied and what can be applied in practise. This discrepancy is even greater to what is delivered by the MPP-vendors. Thus, more sophisticated methods were developed by supercomputing centers serving large MPP systems to a broad user community. For example, an NQS based scheduler for the Intel Paragon was developed by the San Diego Supercomputer Center [20]. A more flexible approach was developed by the Cornell Theory Center to schedule their 512 node IBM SP [17].

In this section we will now motivate a request-scheduling system which alleviates some of the difficulties mentioned. This method has already proved successful in daily operation. A more detailed description is presented in [15].

The scheduling model we are using for the simulation purpose is very close to the constraints described in the previous sections. We assume that the virtual machine-room consists of a number of MPP-systems with similar characteristics. Each is composed of processing nodes of a certain type and a number of user entries. All resource-requests are dedicated to exclusive usage and are limited by the time a virtual hardware environment can be occupied by the application program.

The resulting request-scheduling problem can now be conceived as an n-dimensional bin-packing problem. One dimension corresponds to the continuous time flow and $(n-1)$-dimensions are representing general system characteristics (e.g. the number of processors of a certain type or the number of user-entries). As a high-level decision mechanism must be provided at the QM-D to determine whether a request can ever be fulfilled, we are restricted to level-oriented scheduling algorithms (see [15]). If the first request at a scheduling-point (which corresponds to a new packing-level) is rejected by the MM-Ds, it can never be fulfilled and thus must be removed. To keep the model manageable, only the expected occupation-time and the number of requested processors are considered. All other (architecture-dependent) properties are on the mapping-modules of the MM-Ds. Since the scheduler has the view of ideal MPP-systems it may happen that single machines are over-booked. Thus, an MM-D will reject one or more requests, because they can not be configured any more. Now, it is up to the protocol between the QM-D and the MM-D to solve this conflict.

While doing this, four aims have to be considered: A priority mechanism must be provided, fairness must be guaranteed, the average waiting-time must be small, and the total utilization high. It is up to the scheduler to optimize the latter two. Handling priorities is mainly a question of the waiting-room organization. Fairness in this context means that no resource-request should pend forever. Furthermore, it must be possible to give an estimation of the waiting-time for each pending request. This topic interferes with both the waiting-room and the scheduling-module. Thus, both parts are integrated into the QM-D, whereby the algorithms of the scheduler can be switched by an operator or automatically, as it is done by the Implicit Voting System IVS (3.3). The basic structure of the QM-D is shown in Fig. 3.

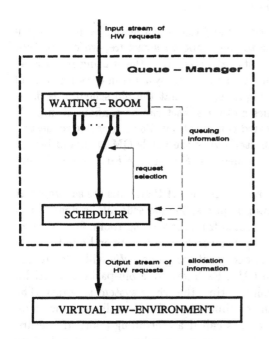

Fig. 3. Structure of the QM-D

The waiting-room is organized in n priority-queues. If the scheduler runs out of work a finite set of pending requests is extracted from the waiting-room. The number of requests to be extracted from each queue $(E_x(p_i) := \left\lceil \frac{N(p_i) * E(p_i)}{E_m} \right\rceil)$ depends on the extraction-order assigned to each queue by the administrator $(E(p_i))$ and its current filling-degree $(N(p_i))$. It is relative to the filling-degree of other priority-classes $(E_m = \max \{1, \max\{E(p_i) \mid N(p_i) \neq 0; 0 \leq i \leq n\}\})$. Using this formula, fairness is guaranteed for the priority-queues of the waiting-room. If fairness can be guaranteed by the scheduler as well (that means even if the scheduler has to handle temporarily rejected requests, non of those requests can be shifted forever), the whole system will behave fairly. If the scheduling algorithm used behaves deterministically, if no new requests of higher priority overtake others in the meantime, if the estimated occupation-times are accurate, and if there is an ideal hardware environment, then we can directly calculate the waiting-time for each request.

However, practise looks somewhat different. Thus, we can only estimate the expected waiting-times. The problem of overtaking within the waiting-room can not be avoided because we have an online system without knowledge of the future. The time-limit given with each resource-request can be treated as an upper bound. But it may happen that an interactively working user will release his resources earlier than promised. If now the management software keeps that partition idle, the time estimations are still valid. We prefer to use this free resources again, which however can result in shorter waiting-times than previously told. Thus, the error-values of the predicted waiting-time (see 4.1 and 4.2) will become negative. In practise this can be alleviated up to a certain degree by also accounting for reserved but unused resources. During the simulations this situation does not occur, as we are using the accounting data of our center as input sequence.

Thus, in our scheduling model we consider a real hardware environment, not known in detail, a waiting-room within which new requests with higher priority can overtake others, together with a deterministic scheduling algorithm.

3.2 Basic Scheduling Primitives

Having introduced the combined priority and queuing scheme, we now concentrate on optimization aspects. Due to the proposed structure, we can use the advantage that the number of requests extracted from the waiting-room is always finite. First of all, let us assume that the MPP-systems in question are not saturated, that there are pending requests, and that the old schedule is done. In this case, most or all of the requests of the subset can be configured immediately. There is no need for sophisticated computations. Passing on the requests is the best we can do. Thus, from the user's view the whole QM-D should behave transparently. This mode is simply called the *First-Come-First-Serve* (FCFS) mode of the scheduler.

From now on, we deal with the case where the MPP-systems are saturated up to a certain degree, there are pending requests, the old schedule is done, and a finite set of pending requests was extracted from the waiting-room. Furthermore, we assume that this set is ordered by the corresponding upper bound of time each hardware request is allowed to occupy its resources. We will refer to this ordered set by the term *request-list* (RL). Each level of a bin-packing algorithm indicates a situation where at a point of time the whole system is empty. This is the case with all vertical lines on the time-axis and if these lines do not cross any rectangle (Fig. 5 – 6). Such a level is called a scheduling-point. If the first (requeued) request can not be configured at a scheduling point, it will never be fulfilled at all and must be removed. By spreading scheduling points into each schedule we can handle temporarily rejected requests resulting from a real hardware environment. At each scheduling-point, at least one decision can be made. Thus the scheduler behaves fairly, too.

The *First-Fit-Decreasing-Height* (FFDH) algorithm [3] computes a sequence of scheduling levels by working through the *RL* in non-increasing order. All rectangles are placed with their left side resting at one of the scheduling points.

The first level is simply the bottom of the bin. At any point of the packing sequence, the next rectangle to be packed is placed on the top of the lowest level on which it will fit, justified to its left border. If none of the current levels will accommodate this rectangle, a new level is created.

To illustrate the behavior of the basic scheduling primitives, we will use the following example. This example is chosen as a wild mixture, ranging from large and short-running to small and long-running requests. Thus, it corresponds to the observed user behavior. Let i denote the request-number as it is inserted

i	1	2	3	4	5	6	7	8	9	10
n_i	6.25	100	6.25	100	12.5	50	12.5	50	25	25
t_i	25	50	10	5	20	40	20	10	15	30

Fig. 4. Sample request sequence

into the waiting-room and n_i (t_i) being the corresponding percentage of the processors (number of time-units) requested. Ordering the requests by the non-increasing time results in $RL = (2, 6, 10, 1, 5, 7, 9, 3, 8, 4)$. Applying the FFDH-algorithm to the example of Fig. 4 results in the schedule shown in Fig. 5 with a total system utilization of

$$UTL_{FFDH}(RL) = \frac{\sum_{i=1}^{N} n_i * t_i}{FFDH(RL)} = \frac{9843.75}{115} = 85.6\%$$

and an average waiting-time of

$$AWT_{FFDH}(RL) = \frac{1}{N} * \sum_{i=1}^{N} \Delta(i) = \frac{1}{10} * 630 = 63.0\,\text{m},$$

with $\Delta(i)$ denoting the absolute waiting-time of request i, and N the length of RL.

If there are two contradictory criteria to be optimized (UTL vs. AWT), it is quite often a good idea to turn things around. Thus, the request list was considered in non-decreasing order. As this modified algorithm increases the height of the bin, it is called *First-Fit-Increasing-Height* (FFIH) algorithm [15]. Applying the FFIH algorithm to the modified list results in packing short rectangles close to the bottom of the bin, and broad rectangles at relatively high x-values. Thus, we get

$$UTL_{FFIH}(RL) = \frac{9843.75}{115} = 85.6\%$$

and

$$AWT_{FFIH}(RL) = \frac{1}{10} * 185 = 18.5\,\text{m}.$$

The resulting schedule is shown in Fig. 6.

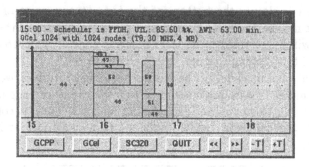

Fig. 5. FFDH packing

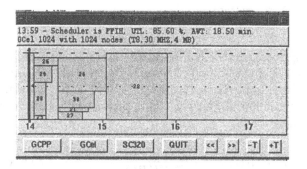

Fig. 6. FFIH packing

All algorithms presented so far can be improved without violating the scheduling-point condition. At first, we consider the FFDH algorithm. Assume that we are working through the *RL* in non-increasing order and that we are computing a location within the bin to place an arbitrary request. Now we abolish the condition that each rectangle must be placed conclusive to the leftmost scheduling point. We allow an arbitrary placement on top of an already placed request without exceeding the scheduling point at the right side, determined by the request which is placed at the lowest y-value. An example of applying this modified algorithm, now called FFDH*, is shown in Fig. 7. This results in

$$UTL_{FFDH*}(RL) = 89.49\%$$

and

$$AWT_{FFDH*}(RL) = 60.5\,m.$$

By applying the same idea to FFIH, (called FFIH*), we can now allow short-running requests to be enqueued dynamically. When preferring these requests to fill the gaps without violating the scheduling points, the average waiting-time and

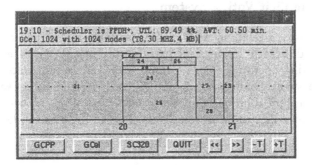

Fig. 7. FFDH* packing

the overall utilization is improved simultaneously. This idea scales to the FCFS algorithm, too. If a new resource request has been enqueued into the waiting-

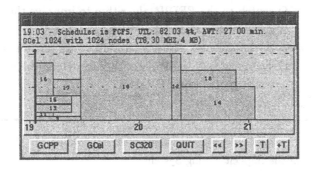

Fig. 8. FCFS* packing

room, it is first checked if this request fits into a gap of the FCFS-schedule. In this case, the request to be planned is allowed to skip all pending requests within the waiting-room. This modification is called FCFS*. An example of applying the FCFS* algorithm results in

$$UTL_{FCFS*}(RL) = 82.03\%$$

and

$$AWT_{FCFS*}(RL) = 27.0\,m$$

(see Fig. 8). However, note that the FCFS* algorithm violates the scheduling-point condition. Thus, when using this algorithm directly, fairness can not be guaranteed anymore.

3.3   The Implicit Voting System

Commonly used scheduling and queuing systems are in general very static. Queues are dedicated to physical parts of the machinery or schedulers rely on time sharing operating-systems running on the resources to be scheduled. Switching between batch and interactive modes is done at a fixed time every day. These custom solutions provide specific capabilities at best, but are not suitable to solve the problem we address. Due to the reasons discussed above,

---

IVS()
>   BEGIN LOOP
>   CASE
>   (the MPP-systems are not saturated)
>   DO switch to the FCFS*-mode and configure immediately OD;
>   BREAK
>   IF (most of the relevant requests were submitted for batch jobs)
>   DO switch to the FFDH* algorithm to improve the overall
>   system utilization OD; BREAK
>   IF (most of the relevant requests submitted are for interactive usage)
>   DO switch to the FFIH* algorithm to reduce the average
>   waiting time OD; BREAK
>   END LOOP

Fig. 9. Outline of the Implicit Voting System

---

we derive that the users themselves (i.e. the most relevant resource requests of the users) should vote dynamically on the characteristics of their favored resource scheduling method. However, they should not vote explicitly. Thus an Implicit Voting System (IVS) was developed to schedule the MPP-systems of a virtual machine-room [15].

The main pre-condition to build such a system is that the set of the requests in question and their main properties can be determined easily and in advance. Using the approach presented, this condition is fulfilled by the scheduling model of (3.1) and the request-list RL. Thus, the basic scheduling algorithms can be dynamically turned by the current mixture of the requests to tradeoff utilization versus response-time.

An outline of IVS is given in Fig. 9. Using the accounting data gathered at the PC^2, IVS was compared to the original FFDH algorithm in [15]. It was shown that using IVS, the system utilization could be improved up to 30 %, relatively to the FFDH scheduling. Simultaneously, the average waiting time could be reduced by 9 %.

We now focus on the methodology to get tight waiting-time estimations. Doing this, we are not fixed on a certain scheduling algorithm, as long as the constraints discussed above are satisfied.

4 Estimating the Expected Waiting-Time

Supercomputers usually show a very high degree of utilization. On machines without time-sharing support, some resource requests may not be fulfilled at once, but have to wait until the required hardware / software is available. Our experience has shown that these waiting-times can last from tens of minutes up to several hours on normal working-days. Since computing time on a supercomputer is very expensive, the availability of results from batch jobs or the start of an interactive parallel program are important events to the user. This is why users have to plan their day at least partially according to the estimated waiting-times of their resource requests, what makes these estimations a very critical parameter.

Unfortunately, there are several reasons why a scheduler can not predict the waiting-time exactly. First, the users' estimations about the expected execution times of their applications are not precise. As a scheduler has to rely on this information without any possibility of verification, we will assume for the rest of this paper that these estimations are correct. This is admissible, because users usually have to pay for their reserved time and are therefore encouraged to minimize the gap between their estimations and the actual execution time. Another reason for estimated waiting-times being inexact is the existence of different priorities. New requests can overtake others within the priority-queues and thus can be configured before requests for which a time prediction was already made. As the previously estimated waiting-time in this case is too short, the resulting error-values are positive (Fig. 10). Finally, an architecture-independent scheduling algorithm has difficulties in finding tight waiting-time estimations due to its limited knowledge of the underlying hardware. The schedule as it is planned by the scheduler may not be valid because of hardware-dependent constraints like limited numbers of I/O-nodes or restricted partition shapes, which further increases the error-values.

In the following, we will show how a scheduler can overcome most of these problems in order to provide the user with waiting-time estimations as tight as possible.

4.1 Using autonomous scheduling algorithms

An autonomous scheduler is a scheduler that sends a request to be configured to the target machine without any knowledge whether they can be fulfilled or not. If, for example, the machine currently has a high internal fragmentation or all I/O-nodes are in use by other applications, the MM-D will have to reject the new request. Afterwards the QM-D has to requeue the rejected request until enough resources are available. If fairness is to be guaranteed, this request will have to be shifted to the next scheduling-point. The time-span for the pending requests within the scheduler (Fig. 3) gets lengthened and the overall throughput gets reduced. Fig. 10 depicts the normalized error-values of the waiting-time estimations that were calculated at the time a request enters the waiting-room. Fig. 11 shows these error-values for estimations made at the time a request enters the scheduler of Fig. 3.

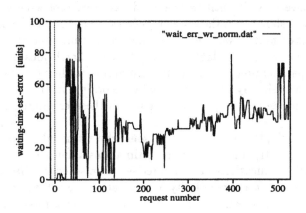

Fig. 10. Estimation errors when entering the waiting-room (without verify-protocol)

Calculating the expected waiting-time for requests already scheduled is straight forward. To determine the waiting-time for a request which is still in the waiting-room (the priority-queues), the system is virtually frozen and the waiting-room is successively cleared, using the formula in (3.1). Each portion extracted is virtually scheduled afterwards, using the IVS (3.3). Thus, we can also estimate the waiting-time for pending requests which are still in the waiting-room. It is obvious that errors resulting from reordering already scheduled requests have the largest impact on the first waiting-time estimation made (Fig. 10), which is also the most important one for the users.

By analyzing the simulation runs for the autonomous scheduling mode, we can see that the error-values resulting from the first 150 requests vary strongly (Fig. 10). Afterwards, the curve stabilizes at a relatively high level. The errors occurring inside the scheduler are of a much lower level. This is due to the fact that there are much more resource requests to be considered from within the waiting-room than from within the scheduler. Note that we have started our simulation with an empty system. Thus, for the first 20 requests nearly no wrong estimations were made.

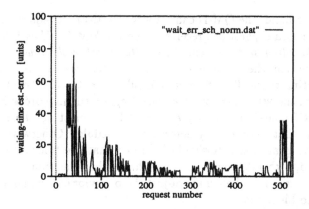

Fig. 11. Estimation errors when entering the scheduler (without verify-protocol)

4.2 Using a verification protocol

In order to overcome the problems of autonomous scheduling algorithms while still being hardware-independent, we introduce a verification protocol between the QM-D and the MM-Ds. The QM-D sends the preplanned schedule to the corresponding MM-D. Afterwards, the MM-D verifies whether this schedule can be configured in the given order on the given hardware or not. In case of conflicts, the MM-D reports the affected requests back to the QM-D and makes a suggestion, for solving the conflicts. The scheduler can then reorganize its schedule according to these suggestions and send it back to the MM-D in order to be verified again. These steps will be iterated until there are no more conflicts within the current schedule. In this way, the predicted waiting-times become deterministic for each set of requests that has been taken out of the waiting-room and inserted into the scheduling-module (Fig. 3).

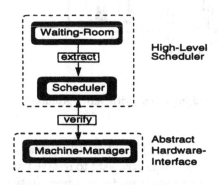

Fig. 12. Scheduling single systems

Fig. 12 depicts the basic structure of this verification protocol as it is currently implemented in CCS. Note that the protocol between the scheduler and the hardware-interface supports the mapping process of the MM-D as well as the scheduling decisions of the QM-D. Since the QM-D sends a complete set of requests to the MM-D for verification purposes, the mapping module of an MM-D can optimize the request placement according to this limited knowledge of the future.

On the other hand, the QM-D can improve its abstract request-schedule by the hardware-related suggestions received from the MM-D. *Thus both, the mapping and the scheduling unit can benefit from this additional knowledge.*

Furthermore, the schedule is deterministic for those resource requests which have left the waiting-room. Therefore, it is possible to extract the next block of applications from the waiting-room when the preplanned time drops below a certain threshold. Of course, the newly extracted block must not be mixed with the applications that have already entered the scheduler. Otherwise, fairness could no longer be guaranteed. It should be noted that the priority mechanism may be weakened, if this threshold is very high. On the other hand, this gives the administrator a good mechanism to adjust the behavior of the management system according to his needs.

Fig. 13 depicts the normalized error-curve of the waiting-time estimations. The measurements were made when the requests were entering the waiting-room and the verification protocol was used. Comparing this diagram with Fig. 10, we can see that there are still some high deviations but most predictions were fairly accurate. Requests that leave the waiting-room and enter the scheduler can now rely on their predicted configuration-times. Thus, the waiting-time estimations made for verified resource requests are absolutely tight.

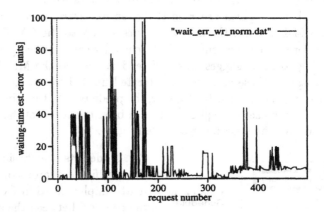

Fig. 13. Estimation errors when entering the waiting-room (with verify-protocol)

In practise, it is very important that this protocol enables CCS to manage reservations, too. Daily use has shown that users frequently want to reserve parts of a dedicated machine for a fixed time. Maybe they want to do a presentation or maybe there is a deadline to be met. The handshake between QM-D and MM-D allows the scheduler to use the remaining parts of the machine and be still able to guarantee that the reservation can be fulfilled at the desired time.

CCS contains a graphical tool to display the verified part of the schedule. This tool enables the users to find out when their requests will be configured and if there are free slots in the current schedule. This encourages the users to submit requests that will fit into free slots of the schedule and thereby to increase the overall throughput.

Another important property is that the scheduling / mapping / verifying activities do not result in additional runtime-overhead for application programs. Only the startup-time of an application may increase by a few seconds. This is because the CCS software is running somewhere in front of the MPP-systems to be managed and not on the compute-nodes themselves.

4.3   Results

Sections (4.1) and (4.2) have shown that the user can more heavily rely on waiting-time estimations, if the high-level scheduler performs a verification handshake with the hardware interface. Thus, the next step is to find out exactly how much better the predictions will be if the extended scheduler is used. In order to do this, there are two parameters to be examined. The first is the frequency of significant errors and the second is the average difference between the predicted and real configuration times. Therefore, we have analyzed the behavior of both schedulers with simulation series of more than 500 resource requests each. The frequencies of the different error-classes are depicted in Fig. 14 and Fig. 15.

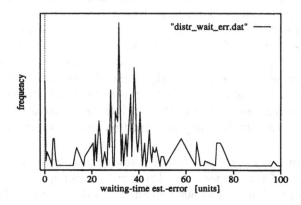

Fig. 14. Error distribution (without verify-protocol)

Without the verification protocol, most of the differences are located around 35 % of the maximum error. In contrast, the extended scheduler has nearly the same maximum error but is able to place most of its predictions within a range of 10 % of the maximum error. Thus, there are only few significant errors if the extended scheduler is used.

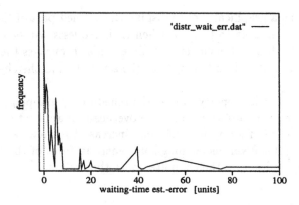

Fig. 15. Error distribution (with verify-protocol)

There are two reasons for estimation-errors to occur, even if the verification protocol is applied. The first one is because we have to schedule an online system. Thus, new enqueued requests with a higher priority can overtake others and therefore interfere with the predictions already made.

The second one is because only the calculated schedule for the requests inside the scheduler (Fig. 3) is verified. Schedules resulting from cleaning the virtually frozen waiting-room, in order to estimate the waiting-time just after request-submission are treated as within the autonomous scheduling mode (see 4.1). Therefore, the predictions made get worse with increasing ratio between the number of pending requests within the waiting-room and those which are already inside the scheduler. Of course one could verify the schedules for all requests in the whole system at any time. In that case, however, we have to pay for the tighter time-values by a significantly increased computation time for the verification task. The compromise we have chosen by only verifying the schedule for requests which are already inside the scheduler can be adapted to the administrator's needs by simply changing the extraction order $E(p_i)$ for the priority-queues (see 3.1).

In the further evaluation of the verification methodology, we have calculated the average difference between predicted and real configuration times. Again, we used a sample of more than 500 requests for both schedulers. For users working interactively the waiting-time estimations become of particular interest, when a request is submitted. Therefore, we have examined the data presented in Fig. 10 and Fig. 13. The normalized mean error-values

$$EV = \frac{100}{N * E_{max}} * \sum_{i=1}^{N} |t_{configured}(i) - t_{estimated}(i)|$$

with

$$E_{max} = \max\{\, |t_{configured}(i) - t_{estimated}(i)|\,;1{\le}i{\le}N\}$$

for all requests were determined and compared. Using the autonomous scheduling approach, a value of $EV = 34.923$ was calculated. This was decreased to $EV = 6.428$ by the verification protocol. Thus, we were able to reduce the uncertainty by 76 % while still maintaining the hardware independence of the algorithm.

5 Towards the Metacomputer Challenge

Metacomputing in its ideal form involves spreading a single application across several HPC systems, allowing a heterogeneous collection of computers to work in concert on a single problem [10, 18]. However, intermediate steps in metacomputer evolution, e.g. using a number of different MPP-systems of a distributed virtual machine-room to achieve a global load-alliance, seem to be more realistic for most applications [12]. Activities are already in process to determine whether such ideas can be transferred into practise and how that might work [1, 5, 13, 19].

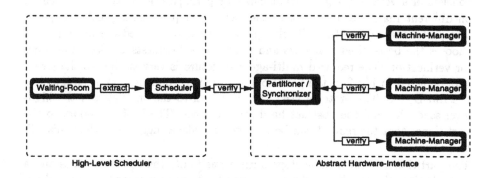

Fig. 16. Scheduler layout for a metacomputer

Building a metacomputer is probably one of the greatest challenges to computer scientists. The required hardware has been available for several years, but we are still far away from a really working metacomputer. In the course of the last years, the WAN technology has made rapid progress. Encouraging global file systems (e.g. AFS, DFS) are emerging. Thus, some important preconditions are fulfilled to establish a general purpose metacomputer. What is needed now is a resource-management layer which can be scaled to these new challenges. By comparing the requirements for such an environment to those of a monolithic HPC system, several additional problems have to be solved. For example, synchronized scheduling and mapping methods using the heterogeneous and architectural possibilities have to be developed. Suitable methods to divide an abstract user-request into subrequests and to select the best suited systems from a virtual machine-room afterwards, while taking the WAN performance into account, are required [9].

Typical applications for a heterogeneous machine-pool will need to have each of their modules running on the best suited computer-system. Some modules may require a vector computer and others may perform best on an SMP machine. A metacomputer scheduler receiving such a request must be able to guarantee that all these modules will be running at the same time. This must of course not decrease the overall throughput to intolerable values.

The CCS approach presented offers a simple and user-friendly interface to the MPP-resources of a service provider. Due to the high-level view of the physical resources, a framework was drawn up to establish a virtual machine-room locally, thus giving a similar shape to various HPC sides.

Fig. 16 shows how the layout of the CCS-scheduler can be extended to meet some of the additional requirements.

The high-level scheduler remains the same as in the single computer case depicted in Fig. 12. The abstract hardware interface now consists of several different MM-Ds, one for each system in the virtual machine-room. The scheduler indirectly communicates with these MM-Ds via a new module which performs the partitioning and synchronizing task. When the scheduler receives a request that consists of several subrequests that can – or perhaps even must – be executed on different machines, it is sent to the partitioner just like any other request. The partitioner notices that all subrequests have to be fulfilled synchronously. It chooses the best-suited machines and sends the subrequests to these machines for verification. The required multi-agent structure is very similar to the structure depicted in Fig. 2, if the partitioning and synchronizing task is assigned to the PM-D, too. The protocol used now is similar to the one between the high-level scheduler and the abstract hardware-interface. The MM-Ds report to the partitioner that the request can be fulfilled or make a suggestion when this will be possible.

The partitioner iterates these steps until it has found the right machines and a suitable time-slot for the synchronous requests. Then, it reports to the scheduler that the schedule is valid or it presents the alternative suggestion. The scheduler itself can later use this additional information as described in (4.2).

Despite the topics purely related to scheduling, there are other important requirements a resource management system has to meet in order to be suitable for a metacomputing environment. For example, there have to be well defined access points for third party products. A metacomputer built from supercomputers of many different vendors must have its own vendor-independent runtime and development tools like debuggers, performance analyzers or load-balancers. Therefore, it is vitally important that the management system provides standardized access points for these tools. However, it takes knowledge about the requirements of these tools to establish the interfaces in a useful way. Thus, computer scientist working on different areas of research have to combine their knowledge in order to build a metacomputer. We think that the design of CCS is a good focal point for these activities.

Acknowledgment

We would like to thank everybody involved in the CCS project. Especially Christian Hellmann for implementing the scheduling strategies and for running the simulations. Finally, we thank the anonymous referees for their helpful comments that improved the presentation.

References

1. A. Bachem, B. Monien, F. Ramme : *Der Forschungsverbund NRW-Metacomputing "Verteiltes Höchstleistungsrechnen"*, Technical Report, Paderborn, 1996
2. M. Campione, K. Walrath : *The Java Language Tutorial: Object-Oriented Programming for the Internet*, ISBN 0-201-63454-6, expected July 1996
3. E. G. Coffman, M. R. Garey, D. S. Johnson, R. E. Tarjan : *Performance bounds for level-oriented two-dimensional packing algorithms*, SIAM J.Comput., Vol. 9, No. 4, pp. 808-826, Nov. 1980
4. A. Colbrook, M. Lemke, H. Mierendorff, K. Stüben, C.A. Thole, O. Thomas : *EUROPORT – ESPRIT European Porting Projects*, Int. Conf. on High-Performance Computing and Networking, Proc. of the HPCN Europe, Springer-Verlag 1994, LNCS No. 796, Vol. I, pp. 46-54
5. E=MC^2 Consortium c/o R. McConnell : *The European Meta Computer Utilizing Integrated Broadband Communications (E=MC^2) Project*, Int. Conf. on High-Performance Computing and Networking, Proc. of the HPCN Europe, LNCS, Springer-Verlag 1995 pp. 54-59
6. D.G. Feitelson : *A Survey of Scheduling in Multiprogrammed Parallel Systems*, Research Report RC 19790 (87657), IBM T.J. Watson Research Center, Oct. 1994
7. D.G. Feitelson, L. Rudolph : *Toward Convergence in Job Schedulers for Parallel Supercomputers*, In IPPS'96 Workshop on Job Scheduling Strategies for Parallel Processing, April 1996
8. R. Funke, R. Lüling, B. Monien, F. Lücking, H. Blanke-Bohne : *An optimized reconfigurable architecture for Transputer networks*, Proc. of 25th Hawaii Int. Conf. on System Sciences (HICSS 92), Vol. 1, pp. 237-245
9. J. Gehring, A. Reinefeld : *MARS – A Framework for Minimizing the Job Execution Time in a Metacomputing Environment*, To appear in spring issue of FGCS 1996
10. A.S. Grimshaw, J.B. Weissman, E.A. West, E.C. Loyot : *Metasystems: An Approach Combining Parallel Processing and Heterogeneous Distributed Computing Systems*, Journal of Parallel and Distributed Computing, Vol. 21, 1994, pp. 257-270
11. R.L. Henderson : *Job Scheduling Under the Portable Batch System*, IPPS Workshop on Job Scheduling Strategies for Parallel Processing, D.G. Feitelson and L. Rudolph (eds), Springer-Verlag 1995, LNCS No. 949, pp. 279-294
12. A.A. Khokhar, V.K. Prasanna, M.E. Shaaban, Cho-Li Wang : *Heterogeneous Computing: Challenges and Oportunities*, IEEE Computer, Vol. 26, No. 6, 1993, pp. 18-27
13. Reagan Moore : *NSF MetaCenter: A White Paper*, San Diego Supercomputing Center, 1995
14. F. Ramme : *Building a Virtual Machine-Room – a Focal Point in Metacomputing*, Future Generation Computer Systems (FGCS), Elsevier Science B. V., Aug. 1995, Special Issue on HPCN, Vol. 11, pp. 477-489

15. F. Ramme, K. Kremer : *Scheduling a Metacomputer by an Implicit Voting System*, 3rd IEEE Int. Symposium on High-Performance Distributed Computing, San Francisco, 1994, pp. 106-113

16. F. Ramme, T. Römke, K. Kremer : *A Distributed Computing Center Software for the Efficient Use of Parallel Computer Systems*, Int. Conf. on High-Performance Computing and Networking, Proc. of the HPCN Europe, Springer-Verlag 1994, LNCS No. 797, Vol. II, pp. 129-136

17. J. Skovira, W. Chan, H. Zhou, D. Lifka : *The EASY – LoadLeveler API Project*, In IPPS'96 Workshop on Job Scheduling Strategies for Parallel Processing, April 1996

18. L. Smarr Ch. E. Catlett : *Metacomputing*, Communications of the ACM, Vol. 35, No. 6, June 1992, pp. 45-52

19. *HIPERCON – High-Performance Computing Network –*, W. Zimmer (ed.), Eine Analyse zum Aufbau und Betrieb eines Höchstleistungsrechnerverbundnetzes in der Bundesrepublik Deutschland, GMD-First, Berlin 1995, im Auftrag des BMBF

20. M. Wan, R. Moore, G. Kremenek, K. Steube : *A Batch Scheduler for the Intel Paragon with a Non-contiguous Node Allocation Algorithm*, In IPPS'96 Workshop on Job Scheduling Strategies for Parallel Processing, April 1996

Packing Schemes for Gang Scheduling

Dror G. Feitelson

Institute of Computer Science
The Hebrew University, 91904 Jerusalem, Israel
feit@cs.huji.ac.il — http://www.cs.huji.ac.il/~feit

Abstract. Jobs that do not require all processors in the system can be packed together for gang scheduling. We examine accounting traces from several parallel computers to show that indeed many jobs have small sizes and can be packed together. We then formulate a number of such packing algorithms, and evaluate their effectiveness using simulations based on our workload study. The results are that two algorithms are the best: either perform the mapping based on a buddy system of processors, or use migration to re-map the jobs more tightly whenever a job arrives or terminates. Other approaches, such as mapping to the least loaded PEs, proved to be counterproductive. The buddy system approach depends on the capability to gang-schedule jobs in multiple slots, if there is space. The migration algorithm is more robust, but is expected to suffer greatly due to the overhead of the migration itself. In either case fragmentation is not an issue, and utilization may top 90% with sufficiently high loads.

1 Introduction

Parallel supercomputers are increasingly being used in preference over the more traditional vector supercomputers. While some of these parallel supercomputers are dedicated to specific applications, a large number are also used as general purpose servers with large and diverse communities of users. As such they must provide convenient scheduling facilities that will handle the allocation of resources to different user jobs.

A large number of scheduling schemes have been proposed for parallel machines [7, 11]. One of these is gang scheduling, where all the threads of a parallel job are scheduled for simultaneous execution on distinct PEs [24]. If the total number of threads in all the jobs exceeds the number of PEs in the system, time slicing is used. However, the context switching is coordinated across the PEs, such that all the threads in a job are scheduled and de-scheduled at the same time. Gang scheduling is a prominent feature of the Connection Machine CM-5 system [28], and is available on the Intel Paragon [17], the Meiko CS-2, and multiprocessor SGI workstations [2]. It has also been used extensively in a home-grown system on a BBN Butterfly at Lawrence Livermore Labs [13], which has recently been ported to their new Cray T3D system.

The main drawback of using gang scheduling is the problem of fragmentation. Specifically, it may happen that a number of jobs are scheduled to run, and a few PEs are left over, but they are insufficient for any of the other queued jobs.

The severity of this problem depends to a large degree on the distribution of job sizes [12]. One solution, used in the CM-5, is to use all the PEs for each job, rather than allowing subsets to be used. In this paper, we investigate alternative solutions based on different schemes for packing the jobs together for scheduling. We show that it is possible to achieve significant improvements over a simple best-fit packing, using either a buddy system to control the mapping, or by migrating jobs so as to re-map them.

As noted above, the experienced fragmentation depends on the workload. Therefore an accurate workload model is essential in order to evaluate the effectiveness of the various packing schemes. To this end we have analyzed a number of accounting traces that include information about many thousands of jobs that have been executed on a number of parallel machines. It is felt that the resulting workload model is much more representative of real workloads than other models that have been used in the literature.

The rest of this paper is organized as follows. Section 2 describes the different packing schemes that we are proposing. Section 3 describes the workload analysis and model. Section 4 then describes the experimental results obtained when using the different packing schemes in conjunction with the workload model. The conclusions are presented in Section 5.

2 Packing Schemes

Our work is done within the framework of a gang scheduling system based on the matrix algorithm by Ousterhout [24]. This algorithm views scheduling space as a matrix, where rows represent time slots and columns represent PEs. Each job is allocated to a single row. If space permits, a number of jobs may be allocated to the same row. Gang scheduling is done by iteratively scheduling the jobs in one row after the other.

The question we wish to investigate is that of packing in this matrix. This includes three sub questions:

1. If multiple slots have enough capacity for a new job, which one should be chosen?
2. When should a new slot be opened?
3. If the chosen slot has more free PEs than required, which ones should be used?

The considerations involved are relatively simple. Relating to the second question, it is generally desirable to pack the jobs into the minimal number of slots possible, because the run fraction[1] for each job is equal to one over the number of used slots. We therefore only consider algorithms that do not open new slots unless there are no used slots with sufficient capacity (or, in one case, if the free processors are not organized as needed).

---

[1] The run fraction is defined as the fraction of wall-clock time that the job is actually running on the CPUs, as opposed to waiting in the run queue or elsewhere.

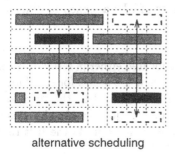 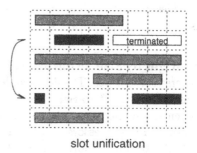

alternative scheduling   slot unification

Fig. 1. *Packing should be done so as to promote alternative scheduling and facilitate slot unification.*

The other two questions can be tied together, by choosing the slot with the optimal choice of PEs. A judicious choice of PEs is important for two reasons (Fig. 1). First, choosing a set of PEs that are free in more than one slot may allow the job to be gang scheduled in multiple slots, thus increasing its run fraction and providing it with better service (this is called *alternative* scheduling). Second, if jobs are in general assigned to disjoint sets of PEs, then when a job terminates it may happen that the remaining jobs in its slot use PEs that are distinct from those used by the jobs in some other slot. This will make it possible to unite the two slots, thus reducing the number of used slots by one, and improving the run fraction of all jobs. Note that alternative scheduling and slot unification are features of the scheduler, and are independent of the packing scheme used. The point made is that better packing schemes will be able to make better use of these features.

A number of algorithms have been devised based on these considerations.

2.1 Capacity Based Algorithms

The first two algorithms just check the slot's capacity.

First Fit In this algorithm, the used slots are scanned in serial order. The first one with sufficient capacity is chosen. If no used slot has sufficient capacity, a new slot is opened. Within the chosen slot, free PEs are allocated in serial order.

Best Fit In this algorithm, the used slots are sorted according to their capacities. The one with the smallest capacity that is sufficient is chosen. If no used slot has sufficient capacity, a new slot is opened. Within the chosen slot, free PEs are allocated in serial order.

2.2 Left-Right Based Algorithms

The next two algorithms are modifications of the best fit algorithm, and modify the way that PEs are allocated within the chosen slot. The idea is to start from both sides, so as to reduce the overlap between sets of PEs assigned to different jobs.

Left-Right by Size In this algorithm, PEs are allocated either in serial order or in reverse serial order. The decision depends on the new job's size: for small jobs, the allocation is left-to-right, and for large jobs it is right-to-left. the threshold between small and large jobs should be near the median job size. In this study we assume 128 processors and use a threshold of 8, which reflects the fact that small jobs are much more common (see Section 3.1).

Left-Right by Slots In this algorithm PEs are again allocated either from the left or from the right, but here the decision depends on the slot. Slots are alternately designated as being filled from the left or from the right. All jobs mapped to a certain slot will therefore be allocated PEs in the same order. When a new slot is opened, its direction is designated so as to make the numbers of slots with the two directions as nearly equal as possible.

2.3   Load Based Algorithms

All the previous algorithms were oblivious of the loads on the different PEs. The next two take this new parameter into account. Again, the motivation is to reduce the overlap between sets of PEs assigned to different jobs.

Minimal Maximum Load The PEs are sorted according to the load on them, measured in jobs that use each PE. For each slot with sufficient capacity, the PEs that are free in that slot are considered. When allocating PEs to a job of n threads, the nth PE in the load order thus defines the maximal load on any PE that will be used in that slot. The slot with the minimal maximal load is chosen. Within that slot, the n least loaded free PEs are then used.

Minimal Average Load This algorithm is similar to the previous one, except that instead of using the load on the nth PE to prioritize the slots, we use the average load on the n least loaded PEs.

2.4   Buddy Based Algorithm

This algorithm is different in the sense that PEs are assigned in groups rather than individually. These groups are organized as a buddy system, based on concepts that were originally developed for memory allocation [18, 25], and following the PE allocation mechanism in the Distributed Hierarchical Control scheme (DHC) [9, 10].

Specifically, the PEs are partitioned recursively into groups that are powers of two. Logically, each group has a controller, thus creating a hierarchy of such controllers. When a job of size n arrives, it is assigned to a controller of size

$2^{\lceil \lg n \rceil}$ (i.e. the smallest power of 2 that is larger than or equal to n). The choice is done by scanning all the used slots, and identifying groups of $2^{\lceil \lg n \rceil}$ contiguous free processors that belong to the same controller. Controllers whose groups of PEs are all free in some slot are candidates for mapping the newly arrived job. If no controller is completely free in any used slot, a new slot is opened[2].

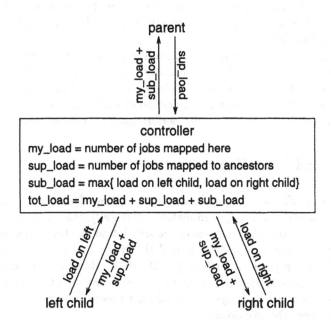

Fig. 2. *Load calculation for controllers in the buddy system approach.*

Out of the free controllers, the one with the least load is chosen. Load on controllers is defined recursively according to the hierarchy as the sum of 3 terms: the number of jobs mapped to this controller, the maximum of the loads on the controller's two children, and the sum of the number of jobs mapped to the controllers ancestors. The data paths needed to compute loads using this scheme are illustrated in Fig. 2. A simplified scheme where load is simply the maximum of the loads on the PEs under the controller was also considered, but proved to be inferior.

If n is not a power of 2, only part of the PEs under the chosen controller are used. These are selected in groups that are powers of two, based on the loads on the controller's descendents. This scheme is equivalent to the "minimal fragmentation" scheme that was shown to be advantageous for DHC [9, 10]. The remaining PEs are not reserved or allocated in any sense, and can later be assigned to other (smaller) jobs. They can also be used to provide additional runtime to jobs that are mapped to other slots, via alternative scheduling.

---

[2] Note that in some cases this may lead to opening a new slot even if there are slots with n free PEs, because the n PEs are not all under the same controller.

2.5 Migration Based Algorithm

The final algorithm solves the problem of PE assignment in a completely different manner. Rather than seeking a good initial placement and then sticking to it, this algorithm migrates jobs from one set of PEs to another as needed in order to unite slots and improve run fractions. Specifically, our algorithm re-maps all jobs upon every job arrival and termination, using a first-fit-decreasing allocation to slots [4] (this algorithm is optimal if all job sizes divide each other, e.g. if they are powers of two [5]).

It is debatable whether this algorithm is realistic, because of the expected overhead, especially on distributed memory machines. It is true that systems that support migration have been implemented successfully [1, 6], but these systems do not attempt to perform migration at such a high rate. However, this algorithm is useful as a bound on the performance that is obtainable.

3 Workload Modeling

The most straightforward way to evaluate scheduling algorithms without a full scale implementation is through simulations. Naturally, the quality of the results depends on the quality of the inputs to the simulation. An important issue is the workload model. It has often been stated that there is no reliable information about workloads on parallel machine [23, 20, 19, 3]. However, this is in fact not true. Like uniprocessor systems, most parallel systems maintain administrative traces of all jobs run on the system. Analyzing these traces reveals a wealth of information about the workload.

For this study we used information derived from traces gathered on 6 different systems, all of which supported a real production workload. The traced systems are summarized in Table 1.

system	trace	comments
128-node iPSC/860 NASA Ames	42050 jobs, 4Q93 10821 parallel user jobs	Intel scheduler [16] analysis described in [8]
128-node IBM SP1 Argonne Natl Lab	19980 jobs, 12/94–6/95 15654 were parallel	home grown scheduler [21] submit trace, not run trace
400-node Paragon San-Diego SC	32500 jobs, 12/94–4/95 25867 were parallel	SDSC/Intel scheduler [29, 17]
126-node Butterfly LLNL	35848 jobs, 1991–1992 >30000 were parallel	home grown gang scheduler [14] no direct access to trace [13]
512-node IBM SP2 Cornell Theory Ctr	17947 jobs, 9/95–11/95 8598 were parallel	Scheduling by IBM LoadLeveler no direct access to trace [15]
96-node Paragon ETH Zürich	1723 jobs	Intel scheduler no direct access to trace [27]

Table 1. *Summary of systems and traces used in workload analysis.*

3.1 Distribution of Job Sizes

An important feature of the workload model is the distribution of job sizes, in terms of the number of nodes used by each job[3]. Histograms of the sizes observed in two of the traces are shown in Fig. 3. Examination of such histograms reveals three distinctive characteristics:

- Small jobs are more common than large ones.
- Some "interesting" sizes appear much more often than others, creating a distribution with pronounced discrete components.
- Practically all possible sizes up to about 100 nodes appear in practice, albeit a small number of times.

system	powers of 2	squares	multiples of 10	full system	sizes plus 1
NASA Ames iPSC/860	yes	(some)	no	(yes)	no
ANL/IBM SP1	yes	some	some	yes	no
SDSC Paragon	yes	some	no	no	no
LLNL Butterfly	yes	yes	some	yes	yes
Cornell SP2	yes	some	no	no	no
ETH Paragon	yes	no	no	yes	no

Table 2. *"Interesting" sizes in the different traces.*

The special sizes that appeared in the different traces are summarized in table 2. The most common one is jobs that use power-of-two nodes — this was a pronounced feature of all the traces. The reasons for using such sizes in preference over others are varied, and include algorithmic suitability (e.g. when using a divide-and-conquer paradigm) and system considerations (e.g. system administrators tend to create batch queues for power-of-two nodes, and system size is often a power of two).

A special case is jobs that require the full machine. In some cases, this is a power of two, but using the full machine was also popular in cases where this is not a power of two. For example, 12.2% of the jobs on the ETH Paragon used all 96 nodes, and these jobs used up 63.8% of the total resources (measured in CPU-seconds). On the LLNL Butterfly, using the whole machine was represented by jobs that used 112 or 113 nodes, which were typical sizes of the parallel cluster (the rest of the nodes were used for login, and did not participate in running parallel jobs). Notable exceptions are the SDSC Paragon and Cornell SP2. For example, the SDSC Paragon had only three 400-node jobs. This is because the system is heterogeneous: 256 nodes have 32MB of memory, and the rest only

---

[3] We assume that the number of nodes does not change during execution, as is the case in many systems that support an SPMD programming model.

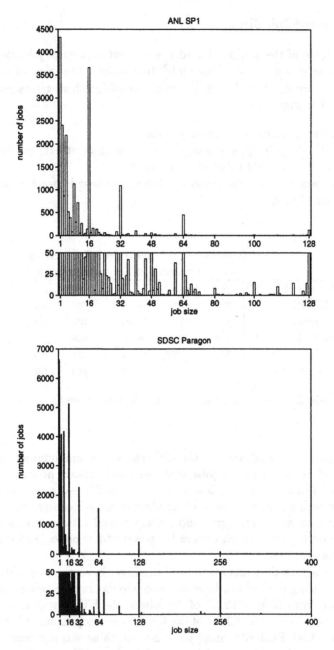

Fig. 3. *Histograms of job sizes on the ANL SP1 and SDSC Paragon.*

16MB, so for many jobs the effective maximum is 256. Also, 32 nodes were typically reserved for interactive use, so using all 400 nodes required turning off interactive use. The Cornell SP2 is also heterogeneous [15], and was never configured for using all 512 nodes.

Other popular sizes are squares (25, 49, 64, 81, 100), used when the algorithm is naturally expressed on a square array of processors (even if the architecture is not a mesh), and multiples of 10 (20, 50, 100), probably used mainly for aesthetic reasons when no other size was specifically warranted. Jobs using a master-workers paradigm sometimes created sizes that are larger by one than another popular size, e.g. $26 = (5 \times 5) + 1$. Of course, several sizes appear multiple times in these lists, and it is hard to know what interpretation to attach to them: 16 and 64 are both squares and powers of two, 50 is a multiple of 10 and one more than the square 49, and 100 is a square, a multiple of 10, and a nice round number.

Finally, in some cases arbitrary numbers seem to appear for no obvious reason. It is possible that this is a result of a specific preference by a single user, that uses a certain size for many repeated executions. Such behavior is discussed in Section 3.3 below.

3.2 Correlation of Runtime with Size

It is largely accepted that the runtimes of jobs in a computer system have a wide distribution, with many jobs that have a short runtime but a few jobs that have very long runtimes. This is typically modeled by a hyperexponential distribution. However, a-priori it was not clear whether or not there is a correlation between the runtime and the size (number of nodes) in parallel systems.

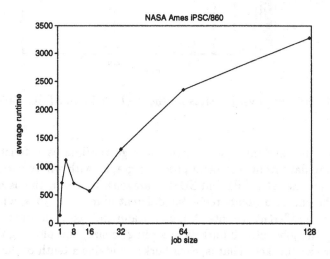

Fig. 4. *Runtimes vs. job sizes on the NASA Ames iPSC/860.*

Plotting the average runtime as a function of the size for the NASA Ames
iPSC/860 trace produces the results shown in Fig. 4. There is an obvious correlation, with larger jobs running longer than smaller jobs.

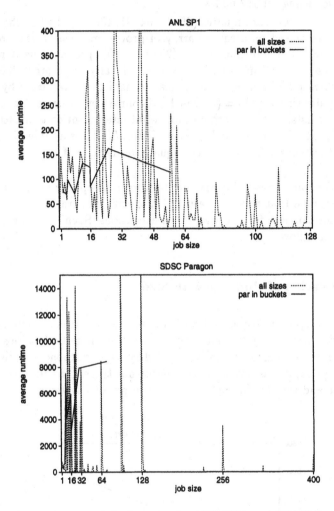

Fig. 5. *Runtimes vs. job sizes on the ANL SP1 and SDSC Paragon.*

For the other systems, plotting the average runtime as a function of the
job size using data from the traces produces graphs with wildly varying shapes
(see Fig. 5 for the ANL SP1 and SDSC Paragon). However, this is misleading,
because different data points represent different numbers of jobs, and therefore
should be give different weights. A more meaningful representation is obtained
by dividing the jobs into 10 buckets according to size, and plotting the average
runtime for each bucket. That is, each bucket contains a tenth of the total jobs,
with the first one containing the smallest jobs, the next bucket containing the

next larger jobs, and so on until the last bucket that contains the jobs using the largest number of PEs. In the plot, the representative size for each bucket is calculated as the average of the sizes of the jobs in the bucket. As there are many more small jobs than large jobs, the plots end at rather small sizes relative to the maximal size possible.

The results, using only parallel jobs, are also shown in Fig. 5. They indicate a weak tendency for larger jobs to have a higher runtime. However, it should be remembered that this is only a general trend, and the runtimes of specific jobs are widely distributed. Also, other studies have noticed differences between the distributions of jobs with "interesting" sizes and jobs that have other sizes, or between interactive and batch jobs. We intend to study such correlations further in the future.

3.3 User Modeling

An important issue in workload modeling is the question of whether jobs are independent of each other. The answer is that very often they are not. Specifically, users tend to submit sequences of similar jobs, one after the other.

In a preliminary effort to study this effect, the runlengths of such sequences were measured. In this context, a sequence is defined as the same user submitting the same job and using the same number of nodes. Results for the NASA Ames trace and the ANL SP1 trace (the two available traces that included user and job information) are shown in Fig. 6. It is seen that some sequences are extremely long (the maximum observed is 402 runs on the ANL SP1). The fact that the slope is a straight line in these log-log plots indicates a generalized Zipf distribution (i.e. $p(n) \propto 1/n^{\theta}$) [30, 26]. Using linear regression, the harmonic order (θ in the equation for the probability distribution) is around 2.2 for both cases, after deleting outliers that appear only a small number of times. Similar results were obtained for the Cornell trace [15].

3.4 Job Classes

In many cases jobs in a system can be classified into a number of classes, and such classification is often an explicit goal of workload analysis. In multiuser parallel systems an obvious classification is the distinction between interactive and batch jobs, as this distinction is supported directly by many systems: interactive jobs are those that are submitted directly and run immediately, while batch jobs are queued for later execution (often using NQS).

The significance of the class distinction is twofold. First, batch jobs tend to run longer than interactive ones. Second, batch queues are often enabled for execution only during the night, thus creating a daily cycle of completely different workloads at prime time and non-prime time. This effect is very pronounced in the NASA Ames trace [8], and can also be seen in the SDSC trace.

The reason to delay batch jobs to non-prime time is that in systems that use space slicing without preemption, the decision to run a batch job might block future requests to run interactive jobs. This consideration is eliminated in time

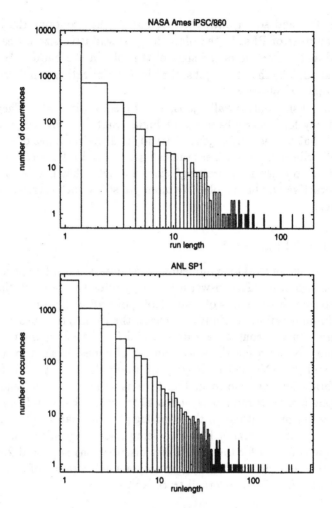

Fig. 6. *Distribution of runlengths of repeated executions on the NASA Ames iPSC/860 and the ANL SP1.*

slicing systems, because a batch job can share the processors with interactive jobs that come later. Moreover, interactive jobs can be demoted automatically to batch status if they run for too long. For example, this is done in the LLNL Butterfly (regrettably, there is no data on how often this actually happened). While such options are interesting, we leave them for future work, and ignore the distinction between batch and interactive jobs in the context of the current gang scheduling study.

3.5 The Model

Based on the above, we model the workload as follows. The distribution of sizes is based on a harmonic distribution, which is then hand tailored to emphasize

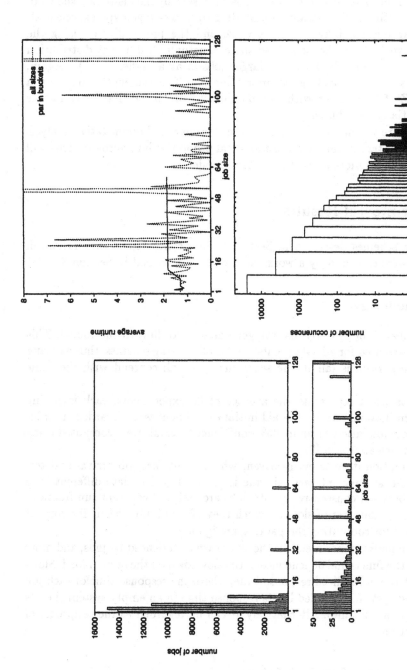

Fig. 7. Histogram of job sizes, correlation of runtimes with job size, and histogram of run lengths for the workload model.

small jobs and interesting sizes. This gives a qualitative approximation to the types of distribution observed in practice, as witnessed by the histogram shown in Fig. 7. The runtimes are distributed according to a two-stage hyperexponential, with a linear relation between the job size and the probability of using the distribution with the higher mean (so there is actually a different distribution for each job size, and the mean for larger jobs is at a higher value). Again, this provides a qualitatively good approximation. The runlengths are from a generalized Zipf distribution with a harmonic order of 2.5. The interarrival times are exponentially distributed.

In the future we plan to conduct a more thorough and quantitative analysis of the workload traces, taking more statistical properties into account. This will be used to create a more accurate workload model.

4 Experimental Results

The packing schemes described in Section 2 were compared by simulation, in which they were exercised by a workload model as described in Section 3.

4.1 Methodology

A single sequence of job arrivals was generated according to the model. This sequence was re-used for all data points and for all packing schemes, thus assuring that the comparison is fair in the sense that they all contend with the same workload.

Each data point represents the average of 30 experiments, each including 1000 job terminations. An additional initial experiment was discarded in order to account for simulation warmup. 95% confidence intervals were computed using the batch means approach [22].

The simulation itself is event-driven, where events are job arrival and termination. The average interarrival time is changed to simulate different load conditions. Between consecutive events, jobs are assigned constant run fractions according to the number of slots in which they can run. Overheads for context switching and for computing the packing are ignored.

The main performance metric is the slowdown experienced by jobs, and more specifically, the functional dependence of the slowdown on the system load. Slowdown is just the normalized response time, where the response time of each job in the loaded system is divided by its response time in an empty system (i.e. its actual computation time). Alternatively, it can be regarded as the reciprocal of the run fraction.

4.2 Comparison of Packing Schemes

The simulation results are shown in Fig. 8. They can be summarized by the following points:

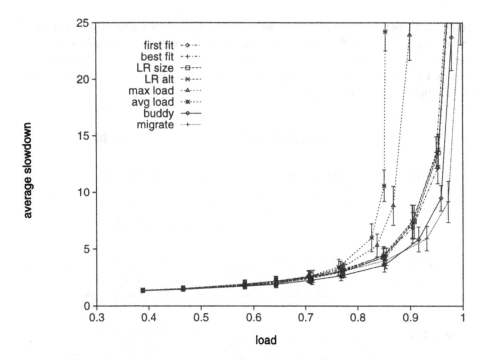

Fig. 8. *Average slowdown as a function of load for the different packing schemes.*

- The first four packing schemes (first fit, best fit, left-right by size, and alternating left-right) produce essentially identical performance.
- The two load-based schemes (minimal maximum load and minimal average load) are significantly worse than the previous four schemes. This is surprising since they take additional pertinent information into account.
- The buddy scheme and the migration scheme are similar to each other, and perform better than all other schemes. Migration has a slight advantage at the highest loads, while buddy has a slight advantage at medium loads.
- When looking at absolute values, rather than just comparing the different schemes, it is apparent that all schemes except the load-based ones can sustain loads leading to over 90% system utilization. The buddy and migration schemes can sustain loads leading to over 95% utilization. This implies that fragmentation is less of a problem than sometimes thought.

Why Load-Based Schemes Are Bad The load based packing schemes were expected to out-perform the oblivious schemes, because they judiciously choose the least loaded PEs to run new jobs. Such a choice was expected to make it easier to unify slots and to run the jobs in alternate slots. However, the simulation results show that choosing lightly loaded PEs leads to poor performance!

The reason for this situation seems to be that choosing PEs individually based on their loads leads to excessive fragmentation. As a result, it actually becomes harder to unite slots, as can be seen in the low unification counts for these two schemes in Fig. 10. Also, it is relatively difficult to schedule jobs to run in additional slots, beyond those to which they are mapped. This can be seen in the low slot counts for these two schemes in Fig. 11, which only improve at the highest sustained loads.

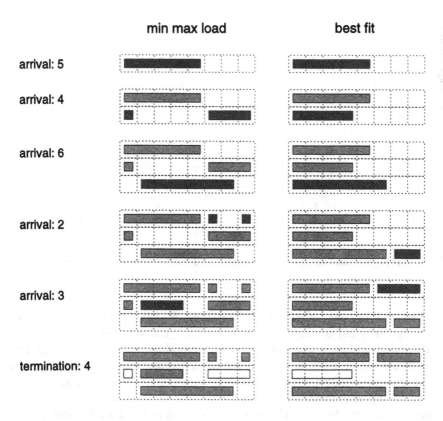

Fig. 9. *Example explaining the poor performance of load-based packing schemes.*

The following example shows how such harmful fragmentation can come about. Consider a sequence of job arrivals with sizes of 5, 4, 6, 2, and 3, in a system with 8 PEs. Fig. 9 shows how these jobs will be mapped by the minimal maximal load scheme and by the best fit scheme. Note that after the third job arrives, it seems that mapping to less loaded PEs leads to good balancing, as no PE has a load of more than two threads, whereas under best-fit some PEs have a load of 3 and some are completely idle. However, the mapping is fragmented, and becomes more so when the two additional jobs arrive. If now the job with size 4 terminates, the best fit scheme will end up with two fully-allocated slots, whereas the minimal maximum load scheme will have three lightly populated slots, and only the 2-PE job will be able to run in an additional slot.

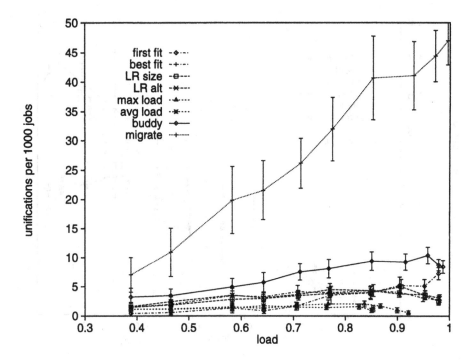

Fig. 10. *Number of slot unification performed with the different packing schemes.*

How Buddy Packing and Migration Achieve Their Good Performance
The simulation results singled out the buddy packing scheme and the migration scheme as those that provide the best performance. It is interesting to note that while the final outcome of these two schemes is very similar, the underlying mechanisms are very different. To show this, we tabulate the number of slot unifications performed by the various schemes (Fig. 10) and the average number of slots in which a job may run under the various schemes (Fig. 11).

The plots show that while buddy packing achieves many more unifications than most other schemes, they are still a rare event: less than one percent of job terminations lead to a unification. With migration[4], this jumps to nearly 5%. Thus by using migration the system may keep the number of used slots close to the minimum necessary, at the price of re-mapping jobs frequently.

Another result of keeping the number of slots down to the minimum is that there is very little free space in each slot, and therefore there is little chance for a job to run in any other slot except the one to which it is mapped. therefore with migration the average number of slots available to each job is lower than in any other scheme. With buddy packing, the average number of available slots

---

[4] The definition of unification under migration is that the number of slots is reduced as a result of a job termination, excluding cases where the terminated job was the only one mapped to the slot.

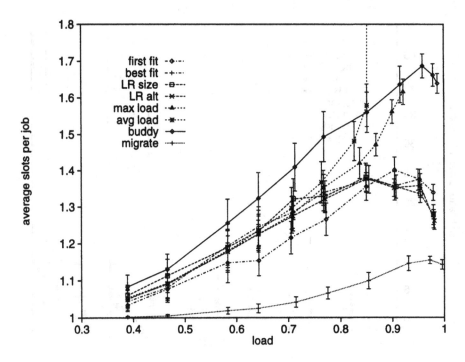

Fig. 11. *Average number of slots in which each job runs under the different packing schemes.*

is higher than in other schemes, because the buddy packing chooses groups of lightly loaded PEs for new jobs. Thus buddy packing achieves its performance not by minimizing the number of slots but rather by using alternative scheduling to allow each job to run in more slots.

The Importance of Unification and Using Alternate Slots As we saw, the performance of buddy packing is achieved by packing jobs so that they have a better chance to run in multiple slots. It is then interesting to check how important it is for the system to support this feature. Also, it is interesting to see how important it is to support slot unification.

The results are plotted in Figs. 12 and 13. Fig. 12, where the system does not support slot unification, is essentially identical to Fig. 8. We can therefore conclude that slot unification is not such an important feature[5] In Fig. 13, where the system does not support the execution of jobs in alternative slots, all the plots show somewhat reduced performance relative to Fig. 8. The most extreme degradation occurs with buddy packing. In fact, when jobs are not allowed to

---

[5] Not allowing unifications at all contradicts the definition of the migration scheme, so it is not plotted. However, note that migration does its unifications itself, and does not rely on the scheduler to do it.

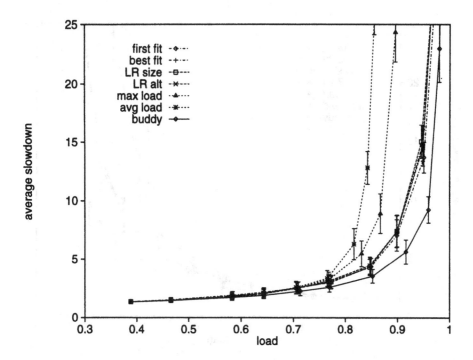

Fig. 12. *Average slowdown as a function of load for the different packing schemes, when no slot unifications are done.*

run in alternative slots, buddy packing performs quite poorly. Thus we see that this is an essential feature if buddy packing is to be used.

5 Conclusions

The current literature does not include any reference to the question of how to pack jobs for efficient gang scheduling. We have developed a number of packing algorithms, and evaluated them using simulations based on a realistic workload model. The results are that two approaches can lead to significant performance improvements over simple best-fit like algorithms: either use mapping based on a buddy system, or use migration to re-map jobs upon each job arrival and termination. Other approaches, such as mapping to the least loaded PEs, proved to be counterproductive.

The relatively good performance of the migration approach is a result of the fact that re-mapping leads to using the minimal number of scheduling slots possible. However, an implementation must then contend with the overhead of the migration process itself, which may be onerous. Therefore it is doubtful whether using migration is a realistic option, but it is still useful as a bound on the performance achieved by a strong on-line algorithm. Mapping based on a buddy system is much simpler and is not expected to involve considerable overhead.

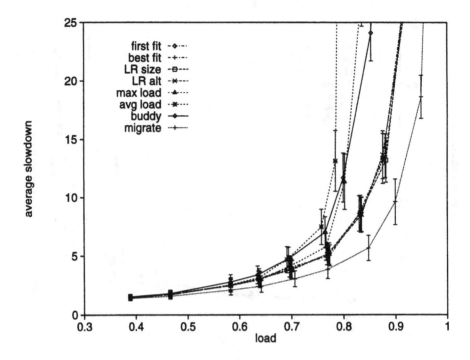

Fig. 13. *Average slowdown as a function of load for the different packing schemes, when jobs only run with their designated slot and do not use free space in other slots.*

However, it requires the system to support gang scheduling of jobs in multiple slots in order to achieve performance benefits. Without such a capability, the performance degrades sharply. Luckily, such support can be provided rather easily by mapping each job to multiple slots to begin with, where one mapping is the "real" one, and the others are tentative and can be deleted when some other job needs the space.

It should be noted that when a good mapping scheme is used, very high system utilization is possible. In our simulations of the buddy and migration schemes, the system only saturated when the utilization was higher than 95%, which is significantly higher than the 50-80% range reported for production systems using static partitioning [8, 29, 15]. This means that fragmentation is less of a concern than is sometimes thought. The high utilization can be attributed to two factors: first, when using time slicing, bad scheduling decisions are less harmful than when using static partitioning, because they only affect one scheduling slot. Other slots that suffer less fragmentation dilute the bad effect, and lead to lower average fragmentation. Second, our workload study indicated that there are many small jobs and many jobs that are powers of two. Both these classes are easier to pack than large jobs with strange sizes.

In the future, we would like to extend this work in the following directions:

- Improve the workload model even further, by making a more quantitative analysis and by studying the arrival process in more detail. For example, is the common assumption of a constant arrival rate a good model, or are there large fluctuations?
- Check what features of the workload model are the most significant ones, in terms of their effect on the results. for example, is user modeling important or can it be ignored?
- Add batch processing both to the workload model and to the gang scheduling algorithm. This is a significant issue because batch jobs, unlike interactive jobs, can be buffered by the system and used to fill in holes that would otherwise be lost to fragmentation.
- Add memory considerations to the mapping schemes. This is hampered at present by the lack of any real data about memory requirements of parallel jobs.

References

1. A. Barak and A. Shiloh, "*A distributed load-balancing policy for a multicomputer*". *Software — Pract. & Exp.* **15**(9), pp. 901–913, Sep 1985.
2. J. M. Barton and N. Bitar, "*A scalable multi-discipline, multiple-processor scheduling framework for IRIX*". In *Job Scheduling Strategies for Parallel Processing*, D. G. Feitelson and L. Rudolph (eds.), pp. 45–69, Springer-Verlag, 1995. Lecture Notes in Computer Science Vol. 949.
3. S-H. Chiang, R. K. Mansharamani, and M. K. Vernon, "*Use of application characteristics and limited preemption for run-to-completion parallel processor scheduling policies*". In *SIGMETRICS Conf. Measurement & Modeling of Comput. Syst.*, pp. 33–44, May 1994.
4. E. G. Coffman, Jr., M. R. Garey, and D. S. Johnson, "*Approximation algorithms for bin-packing — an updated survey*". In *Algorithm Design for Computer Systems Design*, G. Ausiello, M. Lucertini, and P. Serafini (eds.), pp. 49–106, Springer-Verlag, 1984.
5. E. G. Coffman, Jr., M. R. Garey, and D. S. Johnson, "*Bin packing with divisible item sizes*". *J. Complex.* **3**(4), pp. 406–428, Dec 1987.
6. F. Douglis and J. Ousterhout, "*Process migration in the Sprite operating system*". In *7th Intl. Conf. Distributed Comput. Syst.*, pp. 18–25, Sep 1987.
7. D. G. Feitelson, *A Survey of Scheduling in Multiprogrammed Parallel Systems*. Research Report RC 19790 (87657), IBM T. J. Watson Research Center, Oct 1994.
8. D. G. Feitelson and B. Nitzberg, "*Job characteristics of a production parallel scientific workload on the NASA Ames iPSC/860*". In *Job Scheduling Strategies for Parallel Processing*, D. G. Feitelson and L. Rudolph (eds.), pp. 337–360, Springer-Verlag, 1995. Lecture Notes in Computer Science Vol. 949.
9. D. G. Feitelson and L. Rudolph, "*Distributed hierarchical control for parallel processing*". *Computer* **23**(5), pp. 65–77, May 1990.
10. D. G. Feitelson and L. Rudolph, "*Evaluation of design choices for gang scheduling using distributed hierarchical control*". *J. Parallel & Distributed Comput.*, 1996. to appear.
11. D. G. Feitelson and L. Rudolph, "*Parallel job scheduling: issues and approaches*". In *Job Scheduling Strategies for Parallel Processing*, D. G. Feitelson

and L. Rudolph (eds.), pp. 1–18, Springer-Verlag, 1995. Lecture Notes in Computer Science Vol. 949.

12. D. G. Feitelson and L. Rudolph, *"Wasted resources in gang scheduling"*. In 5th *Jerusalem Conf. Information Technology*, pp. 127–136, IEEE Computer Society Press, Oct 1990.

13. B. Gorda and R. Wolski, *"Time sharing massively parallel machines"*. In *Intl. Conf. Parallel Processing*, Aug 1995.

14. B. C. Gorda and E. D. Brooks III, *Gang Scheduling a Parallel Machine*. Technical Report UCRL-JC-107020, Lawrence Livermore National Laboratory, Dec 1991.

15. S. Hotovy, *"Workload evolution on the Cornell Theory Center IBM SP2"*. In *Job Scheduling Strategies for Parallel Processing II*, D. G. Feitelson and L. Rudolph (eds.), Springer-Verlag, 1996. Lecture Notes in Computer Science.

16. Intel Corp., *iPSC/860 Multi-User Accounting, Control, and Scheduling Utilities Manual*. Order number 312261-002, May 1992.

17. Intel Supercomputer Systems Division, *Paragon User's Guide*. Order number 312489-003, Jun 1994.

18. K. C. Knowlton, *"A fast storage allocator"*. *Comm. ACM* 8(10), pp. 623–625, Oct 1965.

19. P. Krueger, T-H. Lai, and V. A. Radiya, *"Processor allocation vs. job scheduling on hypercube computers"*. In 11th *Intl. Conf. Distributed Comput. Syst.*, pp. 394–401, May 1991.

20. S. T. Leutenegger and M. K. Vernon, *"The performance of multiprogrammed multiprocessor scheduling policies"*. In *SIGMETRICS Conf. Measurement & Modeling of Comput. Syst.*, pp. 226–236, May 1990.

21. D. Lifka, *"The ANL/IBM SP scheduling system"*. In *Job Scheduling Strategies for Parallel Processing*, D. G. Feitelson and L. Rudolph (eds.), pp. 295–303, Springer-Verlag, 1995. Lecture Notes in Computer Science Vol. 949.

22. M. H. MacDougall, *Simulating Computer Systems: Techniques and Tools*. MIT Press, 1987.

23. S. Majumdar, D. L. Eager, and R. B. Bunt, *"Scheduling in multiprogrammed parallel systems"*. In *SIGMETRICS Conf. Measurement & Modeling of Comput. Syst.*, pp. 104–113, May 1988.

24. J. K. Ousterhout, *"Scheduling techniques for concurrent systems"*. In 3rd *Intl. Conf. Distributed Comput. Syst.*, pp. 22–30, Oct 1982.

25. J. L. Peterson and T. A. Norman, *"Buddy systems"*. *Comm. ACM* 20(6), pp. 421–431, Jun 1977.

26. D. L. Russell, *"Internal fragmentation in a class of buddy systems"*. *SIAM J. Comput.* 6(4), pp. 607–621, Dec 1977.

27. T. Suzuoka, J. Subhlok, and T. Gross, *Evaluating Job Scheduling Techniques for Highly Parallel Computers*. Technical Report CMU-CS-95-149, School of Computer Science, Carnegie Mellon University, 1995.

28. Thinking Machines Corp., *Connection Machine CM-5 Technical Summary*. Nov 1992.

29. M. Wan, R. Moore, G. Kremenek, and K. Steube, *"A batch scheduler for the Intel Paragon MPP system with a non-contiguous node allocation algorithm"*. In *Job Scheduling Strategies for Parallel Processing II*, D. G. Feitelson and L. Rudolph (eds.), Springer-Verlag, 1996. Lecture Notes in Computer Science.

30. G. K. Zipf, *Human Behavior and the Principle of Least Effort*. Addison-Wesley, 1949.

A Gang Scheduling Design for Multiprogrammed Parallel Computing Environments

Fang Wang[†], Hubertus Franke[‡], Marios Papaefthymiou[†], Pratap Pattnaik[‡], Larry Rudolph[‡*], Mark S. Squillante[‡]

[†]Computer Science Department
Yale University
New Haven, CT 06520-8285
{wang-fang,papaefthymiou-marios}@cs.yale.edu

[‡]IBM Research Division
T.J. Watson Research Center
Yorktown Heights, NY 10598
{frankeh,pratap,mss}@watson.ibm.com

Abstract. Gang scheduling is a resource management scheme for parallel and distributed systems that combines time-sharing and space-sharing to ensure high overall system throughput and short response times for interactive tasks. We recently participated in the design and implementation of a flexible gang scheduling scheme on an IBM SP2 parallel system and a cluster of IBM RS/6000 workstations. In this paper, we present our gang scheduling system and some results of a mathematical model for our system. Using this model, we can obtain exact solutions for measures of system performance as a function of scheduling policy parameters, and thus determine optimal values for several system and policy variables such as the amount of time allocated to the time-slice of each task.

1 Introduction

A good job scheduler in a multiprogrammed, parallel processing environment balances the user's desire to complete its job as quickly as possible with the system's desire to service as many jobs as possible. For example, dedicating all of resources to one job at a time provides the best response time for that job while providing no service time guarantees to any other job.

Many scheduling schemes for multiprogrammed parallel systems have been proposed or implemented and can mostly can be classified as time-sharing, space-sharing, or a mixture of both. In purely time-shared systems, all processors work on a single job for a specified amount of time. Thus, since time-sharing ensures that all jobs will gain some access to the system's resources within a relatively

---

* Larry Rudolph is currently leave from the Hebrew University (Jerusalem) rudolph@cs.huji.ac.il and is visiting the MIT Lab for Computer Science rudolph@lcs.mit.edu

short period of time, it is particularly suitable for interactive tasks. There are situations, however, in which jobs may not need, or cannot efficiently utilize, all of the available processors in the system. It has been argued, for example, that performance does not increase as the number of processors dedicated to a job increases past a certain limit [3, 15]. Thus, simply allocating the total number of available processors to a job can underutilize the system's resources, particularly under workloads with nonuniform resource requirements as can be common in scientific/engineering computing environments [25, 21, 22, 6, 13, 12]. To address this problem, several systems employ different space-sharing strategies in which jobs share the system resources at any given time instead of having each job reserve all of the resources [27, 32, 4, 18, 33, 10, 11, 20, 21, 22, 26, 2, 24, 28]. Space-sharing can provide very efficient resource utilization, decrease resource fragmentation and increase system throughput.

Just as time-sharing on conventional machines provides the user with the fiction of a dedicated machine, a *gang scheduler* can do the same for a parallel machine, by ensuring that all the components of a parallel job execute at the same time. A parallel job or a *gang* consists of a set of processes or *gang members*, with each gang member executing on a different processor. Thus, when a job is gang scheduled, all of its gang members execute in parallel and during a gang context switch, all the members of one gang are suspended and the members of another gang are scheduled. The execution of a gang is time-shared with other gang and when a gang does not fillup the whole machine, several gangs may execute side by side in a space-sharing manner. Such gang scheduling has been shown to be effective when there is fine-grained interaction among the components of a parallel job [7, 8, 9].

Even though gang scheduling can be difficult to implement due to its system-wide context switches, it has several advantages provided that the granularity of the time-sharing component is sufficiently coarse to outweigh the overhead of context switching. It is therefore becoming increasingly popular. In particular, gang scheduling promotes efficient fine-grain interactions among threads in the same gang and provides interactive response time for short jobs.

We have recently participated in the implementation[2] of a scheduling system for the IBM SP–2 computer that features flexible partitions and flexible time slices for each partition [31]. In the scheduler, each job or gang is allocated to a certain configuration of the processors. The gang members of each job execute concurrently and are preempted at the same time when the time slice allocated to the job expires. All jobs are not treated equally; jobs are statically assigned to classes. Each class is allocated a certain fraction of execution time, has its own scheduling strategy, and handles particular ranges of job sizes (in terms of parallelism). Although a job may be guaranteed to be executing a fraction f of the time, the system is free to choose the size of the time slice or the size of the time quantum.

In this paper, we give an overview of our gang scheduling system and its implementation, and analyze some of its key properties, especially the affect of

---

[2] Franke, Pattnaik, and Rudolph are responsible for the design and implementation.

the time quantum size. Our parallel scheduling system is relatively complex and a detailed analysis of its performance characteristics is not straightforward. Fortunately, we recently developed a general model of the gang scheduling system and derived an exact mathematical analysis of some of the properties of our model [29]. Our focus here is not on the complete gang scheduling model and its solution,[3] but instead we use the model in this paper to analyze the performance characteristics of such a parallel system based on various system variables including the workload, arrival rate, and service rate. To our knowledge, such detailed performance analysis results on gang scheduling have not been previously obtained. Most of the previous work on parallel gang scheduling has been empirical and has concentrated on systems issues without analyzing the quantitative properties of the system and their parameters. Our model and related analysis can and is being used to guide additional implementation efforts and performance tuning of multiprogrammed parallel systems.

The remainder of this paper is organized as follows. In Section 2 we review the gang scheduling strategy and summarize the model in Section 3. Section 4 presents a number of experimental results that provide important insights into the implementation and parameterization of gang scheduling in real multiprogrammed parallel computing environments. We conclude with directions for future research.

2   Parallel System Implementation

This section provides an overview of our gang scheduling scheme. We emphasize the flexible partitions and flexible time quantum for each partition. The scheme can be applied to a wide spectrum of parallel and distributed systems. A fuller discription of the scheme, its motivation and implementation challenges appears elsewhere [31].

A parallel job is taken to consist of a collection of processes called a *gang*, where each process maps to a single processor for execution. The scheduling of each of these processes or *gang members* is controlled by the *local schedulers* and the relevant context switching machinery is provided by the local operating systems. If standard communication interfaces (e.g., TCP/IP) are used, context switching can be accomplished by suspending and awakening processes via signal interaction. The presence of high performance communication subsystems (e.g., IBM SP2) can add certain system specific complexity to the context switching, which is described elsewhere [30]. Nevertheless, in this paper we assume that a context switching facility has been provided by the operating system.

The system consists of a *global gang scheduler manager* and a *local scheduler* on each processor. The local scheduler carries out scheduling of processes based on a table that is provided by the global scheduler. The assignment of a job's processes to the local scheduling tables of its assigned processors and the assurance that the tables are consistent (i.e., that the processes of one job are

---

[3] We refer the interested reader elsewhere [29] for these and other technical details.

executing at the same time) is enforced by the global scheduler. In our scheduling scheme, several jobs are allowed to execute at the same time on disjoint processors. Each job is allocated to a certain configuration of processors with a thread of control on each processor. Time-sharing of jobs on the processors is supported. The processes of each job execute concurrently and are preempted when the time quantum for the job is used up. Instead of using a global signalling mechanism, it is sufficient to inform each processor of the time quantums allocated to each process during a scheduling round. The SP–2 system has a reasonably consistent time service based on a synchronous network and an NTP implementation. When load conditions change, then each processor is notified and can recompute the context switch times for all of the processes it controls. Both batch and interactive jobs can be supported in our system.

The global scheduling strategy we employ is based on the distributed hierarchical control (DHC) structure [7, 8] and its corresponding algorithms. The global scheduler is distributed rather than centralized. Jobs submitted to the system are grouped into different *classes* according to the number of processors they require. We have chosen to provide classes for jobs requiring power-of-two processors. Jobs with non power-of-two processes are assigned to the next higher class. That is to say, a job requires p processors will be assigned to class j where $2^j \geq p > 2^{j-1}$. Each class may have its own scheduling policy to provide more flexibility. For instance, a system could have one class with priority scheduling where another class with round robin scheduling. It is possible to have several subclasses with different properties, say one for compute intensive jobs and another for i/o intensive jobs of the same parallelism, but we do not consider this generalization here. An example of an 8-processor system with the corresponding distributed hierarchical control and job classes are shown in Figure 1.

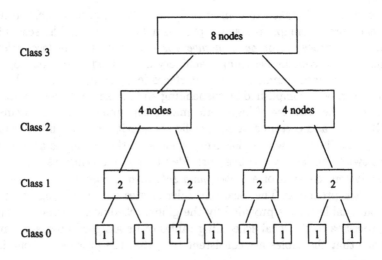

Fig. 1. distributed hierarchical control structure for an 8 processor system

Each class has a corresponding job queue associated with it. A *scheduling round* is a period of time during which each queue executes at least one of its jobs at least once. In the scheduling table maintained by the local scheduler, each row_i of the table contains the queue of processes for class i and a time quantum F_i which represents the time fraction for processes in that queue to execute. By definition $\sum F_i = 1$. It is reasonable to allocate longer time quantum for class with higher context switch cost and class demanding shorter response time. An example scheduling table for an 8-processor system is given in Figure 2.

Class	Fraction (f_i)	Policy
3	.50	Round Robin
2	.25	priority
1	.15	fifo
0	.10	nice

Fig. 2. An example of a scheduling table for a 8 node parallel machine. Each row corresponds to a different "class" of the scheduling tree. Jobs of gang size larger than 4 are described by the top row (class 3). For the system shown in this table, half of the machine resources are given to large jobs by allocating half of the cycle time to that class of jobs.

Conceptionally, we can impose a binary tree of controllers on top of the P processors in the system. Each controller controls the gangs within its subtree. The tree is of height $logP$ and each node is a controller with $2P-1$ controllers in total. In reality, each path in the tree is collected into a gang manager that runs on the processors associated with the leaf node. Hence, any one processor can communicate to any other processor in this layout with the maximum $2(logP)$ communication links.

In our particular system implementation, we have focused on the following First-Come First-Served (FCFS) – Round Robin scheduling strategy. Since class i handles gang sized between 2^{i-1} and 2^i, there can be up to $P/2^i$ gangs executing side by side in a system with P processors. During each time quantum for class p, the first $P/2^p$ jobs on the class p queue are each executed in parallel. Upon the service completion of one such job, the released partition of size 2^p is allocated to the next job on the class p queue (if any). When the number of class p jobs is less than $P/2^p$, the system attempts to allocate the available processors to classes $p-1, \ldots, 0$. If these available processors are not allocated, an arriving job of class p that finds a queue length (including the jobs in service) less than $P/2^p$ is immediately allocated one of the available partitions. From the viewpoint of each class, there is a fixed group of processors and a dedicated fraction of execution time from the scheduling round. Therefore, when a job enters the scheduling system, the upper bound that when the job will be done can be decided. Hence, this scheme guarantees certain service time for accepted jobs.

We have implemented the above scheduling strategy for a cluster of workstations where intra-job communication is performed over TCP/IP. The system has proven to be flexible yet simple. Furthermore the hierarchical infrastructure required to realize the scheduling scheme does not impose heavy messaging traffic among processors, hence the load on the system was limited. Last it satisfies the guaranteed service requirements for users.

The following is concerned with the allocation of time quantum for each class. One method is to have fixed quantum for each class. However, some mechanism is required to assign the idle time of a class with no jobs to other classes with waiting jobs in the queue. Another method of time allocation is to decide the time quantum for each job class depending on the job arrival and service rates for different classes, and the context switch time between classes. We use a mathematical model to determine the optimal time allocation in our system dynamically. This dynamic adjustment of time quanta provides better utilization and higher flexibility. We discuss this time quanta allocation in the next section in somewhat more detail. Another issue needs to consider is to reduce the fragmentation within each class. We are working on some algorithms to move the fragmented nodes in one class up or down the tree to be used by other levels in the tree.

3 Parallel Gang Scheduling Model

In this section we summarize the analytic model used to analyze and determine the optimal time-quanta allocation in our gang scheduling system. The technical details on our mathematical model and its exact solution are presented elsewhere [29].

We model a parallel processing system consisting of P identical processors and L different classes of jobs that are scheduled according to the gang scheduling scheme defined in Section 2. Recall that each job class p, $0 \leq p < L$, divides the processors into partitions of size 2^p on which the jobs of class p are executed, and that a FCFS system queue is associated with each job class from which the processor partitions select work for execution.

We model the following times:

- Time between job arrivals in class p
- Execution Time for class for jobs in p
- Context Switch Overheads between jobs of class p and class $p + 1$
- Time-slice lengths

as independent and identically distributed random variables with a phase-type probability distribution $A_p(\cdot)$ and mean interarrival time $1/\lambda_p$. Each of the four times has is own distribution and mean constants and each are also a function of the job class. The use of phase-type distributions [23] for our model parameters is motivated in part by their important mathematical properties, which can be exploited to obtain a tractable analytic model while capturing the fundamental aspects of our gang scheduling system. Just as important, however, is the fact that any real distribution can in principle be represented arbitrarily close by a phase-type distribution, and a number of algorithms have been developed for fitting phase-type distributions to empirical data [1, 5, 16, 17].

Multiple class p arrivals, multiple class p departures, and both a class p arrival and departure within a small time interval Δt are all assumed to occur with probability of order o(Δt) [14]. Under our assumption of phase-type distributions, this leads to a particular class of Markov chains called *quasi-birth-death processes* [23] which is a generalization of birth-death processes from classical queueing theory [14]. Our mathematical analysis is easily extended to handle batch arrivals and/or departures as long as the batch sizes are bounded, see [29].

The above parallel system employs the gang scheduling policy of Section 2 under which for each job class p, up to $P/2^p$ jobs space-share all of the P system processors. Processors are dedicated to each of the L job classes in a time-sharing manner by rotating the time allocated to the job classes. Without loss of generality, we define a *timeplexing cycle* to be the interval of time between successive time-slices, or *quantums*, for class 0. The nth timeplexing cycle is comprised of a fixed execution quantum for each job class p of length $T_{p,n}$, $0 \leq p < L$, $n \geq 1$, as well as context-switch overheads $C_{p,n}$ for switching between classes p and $(p-1) \bmod L$. The length of the nth timeplexing cycle is therefore given by $T_n = \sum_{p=0}^{L-1}(T_{p,n} + C_{p,n})$.

If the class p queue becomes empty before its quantum expires, i.e., there are no class p jobs in the system, then the system context-switches to the jobs of class $(p-1) \bmod L$. Thus, $T_{p,n}$ is the minimum of the class p time-slice length (having distribution $\mathcal{G}_p(\cdot)$ and mean $1/\gamma_p$) and the time required to empty queue p on its nth time slice, $0 \leq p < L$, $n \geq 1$.

Different methods can be implemented to support this level of context switching in our gang scheduling system, each of which have important implications on system performance both in terms of their mean and variance. Moreover, given specific parameters for a particular implementation (e.g., the time required to context switch between classes), other system parameters must be tuned to achieve the best overall performance and/or to provide guaranteed levels of service for each task executing on the system.

This gang scheduling model is solved for various system parameters and the corresponding measure of the mean number of class p jobs in the system, denoted by $\overline{N}_p$, is computed. The mean response time for class p, denoted by $\overline{T}_p$, is then calculated using Little's result[19] as $\overline{N}_p/\lambda_p$.

4 Results

In this section we present some results from the application of our analytic model to an 8-processor system. We have performed three experiments that illustrate the effects of various system parameters on the mean number of jobs in the system which gives a good indication of the overall system performance. The specific parameters we have investigated are the mean quantum length, the mean service rate, and the relative quantum length of each class within a timeplexing cycle. These experiments illustrate the general utility of our proposed techniques for performance tuning of multiprogrammed parallel systems.

4.1 Number of Jobs as a Function of Mean Quantum Length

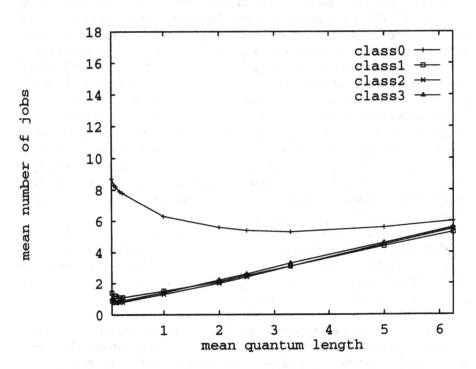

Fig. 3. Mean number of jobs versus mean quantum length for a system with 8 processors and utilization factor $\rho = 0.4$.

Figures 3 and 4 give the mean number of jobs in a lightly and a heavily loaded system, respectively, as a function of the mean quantum length $1/\gamma$. In both figures, data have been obtained for an 8-processor system with four classes $p = 0, 1, 2, 3$ and 2^{3-p} servers in each class. For each p, the mean quantum length $1/\gamma_p$ equals $1/\gamma$, and the mean service rates μ_p satisfy $\mu_0 : \mu_1 : \mu_2 : \mu_3 = 0.5 : 1 : 2 : 4$. For each class p in Figure 3, the mean arrival rate λ_p is 0.4, and therefore, the total utilization factor $\rho = \sum_p \rho_p = \sum_p (\lambda_p \cdot 2^p / \mu_p \cdot P)$ equals 0.4. For each class p in Figure 4, however, the mean arrival rate λ_p is 0.9, and the utilization factor ρ equals 0.9.

Our experiment shows that as quantum lengths start increasing from zero, the mean number of jobs decreases very fast. As quantum lengths increase past a certain point, however, the curves "bend", and the mean number of jobs increases monotonically. The heavier the system load, the closer to each other are the

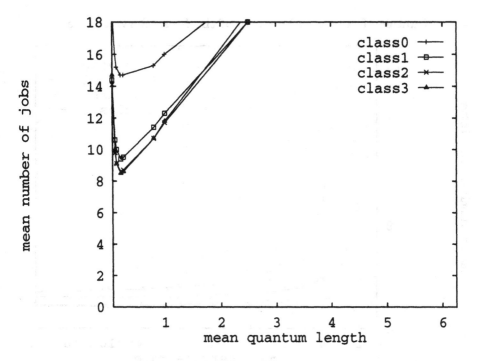

Fig. 4. Mean number of jobs versus mean quantum length for a system with 8 processors and utilization factor $\rho = 0.9$.

"knee" points of the curves. The surprising fact about these curves is that longer quanta result in more jobs in the system.

This seemingly counterintuitive behavior can be explained as follows. When the quantum length is close to zero, the context switch overhead dominates system performance. The steep decrease of the curve for very small quantum lengths is a direct consequence of decreasing this overhead.

As quantum lengths become longer, switching takes a smaller portion of each quantum and more time is allocated to job service. As long as the quantum length of a class does not exceed the mean service time of each job in that class, every server is busy during its time slice, and it pays off to let it run longer.

When the quantum length increases way past the mean service time of each job, however, then the situation becomes similar to an exhaustive service model, where newly arriving jobs in other job classes keep jumping in until the end of the corresponding time quantum. In this case, most of the servers in these classes are idling and switching to another class with a full queue is delayed, thus increasing the average number of jobs in the system.

4.2 Number of Jobs as a Function of the Mean Service Rate

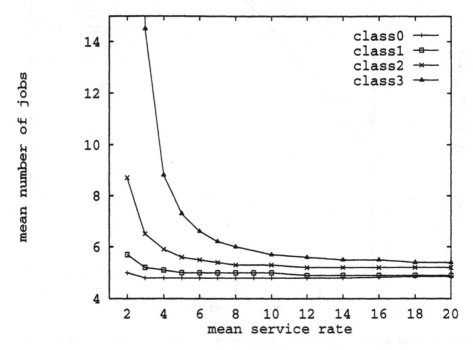

Fig. 5. Mean number of jobs versus mean service rate for a system with 8 processors.

The results of our second experiment are shown in the graphs of Figure 5 which gives the mean number of jobs in an 8-processor system as a function of the mean service rate of each server. For each class p, the quantum length $1/\gamma_p$ equals 5, and the arrival rate λ_p equals 0.6. All classes have the same mean service rate μ_p. Our experiment shows that the mean number of jobs decreases dramatically as the mean service rate starts increasing. After a certain point, however, the rate of decrease becomes very low, and there is no significant benefit from any further increase in the service rate.

4.3 Effect of Context Switch Overhead

Our third experiment focused on the effect of context switch overhead effects on the system performance. The results of our experiment are shown in Figure 6 and Figure 7 which shows the contrast between low vs. high context switch overhead. The graphs in these figures have been obtained assuming that the arrival rates λ_p equal 0.8 for every class p and that the total utilization factor ρ is 0.8. The context switch cost between classes is assumed to be 0.02 in Figure 6 and 0.1 in Figure 7. Therefore, the cost in Figure 7 is five times that in Figure 6. We can see that the larger the switch cost, the more jobs waiting in system before and around the "knee" point. It also changes the position of the "knee" point and

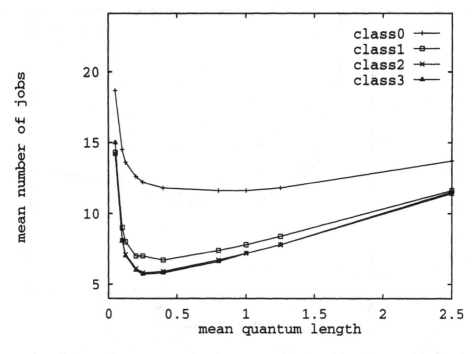

Fig. 6. Mean number of jobs versus mean quantum length for a system with 8 processors and utilization factor $\rho = 0.8$, context switch cost 0.02

the sharpness of the "knee" point. So, coarse-grained gang scheduling, with high context switching overheads, is useful only for "computationally heavy" jobs and for those, it is better to have slightly longer mean quantum times.

4.4 Number of Jobs as Function of Relative Quantum Times

Our fourth experiment focused on the mean number of jobs as a function of the fraction of the quantum lengths of each class over the timeplexing cycle length of the system. The results of our experiment are shown in Figure 8. The graphs in this figure have been obtained assuming that the arrival rates λ_p equal 0.6 for every class p and that the total utilization factor ρ is 0.6. Our data show that for every class, the mean number of jobs decreases monotonically as the quantum length of that class becomes a larger percentage of the timeplexing cycle length. Similar graphs can be obtained for any specified cycle length, arrival times and service times. These graphs can be used to tune the quantum lengths of the given parallel multiprogrammed system in order to maximize its performance. For instance, we can use these results to decide the optimal quantum allocation for each class under heavy traffic conditions. In future, we will also monitor the real system execution with the guidance from the numerical solutions, and compare the actual system behaviors.

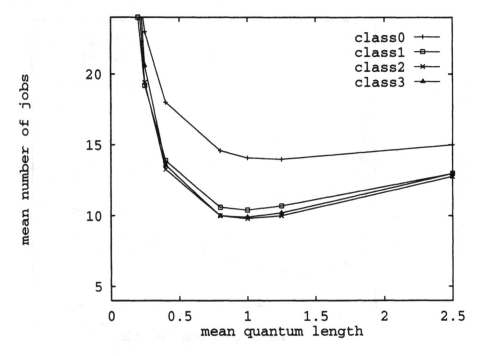

Fig. 7. Mean number of jobs versus mean quantum length for a system with 8 processors and utilization factor $\rho = 0.8$, context switch cost 0.1

5 Conclusion

Designing a job scheduler that is to be used in a parallel machine requires attention to many details. In this paper we have presented a high level design for a gang scheduler in massively parallel processing environments. The distributed, hierarchical control structure allows it to be scalable and distributed in its design. To avoid large latencies and high variations in signal propagation, the system utilizes the local clocks, synchronized by services such as NTP, to control the coordinated context switching of gang members. At the start of each scheduling round, the local schedulers are given the times during which their gang members are to be scheduled. The whole design is layered to support a variety of scheduling policies so that different classes of jobs can be handled in the appropriate manner. For example, large, memory intensive compute-bound jobs have different needs than short, interactive ones. Each job class is allocated a fixed fraction of the scheduling round time. Thus, for particular classes, a bound on the number of jobs and a choice of the right scheduling policy can guarantee a quality of service to the jobs in that class.

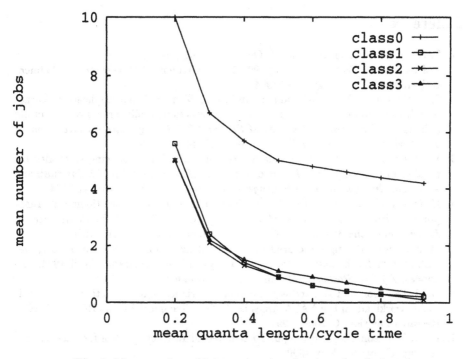

Fig. 8. Mean number of jobs versus time fraction of each class

Furthermore this paper has presented performance results from an analytic queueing model for this scheme, and has shown that one can easily choose parameters of the algorithm that makes the outcome less sensitive to reasonable fluctuations in the job arrival patterns and resource requirement patterns. Although the experiments were run on only an eight node system, it was enough to show that the choice of quantum time is critical to the overall system performance as well as verifying the analytical model. The experiments helped refine the model.

There are many implementation issues that are important and critical to the success of a job scheduler. Among these include allocation of idle time resulting from early job termination or from gang sizes that are not a power of two. These issues are orthogonal to the issue of quantum time and the correctness of the analytical model.

We are examining ways to extent this scheduler to support a wide range of different scheduling policies while retaining its scalability.

Acknowledgement

We would like to thank Kattamuri Ekanadham at the IBM T.J. Watson Research Center for our discussions about the system and general scheduling themes involved.

References

1. S. Asmussen, O. Nerman, and M. Olsson. Fitting phase type distributions via the EM algorithm. Technical Report 1994:23, Department of Mathematics, Chalmers University of Technology, May 1994.

2. S.-H. Chiang, R. K. Mansharamani, and M. K. Vernon. Use of application characteristics and limited preemption for run-to-completion parallel processor scheduling policies. In *Proceedings of the ACM SIGMETRICS Conference on Measurement and Modeling of Computer Systems*, pages 33–44, May 1994.

3. V. D. Cung et al. Concurrent data structures and load balancing strategies for parallel branch-and-bound/a* algorithms. In *The Third DIMACS International Algorithm Implementation Challenge on Parallel Algorithms*, October 1994.

4. K. Dussa, B. Carlson, L. Dowdy, and K.-H. Park. Dynamic partitioning in transputer environments. In *Proceedings of the ACM SIGMETRICS Conference on Measurement and Modeling of Computer Systems*, pages 203–213, 1990.

5. M. J. Faddy. Fitting structured phase-type distributions. Technical report, Department of Mathematics, University of Queensland, Australia, April 1994. To appear, *Applied Stochastic Models and Data Analysis*.

6. D. G. Feitelson and B. Nitzberg. Job characteristics of a production parallel scientific workload on the NASA Ames iPSC/860. Technical Report RC 19773, IBM Research Division, October 1994.

7. D. G. Feitelson and L. Rudolph. Distributed hierarchical control for parallel processing. *Computer*, May 1990.

8. D. G. Feitelson and L. Rudolph. Mapping and scheduling in a shared parallel environment using distributed hierarchical control. In *Proceedings of the International Conference on Parallel Processing*, volume I, pages 1–8, August 1990.

9. D. G. Feitelson and L. Rudolph. Gang scheduling performance benefits for fine-grain synchronization. *Journal of Parallel and Distributed Computing*, 16(4):306–318, December 1992.

10. D. Ghosal, G. Serazzi, and S. K. Tripathi. The processor working set and its use in scheduling multiprocessor systems. *IEEE Transactions on Software Engineering*, 17:443–453, May 1991.

11. A. Gupta, A. Tucker, and S. Urushibara. The impact of operating system scheduling policies and synchronization methods on the performance of parallel applications. In *Proceedings of the ACM SIGMETRICS Conference on Measurement and Modeling of Computer Systems*, May 1991.

12. S. Hotovy. Cornell Theory Center workload measurements. Personal Communications, 1995.

13. S. Hotovy, D. Schneider, and T. O'Donnell. Analysis of the early workload on the Cornell Theory Center IBM SP2. Technical report, Cornell Theory Center, 1995.

14. L. Kleinrock. *Queueing Systems Volume I: Theory*. John Wiley and Sons, 1975.

15. A. Krishnamurthy et al. Connected components on distributed memory machines. In *The Third DIMACS International Algorithm Implementation Challenge on Parallel Algorithms*, October 1994.

16. A. Lang. Parameter estimation for phase-type distributions, part I: Fundamentals and existing methods. Technical Report 159, Department of Statistics, Oregon State University, 1994.

17. A. Lang and J. L. Arthur. Parameter estimation for phase-type distributions, part II: Computational evaluation. Technical Report 160, Department of Statistics, Oregon State University, August 1994.

18. S. T. Leutenegger and M. K. Vernon. The performance of multiprogrammed multiprocessor scheduling policies. In *Proceedings of the ACM SIGMETRICS Conference on Measurement and Modeling of Computer Systems*, pages 226–236, May 1990.

19. J. D. C. Little. A proof of the queuing formula $L = \lambda W$. *Operations Research*, 9, 1961.

20. C. McCann, R. Vaswani, and J. Zahorjan. A dynamic processor allocation policy for multiprogrammed shared-memory multiprocessors. *ACM Transactions on Computer Systems*, 11(2):146–178, May 1993.

21. V. K. Naik, S. K. Setia, and M. S. Squillante. Performance analysis of job scheduling policies in parallel supercomputing environments. In *Proceedings of Supercomputing '93*, pages 824–833, November 1993.

22. V. K. Naik, S. K. Setia, and M. S. Squillante. Scheduling of large scientific applications on distributed memory multiprocessor systems. In *Proceedings Sixth SIAM Conference on Parallel Processing for Scientific Computing*, pages 913–922, March 1993.

23. M. F. Neuts. *Matrix-Geometric Solutions in Stochastic Models: An Algorithmic Approach*. The Johns Hopkins University Press, 1981.

24. E. Rosti, E. Smirni, L. W. Dowdy, G. Serazzi, and B. M. Carlson. Robust partitioning policies of multiprocessor systems. *Performance Evaluation*, 19:141–165, 1994.

25. R. Schreiber and H. D. Simon. Towards the teraflops capability for CFD. In H. D. Simon, editor, *Parallel CFD - Implementations and Results Using Parallel Computers*. MIT Press, 1992.

26. S. K. Setia and S. K. Tripathi. A comparative analysis of static processor partitioning policies for parallel computers. In *Proceedings of MASCOTS '93*, January 1993.

27. K. C. Sevcik. Characterizations of parallelism in applications and their use in scheduling. In *Proceedings of the ACM SIGMETRICS Conference on Measurement and Modeling of Computer Systems*, pages 171–180, May 1989.

28. K. C. Sevcik. Application scheduling and processor allocation in multiprogrammed parallel processing systems. *Performance Evaluation*, 19:107–140, 1994.

29. M. S. Squillante, F. Wang, and M. Papaefthymiou. An analysis of gang scheduling for multiprogrammed parallel computing environments. Technical report, IBM Research Division, January 1996. To appear in *Proceedings of the Eighth Annual ACM Symposium on Parallel Algorithms and Architectures (SPAA)*, June 1996.

30. H. Franke, P. Pattnaik. Technical report in preparation, IBM Research Division, January 1996

31. H. Franke, P. Pattnaik. Technical report in preparation, IBM Research Division, January 1996

32. A. Tucker and A. Gupta. Process control and scheduling issues for multiprogrammed shared-memory multiprocessors. In *Proceedings of the Twelfth ACM Symposium on Operating Systems Principles*, pages 159–166, December 1989.

33. J. Zahorjan and C. McCann. Processor scheduling in shared memory multiprocessors. In *Proceedings of the ACM SIGMETRICS Conference on Measurement and Modeling of Computer Systems*, pages 214–225, May 1990.

Implementation of Gang-Scheduling on Workstation Cluster

Atsushi Hori[1], Hiroshi Tezuka[1], Yutaka Ishikawa[1], Noriyuki Soda[2],
Hiroki Konaka[1], Munenori Maeda[1]

[1] Tsukuba Research Center, Real World Computing Partnership,
Tsukuba Mitsui Building 16F, 1-6-1 Takezono, Tsukuba-shi, Ibaraki 305, JAPAN
URL:http://www.rwcp.or.jp/people/mpslab/score/scored/scored.html
[2] Software Research Associates, Inc.

Abstract. The goal of this paper is to determine how efficiently we can implement an adequate parallel programming environment on a workstation cluster without modifying the existing operating system. We have implemented a runtime environment for parallel programs and gang-scheduling on a workstation cluster. In this paper, we report the techniques used to implement an efficient runtime environment and gang-scheduling on a workstation cluster. The most important technique is "network preemption." A unique feature of our approach is that the gang-scheduling is also written in a parallel language. Our evaluation shows that gang-scheduling on workstation clusters can be practical.

1 Introduction

Workstation clusters are gathering attentions as an alternative to parallel machines [1, 2, 14]. If a workstation cluster can be made to imitate a parallel machine, then it would be a cost-effective and familiar-to-use parallel execution environment. To prove this, we have implemented a parallel program execution environment on a workstation cluster.

Gang-scheduling is known to be efficient for job scheduling parallel programs [11, 4, 16, 5, 2]. However, most of the work has been done by simulation and gang-scheduling overhead has not been taken into account. Further, it is not obvious how efficient it will be when implemented on workstation cluster.

Gang-scheduling is thought to be efficient for fine-grain parallel programs [11, 4, 16, 5, 2]. FM [12] and U-Net [17] put the communication layer at the user level to reduce communication overhead, and thus can handle finer grain parallel programs. We have also developed a communication layer at user level, called PM. However, user-level communication may result in inter-process interference problems during communication [6]. We avoid this problem by implementing "network preemption."

The goal of this paper is to determine how efficiently we can implement an adequate parallel programming environment on a workstation cluster without modifying the existing operating system. We have implemented an efficient runtime environment for parallel programs and gang-scheduling on a workstation cluster. In this paper, we report on the techniques we used to implement gang-scheduling on a workstation cluster, and the measured overhead of the gang-scheduling. A unique feature of our approach is that the gang-scheduling is also written in a parallel language.

2 Assumptions and Terminology

Parallel Process. A "parallel process" is a set of processes that are execution entities derived from the same single SPMD program. When parallel processes are switched, all parallel processes are assumed to be scheduled simultaneously (gang-scheduled).

Workstation Cluster. A workstation cluster is a set of workstations connected by a high-speed network. Here, the workstation cluster is a computation server for parallel (and sequential) programs. If a user requests n processors to run a parallel program, the system provides at least n processors out of N processors in the cluster ($n \leq N$). We assume that every workstation in the cluster is dedicated for use as a computation server. And we assume that none of the workstations are available for use as a personal computer.

This usage model is almost the same as the *Processor Pool Model* [15], except that our model can provide a "virtual parallel machine." The workstation cluster can be multiplexed in processor space and/or time to serve as a virtual parallel machine.

The current configuration of our workstation cluster is shown in Figure 1. Nine SS20s are connected by a Myrinet [3], a gigabit class high-speed LAN. All the evaluations in this paper are measured on this workstation cluster.

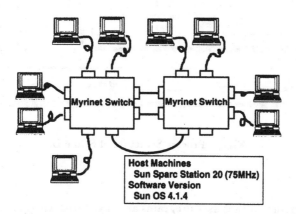

Fig. 1. Myrinet and SS20 Cluster

Processor. We assume all workstations have exactly one processor. This assumption simplifies the model used for explanation, and this is true of the workstation cluster we used.

3 SCore-D

SCore-D provide the execution environment for the workstation cluster. SCore-D is also a parallel process. Figure 2 shows the process structure on a workstation cluster with SCore-D. One of the SCore-D daemon processes is a dedicated server that is the entry point (connection host) from user programs. This process is called the "Server Process." The rest of the processes are called "SCore-D Processes."

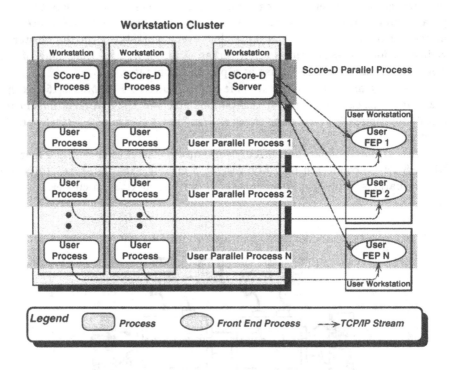

Fig. 2. Process Structure of SCore-D

Here, it is assumed that user programs are linked with an appropriate runtime library. When the user program is invoked on the user's local workstation, the runtime tries to make a TCP connection with the SCore-D server. The process running on the user's workstation is called the "Front End Process (FEP)." When the connection is established, the runtime passes information on the user's program to the SCore-D server, and the server broadcasts the information to the rest of the SCore-D processes. Then SCore-D processes spawn (**fork** and **exec**, in UNIX) the user processes, and the user processes now become a parallel process. When spawned, each user process make a TCP connection with the FEP. This TCP stream becomes the standard output of the user parallel process, and the FEP passes the streamed data to its standard output. Due to the limitation of the current version, one of the workstations in the cluster is a dedicated SCore-D server.

The user parallel process can be stopped, run, and killed, when the SCore-D processes send SIGSTOP, SIGCONT, and SIGKILL signals respectively to the child processes. SCore-D processes can also detect an abnormal termination in a user process. Using the signal functions of UNIX, SCore-D can schedule user parallel processes.

From the user's viewpoint, it looks as if the invoked user program spawns itself onto the workstations in the cluster. Further, when the FEP is suspended, resumed or killed by the user, the corresponding user parallel process is suspended, resumed or killed by SCore-D. Thus the FEP and spawned parallel process look seamless.

3.1 MPC++

The SCore-D program is written in MPC++ . The user parallel programs running under SCore-D are assumed to be written in MPC++ . Since SCore-D itself is a parallel program, it is natural to write in a multi-threaded parallel programming language.

MPC++ is a multithreaded parallel language based on C++[8; 10]. MPC++ provides a SPMD parallel programming model and threads of control to extract the full power of parallel machines or workstation clusters. One of the most unique features of MPC++ is meta-level programming which enables users to extend its language features [7, 9].

The MPC++ compiler consists of a front-end processor and a back-end processor. The front-end can also generate C++ source code and the generated C++ code can be compiled with the GNU g++ compiler. The MPC++ language features and the meta-programming results are thus compiled and will run on most computers.

3.2 MPC++ runtime library

The evaluated programs described in this paper are compiled with the MPC++ front-end processor and the GNU g++ compiler as a backend. The compiled codes are linked with the MPC++ runtime library. The library is designed to have low overhead and to support the functions required by MPC++ programs.

There are two kinds of runtime library for the MPC++ program. One is stand-alone and the other is assumed to run under SCore-D. The stand-alone version forks processes using the UNIX rsh command. We also implemented two versions to wait for incoming messages from remote processors, block-wait and busy-wait. The MPC++ process is blocked when there is no current message using block-wait. The MPC++ process continues spinning around until a remote message arrives by busy-wait. SCore-D uses the stand-alone, block-wait runtime library, while user parallel processes use the busy-wait runtime library. To do so, the blocking overhead in user processes can be avoided, and user processes can get more CPU time.

In the thread model of MPC++, when a thread suspends and waits at a synchronization point, its execution stack should be kept. This is a familiar thread model and setjmp and longjmp subroutines are used to implement thread context switching. It is known that longjmp takes a longer time on processors with register windows than on other kinds of processors. We have succeeded to fasten longjmp several times faster, writing our own setjmp and longjmp subroutines in assembler for SPARCstations.

The other key technique used in the MPC++ runtime library is our own Myrinet driver software, described in the next subsection. With our Myrinet software driver and the fast thread implementation, the MPC++ runtime library realizes a very efficient multi-threaded programing environment.

3.3 PM Communication library

The Myrinet LAN interface board has a dedicated processor, called LANai [3]. LANai software is also provided by Myricom, Inc. Their focus is, however, on achieving high bandwidth. The latency from the user level Myrinet LAN is only a few times faster than UDP with 10 base-T. This is not surprising as they are targeting users using Myrinet as an alternative to Ethernet.

FM [12] achieved 22 μ sec in one-way latency with the same Myrinet, using their own LANai program. We have also developed our own LANai program and driver program, called PM. PM achieved 24 μ sec in one-way latency. Both FM and PM implement the communication layer at user-level, and use neither system calls nor interrupts. In the order of micro-seconds, the overheads incurred by system calls or interrupts are prohibitive.

PM can support a multi-process environment, while FM cannot. PM has several communication channels[3]. A channel consists of two FIFO buffers for receiving and sending messages. Since these channels are memory-mapped, copying messages is avoided. These channels can be used to implement priority in message sending and receiving, or to realize a multi-process environment. In SCore-D, SCore-D processes use one channel, and the user processes use the other channel(s). If those channels are memory-mapped in each user address space, then the inter-process protection can be guaranteed.

For flow-control, an Ack message is sent back to the sender when the receiving is successful. If the receive buffer is full, a Nack message is sent back. At the sender, when the Ack message is received, PM just frees the sending message area of memory. Thus this flow-control mechanism does not result in doubling

---

[3] Currently three channels are implemented in PM.

the latency. If the sender receives a Nack message, then it sends the same message again. Note that this PM's flow-control strategy keeps message flying even if the receiver's buffer is full. Therefore dameon processes can communicate at any time, because no messages stay and block in the network for an infinite time.

Due to the multi-channel support and the flow-control, the PM performance is slightly degraded compared with FM. However, these are the keys to developing a multi-process environment, as described in the next subsection.

3.4 Support for gang-scheduling

The number of channels limits the number of simultaneously running processes. To support a multi-process environment, it is not enough to have multiple channels. Even if there were a sufficient number of channels, one should guarantee that there is no message in all those channels involved in the parallel process in the network, when the channel is reused. Otherwise a message being sent in a parallel process may be lost and the other parallel process may receive the message instead. This means that the numer of channels should be larger than the number of generated processes in the lifetime of the scheduling system.

If a message protocol layer exists in the operating system kernel, then this situation can be avoided. In this way, however, one can suffer from large communication overhead and can only handle coarser-grain parallelism. To avoid the communication overhead, all the message protocol layers should be implemented at user level [17]. Therefor we need a mechanism to detect when the messages for a parallel process in a network are flushed. If this is possible, then parallel processes can be preemptable, time-sharing of parallel processes can be implemented, and fast user-level communication is achieved at the same time.

To implement this requirement, we apply the Ack based protocol of PM to guarantee the non-existence of a message for a process in the network. It is necessary to sense the state in which PM (and LANai) has received all the Ack or Nack messages corresponding to the sending messages. We call this the "quiet state." Further, PM provides the other functions to save and restore the channel context.

However, we must still guarantee that no message comes while or after the channel context is being saved. Otherwise loss of message or an inconsistent channel status would result. Figure 3 shows the procedure to switch processes in gang-scheduling which guarantees this. This procedure exactly mirrors the SCore-D process. We assume that the SCore-D server process has control of process scheduling.

1. The server process decides to switch processes, and tells all SCore-D processes to stop currently-running user processes (FREEZE message in Figure 3).
2. Each SCore-D process sends SIGSTOP, and knows that the user process has stopped when it receives the SIGCHLD signal. Then SCore-D processes wait until the user's PM channel is in the quiet state.

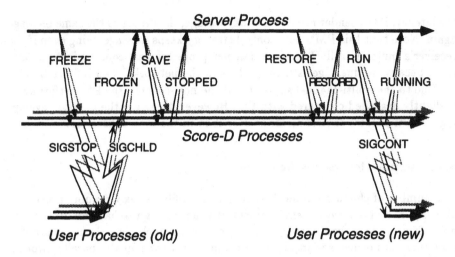

Fig. 3. Parallel Process Switching

3. The server process is informed each processor is now in the quiet state (FROZEN message). The server process waits until it receives a FROZEN message from each of the processors involved in user processes. This finally guarantees that there are no messages from user processes in the network.

4. After this guarantee, the server process tells all SCore-D processes to save the channel context (SAVE message).

5. Each SCore-D process saves its channel context. Completion of saving is reported to the server process (STOPPED message).

6. The server process waits for all STOPPED messages, to confirm that all user processes have been stopped. Then the server process tells user processes to restore the context of the next process to run with the RESTORE message.

7. Each SCore-D process restores the channel context, and reports to the server process when done (RESTORED message).

8. When the server process has received all RESTORED messages, the server tells all SCore-D processes to run the new user processes (RUN message).

9. The SCore-D process sends a SIGCONT signal, and reports to the server process (RUNNING message).

10. The server process now knows that all new user processes are running.

The above procedure can be thought of as "network preemption." We have already proposed that this network preemption can be used not only for gang-scheduling, but also to detect an idle or terminated status in a parallel process, checkpointing, or global GC [6].

4 Evaluation

Figures 4 and 5 are the MPC++ programs used to evaluate the SCore-D scheduling. Figure 4 is a fibonacci program to calculate the nth number in the fibonacci series. In this program, two threads are forked in a thread recursively (lines 8 and 9). The @ symbol at the end of the function call and the expression in square brackets indicates a synchronous remote function call of the function on the processor specified by the expression.

The first thread to calculate the $(n-1)$th term in the fibonacci series is forked and waits for its answer. Then the second thread to calculate the $(n-2)$th term is forked and waits again. Finally the answers return to their parent thread. Those threads are distributed simply in a round-robin fashion. The fib() function is the top level function to be used in the evaluation. It simply iterates to calculate the fibonacci term for the number of times specified in the loop argument.

Figure 5 is the other MPC++ program used in the evaluation. In this program, threads are forked to the next processor sequentially. A thread forks another thread to the next processor and terminates. In the notation of thread invocation in this program, the function is forked asynchronously (line 3). For more details, refer [7, 9, 10].

```
1 int pe;
2 int dist() {
3   return( pe = ( pe + 1 ) % NPE );
4 }
5 int fibonacci( int n ) {
6   if( n < 2 ) return( n );
7   else
8     return( fibonacci( n-1 )@[ dist() ] +
9             fibonacci( n-2 )@[ dist() ] );
10 }
11 void fib( int n, int loop ) {
12   int i;
13   for( i=0; i<loop; i++ )
14     fib( n );
15 }
```

Fig. 4. Example of MPC++ program

```
1 void rt( int hop_count ) {
2   if( hop_count == 0 ) exit( 0 );
3   rt( hop_count - 1 )@()[ next_pe() ];
4 }
```

Fig. 5. Round-Trip program

We chose those two evaluation programs because they are positioned on opposite sides in the execution pattern. The fibonacci program forks a number of threads almost explosively. In the round-trip program, however, there is no more than one running thread and no more than one message during the execution of the program.

4.1 MPC++ runtime performance

Table 1 shows the execution time for each evaluation program on our workstation cluster. For the fibonacci program, the larger the number of processors, the longer the execution time. This is because the granularity of the thread is too fine. In this paper, however, the communication and thread invocation pattern is the focus, not the speed. Supposedly, the execution time of a round-trip program is almost constant, independent of the number of processors, except in the case of one processor.

From the execution time of the round-trip program we can estimate the overhead for MPC++ runtime. It takes about 4 μsec. to fork a local thread. For a remote thread, it takes about 35 μsec. including 24 μ sec. one-way latency at the PM level. With the fibonacci program, we found that our MPC++ runtime is about 17 times faster than implementing the thread using LWP provided with the SunOS.

Table 1. Execution time of evaluation programs [*sec.*]

	Number of processors			
	1	2	4	8
fib(15,1000)	15.47	77.7	105.1	121.5
rt(1000000)	4.09	34.55	35.56	34.94

Table 2 shows the time to save or restore the network context at the PM level. In this table, buffer "empty" means that there is no message in the buffer, and "full" means that the buffer is almost full. A full receive buffer contains 2,730 messages in 32 KBytes. A full send buffer contains 511 messages in 12 KBytes.

As expected, the time to save or restore depends on the number of messages in the buffers. In this table, context saving takes more time than restoring. This is because reading from the S-Bus memory space is slower than writing to the S-Bus memory space.

Table 3 shows a comparison of elapsed time between the program linked with stand-alone runtime and the program running under SCore-D linked with SCore-D runtime. In this table, the time quantum of gang-scheduling is infinite. Since there is no reason for a slow-down in program execution under SCore-D, the speeds of the evaluation programs are the same.

Table 2. Network preemption time [$10^{-3} sec.$]

Buffer		Time	
Receive	Send	Save	Restore
empty	empty	0.13	0.11
empty	full	1.88	1.40
full	empty	3.39	1.95
full	full	5.15	3.22

Table 3. Elapsed Time Ratio under SCore-D

SCore-D/	Number of processors			
stand-alone	1	2	4	8
fib(15,1000)	1.00	0.99	1.01	1.01
rt(1000000)	1.00	1.01	0.97	1.00

Time Quantum : Infinite

4.2 Gang-scheduling performance

Figure 6 show the slow-down curves due to the gang-scheduling overhead on each evaluation program. The time quantum is varied between 200, 300, 500, and 1,000 msec. In each time quantum, the number of processors is also varied between 1, 2, 4 and 8.

The slow-down due to the scheduling overhead can be calculated as,

$$T_{Elapsed} = \frac{T_{Quantum}}{T_{Quantum} - T_{Overhead}} T_{Process}$$

where $T_{Elapsed}$ is the elapsed time, $T_{Quantum}$ is the time quantum, $T_{Overhead}$ is the scheduling overhead, and $T_{Process}$ is the processing time. Using this formula, the scheduling overhead times calculated from the evaluation results are shown in Table 4.

The possible reasons for scheduling overhead are, i) SCore-D overhead, ii) refilling the cache (flushed out by SCore-D), iii) saving and restoring the network context (network preemption), and iv) process switching at the UNIX level. The SCore-D overhead includes the costs of broadcasts and synchronizations. Thus the scheduling overhead can depend on the number of processors involved. The cost of network preemption depends on the number of messages and the total message size, as shown in Table 2. As with the round-trip program and any program with one processor, the overhead from network preemption can be neglected.

As shown in Figure 6, and also in Table 4, the scheduling overhead depends on the number of processors. According to our investigation, most of the overhead

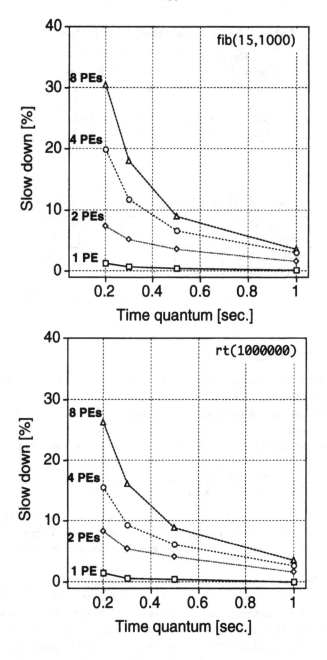

Fig. 6. Gang-scheduling Overhead

Table 4. Gang-scheduling Overhead [10^{-3} sec.]

	TQ	\multicolumn{4}{c}{Number of processors}			
		1	2	4	8
fib(15,1000)	200	2.6	13.9	33.1	46.6
	300	2.3	14.7	31.5	45.5
	500	2.3	14.7	31.5	45.5
	1000	1.6	16.1	29.9	35.1
rt(1000000)	200	3.0	15.3	27.0	41.6
	300	1.9	15.2	25.6	41.5
	500	2.5	19.5	28.8	41.0
	1000	0.2	15.8	25.8	34.5

comes from the delay of the SIGSTOP signal. Curiously the SIGSTOP signal to suspend other processes is delayed, and the delay time varies up to 50 msec. This phenomenon can not be found in the IRIX System V.4 (SiliconGraphics) or FreeBSD 2.0.0. We suppose that the SunOS (version 4.1.4) intentionally delays delivery of the SIGSTOP signal until the end of the time quantum. Since the server process should wait for all processes to stop, the time to stop a running parallel process depends on the number of processors involved, and is costly. Furthermore, the variance in SIGSTOP delivery creates a "coscheduling skew"[2]. Both of these can be severe problems when implementing gang-scheduling on a workstation cluster.

4.3 Voluntary gang scheduling

To avoid the delay in signal delivery, we implemented another version of gang-scheduling. The runtime library of user processes yields by itself when the time quantum ends. We call this version "voluntary gang-scheduling." Table 5 shows the overhead calculated in the same way as for Table 4. The overhead is reduced roughly three times or more at 8 processors. The dependence on the overhead with the number of processors is weakened. When the time quantum is one second, the slow-down due to the scheduling overhead is less than 1.4 %.

5 Concluding Remarks

SCore-D and the MPC++ runtime contribute to an efficient parallel program execution environment. The gang-scheduling of SCore-D realizes multi-user, multi-parallel-process environment. To implement efficient and practical gang-scheduling, we developed "network preemption."

It is very difficult to estimate and guarantee the maximum time for network preemption in a large network, considering the effect of hot-spots [13]. This situation becomes a severe problem in implementing real-time scheduling. We have

Table 5. Voluntary Gang-scheduling Overhead $[10^{-3} sec.]$

	TQ	Number of processors			
		1	2	4	8
fib(15,1000)	200	3.4	6.4	13.4	15.3
	300	2.7	4.5	13.2	14.3
	500	2.7	6.7	11.0	11.7
	1000	3.7	5.0	13.3	11.0
rt(1000000)	200	2.8	5.2	11.6	11.9
	300	2.3	5.6	11.7	11.2
	500	2.3	7.3	8.7	10.5
	1000	4.1	8.6	12.2	8.8

already proposed an architectural support for gang-scheduling, called "Drain" [6]. The Drain mechanism can guarantee the maximum time to reach the quiet state.

We found that the signal delivery of the SunOS can be an obstacle when implementing gang-scheduling. However it can be avoided with voluntary gang-scheduling. With network preemption and voluntary gang-scheduling, we believe that gang-scheduling on a workstation cluster can be made sufficiently practical and scalable.

The target of SCore-D is very similar to that of GLUnix [1, 2]. In [2], some simulated results of gang-scheduling on a workstation cluster are shown. However, this paper is the first report on implementing gang-scheduling on a workstation cluster as far as we know.

The other unique feature of SCore-D is that SCore-D itself is written in MPC++, a multi-threaded programming language. All the functions described in this paper have been implemented in only 1,600 lines of code.

SCore-D will support global resource management including parallel I/O. We intend to move onto a larger workstation cluster, and we will continue to investigate the implementation of gang-scheduling.

References

1. Thomas E. Anderson, David E. Culler, David A. Patterson, et al. A Case for NOW (Networks of Workstations). *IEEE Micro*, 15(1):54–64, February 1995.
2. Remzi H. Arpaci, Andrea C. Dusseau, Amin M. Vahdat, Lok T. Liu, Thomas E. Anderson, and David A. Patterson. The Interaction of Parallel and Sequential Workloads on a Network of Workstations. UC Berkeley Technical Report CS-94-838, Computer Science Division, University of California, Berkeley, 1994.
3. Nanette J. Boden, Danny Cohen, Robert E. Felderman, Alan E. Kulawik, Charles L. Seitz, Jakov N. Seizovic, and Wen-King Su. Myrinet: A Gigabit-per-Second Local Area Network. *IEEE Micro*, 15(1):29–36, February 1995.

4. Dror G. Feitelson and Larry Rudolph. Distributed Hierarchical Control for Parallel Processing. *COMPUTER*, 23(5):65–77, May 1990.
5. Dror G. Feitelson and Larry Rudolph. Gang Scheduling Performance Benefits for Fine-Grain Synchronization. *Journal of Parallel and Distributed Computing*, 16(4):306–318, 1992.
6. Atsushi Hori, Takashi Yokota, Yutaka Ishikawa, Shuichi Sakai, Hiroki Konaka, Munenori Maeda, Takashi Tomokiyo, Jörg Nolte, Hiroshi Matsuoka, Kazuaki Okamoto, and Hideo Hirono. Time Space Sharing Scheduling and Architectural Support. In D. G. Feitelson and L. Rudolph, editors, *Job Scheduling Strategies for Parallel Processing*, volume 949 of *Lecture Notes in Computer Science*, pages 92–105. Springer-Verlag, April 1995.
7. Yutaka Ishikawa. MPC++: Massively Parallel, Message Passing, Meta-Level Programming C++. In *Parallel Object Oriented Methods and Application'94*, 1994.
8. Yutaka Ishikawa. The MPC++ Programming Language V1.0 Specification with Commentary Document Version 0.1. Technical Report TR–94014, RWC, June 1994.
9. Yutaka Ishikawa. Meta-Level Architecture for Extendable C++. Technical Report TR–94024, RWC, January 1995.
10. Yutaka Ishikawa, Atsushi Hori, Hiroshi Tezuka, Motohiko Matsuda, Hiroki Konaka, Munenori Maeda, Takashi Tomokiyo, and Jörg Nolte. MPC++. In Gregory V. Wilson and Paul Lu, editors, *Parallel Programming Using C++*. MIT Press, 1996.
11. John K. Ousterhout. Scheduling Techniques for Concurrent Systems. In *Proceedings of Third International Conference on Distributed Computing Systems*, pages 22–30, 1982.
12. Scott Pakin, Mario Lauria, and Andrew Chien. High Performance Messaging on Workstations: Illinoi Fast Messages (FM) for Myrinet. In *Supercomputing'95*, December 1995.
13. Gregory F. Pfister and V. Alan Norton. "Hot Spot" Contention and Combining in Multistage Interconnection Networks. *IEEE Transactions on Computers*, pages 943–948, October 1985.
14. Jim Pruyne and Miron Livny. Parallel Processing on Dynamic Resources with CARMI. In D. G. Feitelson and L. Rudolph, editors, *Job Scheduling Strategies for Parallel Processing*, volume 949 of *Lecture Notes in Computer Science*, pages 259–278. Springer-Verlag, April 1995.
15. Andrew S. Tanenbaum. *Modern Operating Systems*. Prentice-Hall, 1992.
16. Gupta A. Ticker and Shigeru Urushibara. The Impact of Operating System Scheduling Policies and Synchronization Methods on the Performance of Parallel Applications. In *ACM SIGMETRICS*, pages 120–132, 1991.
17. Thorston von Eicken, Anindya Basu, and Werner Vogels. U-Net: A User Level Network Interface for Parallel and Distributed Computing. In *Fifteenth ACM Sumposium on Operating Systems Principles*, pages 40–53, 1995.

Managing Checkpoints
for Parallel Programs

Jim Pruyne and Miron Livny

Department of Computer Sciences
University of Wisconsin–Madison
{pruyne, miron}@cs.wisc.edu

Abstract. *Checkpointing is a valuable tool for any scheduling system to have. With the ability to checkpoint, schedulers are not locked into a single allocation of resources to jobs, but instead can stop running jobs, and re-allocate resources with out sacrificing any completed computations. Checkpointing techniques are not new, but they have not been widely available on parallel platforms. We have implemented CoCheck, a system for checkpointing message passing parallel programs. Parallel programs tend to be large in terms of their aggregate memory utilization, so the size of their checkpoint is also large. Because of this, checkpoints must be handled carefully to avoid overloading the system when checkpoints take place. Today's distributed file systems do not handle this situation well. We therefore propose the use of checkpoint servers which are specifically designed to move checkpoints from the checkpointing process, across the interconnection network, and on to stable storage. A scheduling system can utilize numerous checkpoint servers in any configuration in order to provide good checkpointing performance.*

1 Introduction

The ability to checkpoint a running program, whether it be a sequential or parallel program, is a valuable tool for a scheduling system. One common use for checkpointing is to provide fault tolerance. Checkpointing also allows the scheduler to re-allocate resources among both running and queued jobs without sacrificing any computations already performed. For example, Condor's [1] ability to checkpoint sequential programs has allowed it to effectively utilize the idle time of privately owned workstations for long running jobs. By checkpointing a program when an owner reclaims a machine, Condor is able to run programs which take much longer than any single idle interval at a workstation.

Parallel scheduling systems may also benefit from the ability to checkpoint programs in many ways. For example, most current parallel schedulers require the user to specify how long a job will run, and the scheduler simply kills jobs which do not complete in the specified time. By killing the job, the entire current state of the computation is lost, and therefore the resource time allocated to the job has been wasted. A more desirable approach would be to checkpoint the entire parallel application. The checkpointed program could then be re-submitted to the system, and computation would continue from the point where the job was forced to vacate the machine. In this way, the time already invested in the job will be preserved.

Another use for checkpointing in a parallel system is to perform *dynamic partitioning* which has been shown [2] to be more effective than static methods of scheduling parallel programs. In a dynamic partitioning scheme, the number of resources allocated to a job is changed while the job is running based on changes in load on the overall system. Without the ability to checkpoint and save the state of running processes, it would not be possible to move processes to perform a dynamic partitioning resource reallocation. The conditions under which dynamic partitioning is beneficial depend greatly on the overhead involved in doing resource re-allocation. When this overhead becomes high, the benefits of dynamic partitioning are lost. It is therefore important to perform checkpoint and restart operations as quickly as possible.

Techniques for checkpointing of parallel and distributed programs have been understood for quite some time. For example, Chandy and Lamport proposed a "distributed snapshot" protocol in 1985 [3]. Thus far, however, implementations of these techniques for real parallel systems have been rare. Building on the theory and the experience gained doing checkpointing for single process jobs in Condor, we have developed a system for checkpointing message passing parallel programs called CoCheck (for Consistent Checkpointing). CoCheck implements a network consistency protocol much like Chandy and Lamport's distributed snapshot protocol, and utilizes the single process checkpoint ability of Condor to save the state of each process in a parallel application.

In practice, checkpointing a parallel program tends to be a time consuming operation. The exact attribute which makes parallel programs desirable, their ability to perform computations which are extremely large in both computation and memory requirements, makes them difficult to checkpoint. In particular, a checkpoint must by definition include the entire state of the running program. A parallel program's state consists of the state of the interconnection network as well as the address space of each process. The combined memory of all of the processes often amounts to a huge overall state which must some how be moved into secondary storage. There are two potential bottlenecks in saving this data: the interconnection network over which the data must travel, and the secondary storage devices on which the data will be stored. Because the scheduling system makes decisions related to checkpointing, it must determine how and where the checkpoints will be stored. To give the scheduler flexibility in making these decisions, we have implemented a *checkpoint server* which performs checkpoint file store and retrieve operations at the request of the scheduler. Using checkpoint servers, the scheduler is able to precisely direct the movement of checkpoints, and is not at the mercy of an external mechanism, such as a distributed file system, in which it cannot impose policy.

The rest of this paper is organized as follows. The next section describes the design of CoCheck. Section 3 provides discussion of alternatives which led to the development of the checkpoint server, and how it may be used by a scheduler. This is followed by some practical experience with the overall system and some conclusions and thoughts on future work.

2 CoCheck

CoCheck [4] is a freely available system for creating checkpoints of parallel programs which communicate via a Message Passing Environment (MPE). It has been developed via a collaboration between researchers at the Technical University of Munich and ourselves. The implementation available today works with PVM [5] on workstation clusters. Work is ongoing in Munich to extend CoCheck to support MPI [6].

We started with a number of important design goals when developing CoCheck. The first goal of CoCheck was to remain portable. That is, although the first implementation was done on top of PVM, the concepts used in CoCheck should be applicable to any MPE. Another important aspect of CoCheck is that it does not require modifications to the MPE implementation. This helps with portability both across different message passing systems, and for maintaining compatibility with updated releases of a single system. It also permits us to implement CoCheck on systems for which source code is not available. Additionally, we required flexibility in the degree of checkpointing to be performed. For example, it may be desirable to create a global checkpoint all processes in a parallel application, or it may only be necessary to checkpoint a little as one process to perform a migration. The degree of checkpointing to be performed is put under the control of the application or the scheduling system. Finally, CoCheck must have no *residual dependencies* on resources after a checkpoint is complete. This is to say that it is unacceptable to require continued participation in the life of a parallel program by a resource on which all processes have been checkpointed.

2.1 CoCheck Components

The state of a message passing parallel program at any given time consists of the state of each process in the application as well as the state of the communication network which may be carrying or buffering messages in transit. To capture this state, and to meet our design goals, CoCheck has been designed in three components: an overlay library for the message passing API, a single process checkpointing library, and a resource management (RM) process which coordinates the checkpointing protocol. The two libraries are linked into every application process generating a service layering as shown in figure 1. External to the application is a RM process which runs as part of the scheduling system. By using these three components, we have been able to meet our design goals, and at the same time leverage much pre-existing technology.

The overlay library is the key to doing checkpointing without modification to the underlying MPE. This library provides a stub for every function defined by the MPE. These stubs trap all application calls to the MPE, and perform communication identifier or other translations which must be made as a result of previous checkpoints and restarts. In most cases, the stub will in turn call the

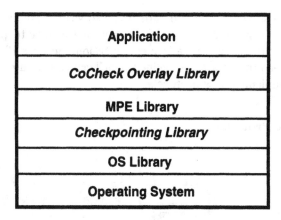

Fig. 1. Layering of the CoCheck components

original MPE function to get the actual service performed. The overlay library also implements the protocol to capture the network state which is described below.

Single process checkpointing libraries have existed for quite some time. CoCheck utilizes the checkpointing library which was developed as part of Condor [7, 8] which, among others, provides this functionality without any modifications to the operating system on which it runs. The technique used for performing single process checkpointing is similar to the message passing overlay library described above (indeed, the techniques used in single process checkpointers were an inspiration for CoCheck's overlay approach). The state of a single process includes its memory (the bounds of its address space), the state of the processor registers, and any state within the operating system kernel such as the set of open files and their current seek position. Determining the bounds of the address space and saving the registers of a process are typically easy to perform. However, the increasing use of techniques such as dynamically loaded libraries have made address space lay-outs more complex making this a more difficult task. The overlay functions in a checkpointing library catch calls to the kernel which modify the kernel state of a process (for example, opening a file), and record this information so that it can be saved in the checkpoint and restored upon restart. Not all state of a process can be saved. For example, the parent-child relationship of processes following a fork() system call, or inter-process communication outside the scope of the MPE (e.g. pipes or sockets) cannot be retained. The Condor checkpointing library therefore disallows these system calls by trapping them and returning an error.

The final component of CoCheck, the resource manager process is the co-ordinator for the entire system. The RM process provided with CoCheck is an extension to the external RM process first designed for use with PVM [9]. This process receives requests for checkpointing services, and initiates the CoCheck protocol between itself and the overlay library of each the application processes to perform these services. The standard RM also writes a meta-checkpoint file which can later be re-read by a new instance of the RM to provide the information needed to restart the entire computation. Because PVM allows new resource manager processes to be defined, CoCheck can be used with any RM process which implements its protocols.

2.2 CoCheck Protocol

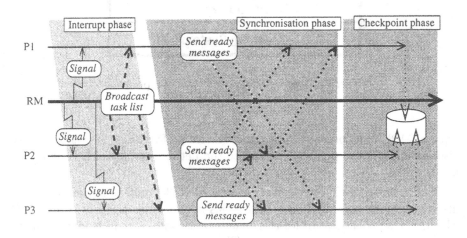

Fig. 2. CoCheck's network cleaning protocol

The CoCheck protocol (shown in figure 2) is responsible for ensuring that the entire state of the network is saved during a checkpoint, and to insure that communication can be resumed following a checkpoint. The CoCheck protocol begins when the RM determines that a checkpoint is required. This may be due to an application request, or because of a change in the state of a resource or due to a scheduling decision (such as the end of the time quanta allocated to a job). The RM begins by sending a signal and a message to each of the application processes. The combination of signal and message is required because each process may be either computing or communicating. The signal will interrupt a process which is computing causing it to enter the CoCheck library to participate in the checkpoint protocol. The overlay library of a process which is communicating will simply see the checkpoint request message, and interpret it as a request to begin checkpointing.

The checkpoint request message sent from the RM to each process contains two pieces of information. The first is how this process should participate in the checkpoint. The most common alternative is for the process to checkpoint itself. In this case, the message contains a World Wide Web style Universal Resource Locator (URL) which specifies where the checkpoint is to be written. This may be simply a file, an ftp site, or it may specify a *checkpoint server* which will be described later. When the URL does not specify a local file, the checkpoint is written directly to the network, and is never stored on the local disk. Avoiding the local disk operation allows checkpoints to occur at the maximum speed the network protocols permit. Instead of specifying a checkpoint destination, the message may tell the process not to checkpoint at all, or it may request that the process generate a new, CoCheck specific, URL from which another process may read its checkpoint. This last alternative provides a means of performing a direct process migration without the need to create an intermediate checkpoint file.

The checkpoint request message sent by the RM also includes a list of communication identifiers of processes which are also checkpointing. The checkpointing processes sends a *ready* message to each of these processes, and then waits for ready messages from all the other processes. Any other messages which are received while waiting for readys are assumed to be part of the application's communication, and will be buffered in the process' address space so they become part of the process' checkpoint. With the provision that messages are delivered in order between any two processes, it can be assumed that the network has been drained when all of the ready messages are received. At this point, it is safe for each process to disconnect from the MPE (if the MPE requires it), and to invoke the Condor checkpointing library to save its state.

To restart from a CoCheck checkpoint each process is provided with a URL from which to read its individual checkpoint by the RM. Prior to performing a restart operation, the process connects itself with the MPE to establish a new communication identifier. It next performs a single process restart operation while preserving its new communication id. Following the restart, each process sends its new communication id to the RM process. The RM collects all of these ids from the restarting processes, and sends a mapping of old ids to new ids to each process. When this is received, it is installed in the CoCheck library, and all future communications will go through this mapping before passing into and out of the MPE implementation. In this way, processes are able to continue to use the original communication ids which were in use prior to the checkpoint. After the new mapping is installed, the application processes resume from the point at which the initial checkpoint notification was received.

2.3 CoCheck API

CoCheck was designed to be flexible in the number of processes to be checkpointed and in where the checkpoint is to be written. To leverage this flexibility, the interface to CoCheck must also be flexible. The basic interface to CoCheck is with the `GeneralCkpt()` function. `GeneralCkpt()` takes arguments for specifying three groups of processes: those that should be checkpointed, those that should block while the processes remain checkpointed in order to maintain a consistent communication identifier space, and those processes which should neither checkpoint nor block. This last group simply insures that the network is clear between itself and the checkpointing processes before continuing. The complement to the `GeneralCkpt()` function is `GeneralRestart()` which requires only specifying the first two groups of processes in order to get the checkpointed ones restarted, and to get the blocking ones new communication identifier mappings.

The checkpoint and restart functions are asynchronous remote procedure calls against the resource manager process. As with CARMI [10], they immediately return an integer request identifier. In this way, a process requesting a checkpoint need not block while the CoCheck protocol is running, and while the individual checkpoints are being stored. Processes may, though, include themselves in any of the set of processes defined by `GeneralCkpt()`. When a request is complete, the RM sends a completion notification message to the requesting processes.

Using these two functions as a basis, a variety of more special case checkpointing functions can be developed. For example, it is easy to design calls which checkpoint an entire parallel application or a single process. With only slight extensions, it has been possible to provide requests for migrating a single process, requesting a checkpoint to take place when another event occurs (such as a privately owned workstation being revoked), or allowing the user to specify where checkpoints should be written.

3 Methods of storing Checkpoint Files

When a scheduler makes a decision that an application must be checkpointed, it must also determine how that checkpoint will be stored. Checkpointing a parallel application creates a very large burst of data which must be stored reliably and as quickly as possible. This bursty pattern is exactly the set of circumstances under which most communication and storage systems perform poorly.

The tolerance to latency in performing a checkpoint will depend on the environment in which the parallel application is running. In a situation in which use of a resource may be revoked (such as for privately owned workstations), there is a degree of real-time constraint in saving the data. Condor, for example has a user configurable upper bound on the time allowed for a checkpoint when a workstation is reclaimed. If the checkpoint is not complete within this interval, Condor kills the job rather than waiting for the checkpoint to complete. In an environment where resources are completely under the control of the scheduling system there may be no hard constraint, but it is still very important to complete the checkpoint as quickly as possible in order to free the resources for other jobs. Time spent checkpointing is time when useful computation is not taking place.

The simplest, and perhaps most desirable method of storing a checkpoint of a parallel program is to simply use an existing distributed file system. Examples of these include the Network File System (NFS) [11] and the Andrew File System (AFS) [12]. Using these systems for storing checkpoints is quite attractive because it allows them to be stored in the same way as other files. The problem of where and how data is stored is handled by the file system. Unfortunately, these systems were not designed to perform well on operations which involve one time transfers of large files such as checkpoints.

NFS has stateless servers which handle file requests a single page at a time. This leads to poor performance because the file must be moved across the network via a series of page size requests to the server. AFS uses a more complex, full file caching scheme in which all files accessed are moved in their entirety between the server and client disks. Practice has shown that AFS is not adequate for parallel systems. For example, the Cornell Theory Center recommends that AFS not be used when data transfers become large [13]. The caching scheme used by AFS is particularly poor at writing results such as checkpoint files. These results generally will not be re-used on the node where they are generated, so caching them locally provides no future benefit, and in fact may cause other, useful data to be flushed from the cache. The AFS scheme also ends up causing two disk writes (one locally and one on the server) for the entire file. With fast interconnection networks, the latency of disk accesses becomes a bottleneck. A final difficulty with AFS is the inflexibility in placing file servers. AFS servers are considered insecure unless placed in a "locked room" to which users do not have access. This limits the ability to place AFS servers such that they will be close to the processes generating checkpoints.

3.1 Checkpoint Servers

Due of the perceived shortcomings of the existing solutions, we have developed a *Checkpoint Server* specifically suited for the problem of storing and retrieving checkpoints. The goal of the checkpoint server is simply to move data between the network and the local disk as quickly as possible. It is the scheduler's job to determine when a checkpoint should take place, and what checkpoint server should be used for storing which checkpoint files. When a checkpoint or restart is to be performed, the RM process, as the schedulers representative in the CoCheck protocol, starts by contacting the required servers to request a store or retrieve operation. The server responds by generating a URL on which it will transfer the checkpoint, and forks a child process to perform the transfer. The URL service prefix (e.g. "http:" or "ftp:") is unique to our checkpoint server, and is understood by the Condor checkpointing library (as described previously). This URL contains an Internet Protocol (IP) address and port number pair to perform a TCP transfer of the checkpoint. TCP is used because it is the fastest reliable protocol available in our network of workstations environment. In other environments, other transport protocols could be used by generating URL's with different service prefixes, and implementing them in the URL component of the Condor library. The checkpoint server uses a child process to perform the transfer to insure that it will be ready to receive the next service request.

Like other simple components, checkpoint servers can be combined to form more complex structures. A scheduling system can use multiple checkpoint servers as building blocks to provide good checkpointing performance. In putting the blocks together, one must consider a number of factors. Perhaps most important is the topology and characteristics of the underlying communication network. In a large, fragmented network with high latencies and low bandwidth, checkpoint servers should be scattered about to insure that any checkpointing process has as fast a link as possible to some checkpoint server. In a smaller, more tightly connected network, it may not be necessary to have many checkpoint servers since every potential checkpointing process will always have a fast path to a server.

One must also consider the characteristics of the checkpoint servers themselves. Particularly when attempting to reduce the total number of checkpoint servers, it is important to look at issues such as the bandwidth of the disk. When a fast network delivers many checkpoints to the same server, the disk will become the bottleneck. Also, the capacity of the disk is important. A server with a small disk should not be placed in a location where it will be expected to store many checkpoints. A scheduling system must understand these sorts of characteristics of its checkpoint servers, and schedule the checkpoint servers much like it would schedule compute or other resources.

A final consideration when deciding how to use checkpoint servers is how frequently checkpoint operations take place. In an opportunistic system such as Condor, the return of a single user may cause a multi-node parallel application to checkpoint. For this environment, it is worthwhile to allocate significant resources to checkpointing because they will be needed frequently. In all environments the frequency of checkpoint operations is going to be determined by the way in which the scheduler utilizes checkpointing.

A scheduler may trigger checkpoints periodically to provide fault tolerance. The degree of checkpointing in this case is going to depend on the scheduler's level of trust for its resources. When resources are reliable, the interval between checkpoints may be large, and there will be little load placed on the checkpoint servers. When the resources are less reliable, checkpoints may be taken more often in order to reduce the amount of computation lost due to a failure. A checkpoint may also be invoked based on the priority of jobs in a queue. There may be a preemption policy that running jobs will be checkpointed and replaced by newly submitted jobs with higher priority. Checkpoints may also be used to perform re-allocation of resources among running jobs to implement a dynamic partitioning strategy or, for example, to move processes which communicate frequently close to one another. In all of these cases, the variety of jobs is going to influence the frequency of checkpoints and therefore the level of checkpoint servicing required. It is therefore extremely important that the scheduler have flexibility in the number and placement of checkpoint servers.

Parallel schedulers also need to take the placement of checkpoint servers into consideration when they are allocating processes to compute nodes. Processes should be spread around the resources such that no single checkpoint server will be overloaded in case there is a need to checkpoint. Knowledge of the characteristics of the checkpointing infrastructure should be used. The scheduler must balance its desire to distribute checkpoints evenly with the application's need for high bandwidth and low latency communication which generally are achieved by clustering the application processes. Applications which do not do intensive

communication may be scheduled based on the expected checkpointing requirements, while communication intensive applications may be scheduled to reduce
application communication time at the cost of higher checkpoint times.

4 Experience with the deployment of checkpoint servers

As described in the previous section, before deploying checkpoint servers in our
department, we had to understand the need for checkpointing services as well as
the characteristics of our communication infrastructure. The Computer Sciences
department at the University of Wisconsin has around 200 desktop workstations
most of which are available to the Condor resource management system for
executing long running sequential applications. Each of these workstations is
also available to users via CARMI [10] the resource management and parallel
programming interface to Condor. Condor has always supported checkpointing of
sequential applications, and CoCheck has recently been integrated with CARMI
to provide checkpointing services to parallel applications. Because checkpoints in
this environment are triggered by owners returning to their workstations, they
occur relatively frequently. We therefore require a checkpoint server architecture
which can service numerous checkpoints.

Checkpoint Route	Time to Checkpoint
Checkpointer and server on same sub-net	46
Checkpointer and server on different sub-nets, same router	64
Checkpointer and server on FDDI connected sub-nets	79
Checkpointer on Ethernet, server on FDDI	49

Table 1. Times, in seconds, to write a 32Mb checkpoint file

The principle limitation in our environment, as in many other environments,
is the available network bandwidth. Each of our workstations lies on an Ethernet
class sub-net. Each Ethernet is connected to one or two routers which in turn
directly connect each sub-net to three to five other sub-nets as well as an FDDI
backbone. The path between any two workstations, therefore, is at best at the
Ethernet rate of 10 $\frac{Mbit}{sec}$, and may require crossing one or two routers. The
department also has AFS available to all of the workstations, and the AFS
servers are connected directly to the FDDI ring. We therefore wish to explore
the alternatives in placing checkpoint servers on sub-nets as well as sharing the
AFS servers which are directly on the FDDI ring.

Table 1 summarizes the results of experiments to determine how the network
topology affects the time to write a checkpoint. In each of these experiments,
a 32Mb checkpoint file was generated on a SPARC workstation running SunOS
4.1.3. The checkpoint files were received at checkpoint servers running on Dec
Alpha workstations running OSF/1 V2.1. The results reported are the average

of a number of checkpoint operations. In all cases, the variance in the time to checkpoint was low. As would be expected, placing the checkpoint server and checkpointing process on the same sub-net produced the best results. Placing the checkpoint server on FDDI performed nearly as well. In the tests where the checkpoint had to move off of one sub-net and onto another, the time increased markedly.

From these results, it seems that the most desirable method of placing checkpoint servers would be one per sub-net. In this way, every workstation will have the fastest available path to a server. There are two disadvantages to this. First, the number of sub-nets is large (approximately a dozen containing user's workstations), so many resources would have to be established as checkpoint servers. Also, although placing a checkpoint server on each sub-net will improve checkpoint times, to gain the same advantage at restart time would require re-scheduling a job on the same sub-net as when it last checkpointed. This severely limits the number of resources available for a restarting job. We wish to investigate ways to circumvent this problem by building hierarchies of checkpoint servers. A small checkpoint server could be placed near to the resource on which the checkpoint is taking place, but after the checkpoint is complete, it could be moved to some larger higher level server from which the restart will occur. This movement to the higher level server could take place off-line, when there is no immediate need for the checkpoint at any particular site.

Placing checkpoint servers directly on the FDDI ring appears to be nearly as desirable as having a checkpoint server per sub-net. In our environment, there are administrative barriers to this, but it appears that, in general, it would be wise to dedicate some resources on the highest bandwidth portion of a network to provide good checkpoint performance.

Our second set of tests was intended to determine if checkpointing performance scales as the number of checkpointing processes, servers and size of individual checkpoints is increased. We also wanted to see exactly how well an existing file system, AFS, performs on these operations. Once again, our tests were limited by the bandwidth on our network. It is clear that no single checkpoint can occur faster than the bandwidth of a single sub-net, so we did not want any two checkpointing processes to lie on the same sub-net. This constraint limited us to checkpointing no more than two processes simultaneously. Figure 3 shows the results of different checkpoint server configurations and checkpoint sizes.

In all cases, the time to checkpoint scaled nearly linearly with the size of the checkpoint files. The most striking result is how poorly AFS performs for checkpoint operations. As mentioned previously, this is due to the method in which AFS caches files. As a checkpoint is being written, it is stored entirely on the local disk. When the file is closed, it is read off of the disk, and transfered across the network to the file server where it is written to the server's disk. This requires three disk I/O's as opposed to one for the checkpoint server. Nonetheless, it is surprising that AFS required approximately an order of magnitude more time to produce a checkpoint.

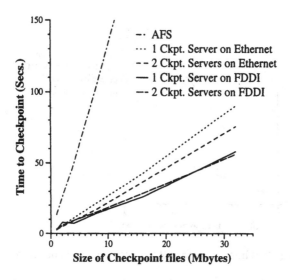

Fig. 3. Time to checkpoint 2 processes of various sizes

In the checkpoint server cases, the results are what one might expect by extrapolating from the single checkpoint tests. Sending two 32Mb checkpoints to the same checkpoint server, takes almost exactly twice as long (90 seconds) as sending one checkpoint to one server. When sending to two checkpoint servers on separate sub-nets, we were constrained by our environment to go across the FDDI ring. The last of two checkpoints completed in virtually the same time as one checkpoint taking a route across FDDI. Sending two checkpoints to one server on FDDI took only slightly longer (58 seconds) than sending one checkpoint onto FDDI (49 seconds). This implies that the network is still the bottleneck in this operation, and that the processor and disk are still able to keep up. As more sub-nets feed the same FDDI connected checkpoint server, we would expect the disk to become the bottleneck. The fact that an additional server on the FDDI ring does not improve checkpoint performance further shows that the single server is not yet a bottleneck.

Figure 4 shows results of similar experiments for restarts. The same configurations of checkpoint servers and checkpoint sizes were used for the restart tests as for the checkpoint tests. The results for restarts are similar to those for checkpoints. Once again, AFS performs poorly, though restarts are significantly better than checkpoints. Typically, restart times are slightly higher than checkpoint times. This is due to the fact that in order to perform a restart, the executable file for the restarting process must first be moved to the executing machine. Executables are moved from the checkpoint server to the local disk of the executing machine using the same mechanism as checkpoint files.

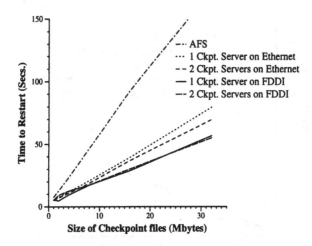

Fig. 4. Time to restart 2 processes of various sizes

5 Conclusions and future work

Parallel job schedulers are faced with an increasingly difficult task because the type of jobs and the types of resources are becoming more and more diverse. By providing schedulers with new techniques, such as checkpointing, we make it possible for more efficient schedules to be created. With each new technique, however, comes additional complexity of determining when and how to use it. For checkpointing, the problem is determining both when to checkpoint and how to most efficiently move large checkpoint images.

Today's methods of storing files on parallel systems, namely distributed file systems, do not provide adequate performance for storing checkpoints. These file systems are also implemented completely outside of the scheduling system, so the scheduler has very little means of controlling how they move data. By implementing checkpoint servers, we have given the scheduling system control over where and when data will be transferred. The scheduler can then treat the checkpoint servers like other resources which must be scheduled. Checkpoint servers provide the scheduler a great deal of flexibility in how checkpoints are stored. Techniques such as hierarchical checkpoint servers or striping a single checkpoint across multiple servers have not yet been investigated, but may provide higher levels of performance.

Initial experience with CoCheck has been very good, and the current work to support MPI with CoCheck is a good sign of its portability. Further experience with the checkpoint servers, and how best to utilize them is needed. Our existing testing environment is severely limited by the bandwidth of our network. We hope to gain further experience with the checkpoint servers on hardware which is dedicated to parallel processing and which contains a faster interconnect. Our department's Cluster Of Workstations (COW) which consists of forty dual processor SPARC workstations connected by a Myrinet is a likely target. The current obstacle to this is porting the Condor checkpointing library to the Solaris operating system which runs on these nodes. The simplicity of the checkpoint server should allow us to easily tailor it to use the best available communication protocol as we move to new hardware.

In addition to checkpoints, users' data sets must be distributed among the nodes of a parallel system. Integrating the distribution of this data into a scheduling system may allow faster start up of jobs. Instead of jobs waiting for the nodes to be loaded after being scheduled, the scheduler could load the data using techniques similar to the checkpoint server. This would require additional submit time information from the user specifying what data is needed on which node. Further integration with parallel I/O systems would also be desirable.

Acknowledgements

We wish to thank Georg Stellner of the Technical University of Munich for his initial design and collaboration during the development of CoCheck. The principle work on the implementation of the Checkpoint Server was done by Hsu-lin Tsao as part of a class project for Prof. Marvin Solomon.

References

1. M. J. Litzkow, M. Livny, and M. W. Mutka, "Condor: A hunter of idle workstations," in *Proceedings of the 8th International Conference on Distributed Computing Systems*, pp. 104–111, June 1988.
2. M. Squillante, "On the benefits and limitations of dynamic partitioning in parallel computer systems," in *Job Scheduling Strategies for Parallel Processing* (D. G. Feitelson and L. Rudolph, eds.), vol. 949 of *Lecture notes in Compter Science*, Springer-Verlag, 1995.
3. K. M. Chandy and L. Lamport, "Distributed snapshots: Determining global states of distributed systems," *ACM Transactions on Computer Systems*, vol. 3, pp. 63–75, Feb. 1985.
4. G. Stellner and J. Pruyne, "Resource management and checkpointing for PVM," in *Proceedings of the 2nd European Users' Group Meeting*, pp. 131–136, Sept. 1995.
5. A. Geist, A. Beguelin, J. Dongarra, W. Jiang, R. Manchek, and V. Sunderam, *PVM: Parallel Virtual Machine – A Users' Guid and Tutorial for Networked Parallel Computing*. Cambridge, MA.: The MIT Press, 1994.
6. G. Stellner, "CoCheck: Checkpointing and process migration for MPI," in *Proceedings of the International Parallel Processing Symposium*, IEEE, April 1996.
7. M. J. Litzkow and M. Solomon, "Supporting checkpointing and process migration outside the Unix kernel," in *Proceedings of the Winter Usenix Conference*, (San Francisco, CA), 1992.
8. T. Tannenbaum and M. Litzkow, "The Condor distributed processing system," *Dr. Dobb's Journal*, pp. 40–48, February 1995.
9. J. Pruyne and M. Livny, "Providing resource management services to parallel applications," in *Proceedings of the Second Workshop on Environments and Tools for Parallel Scientific Computing* (J. Dongarra and B. Tourancheau, eds.), SIAM Proceedings Series, pp. 152–161, SIAM, May 1994.

10. J. Pruyne and M. Livny, "Parallel processing on dynamic resources with CARMI," in *Job Scheduling Strategies for Parallel Processing* (D. G. Feitelson and L. Rudolph, eds.), vol. 949 of *Lecture notes in Compter Science*, Springer-Verlag, 1995.

11. R. Sandberg, D. Goldberg, S. Kleiman, D. Walsh, and B. Lyon, "Design and implementation of the Sun network file system," in *Proceedings of the Summer Usenix Conference*, pp. 119–130, 1985.

12. J. H. Howard, M. L. Kazar, S. G. Menees, D. A. Nichols, M. Satyanarayanan, R. N. Sidebotham, and M. J. West, "Scale and performance in a distributed file system," *ACM Transactions on Computer Systems*, vol. 6, pp. 51–81, February 1988.

13. J. Gerner, "Input/output on the IBM SP2–an overview." http://www.tc.cornell.edu/ SmartNodes/Newsletters/IO.series/intro.html.

Using Runtime Measured Workload Characteristics in Parallel Processor Scheduling

Thu D. Nguyen, Raj Vaswani, and John Zahorjan

Department of Computer Science and Engineering, Box 352350
University of Washington, Seattle, WA 98195-2350 USA

Abstract. We consider the use of runtime measured workload characteristics in parallel processor scheduling. Although many researchers have considered the use of application characteristics in this domain, most of this work has assumed that such information is available *a priori*. In contrast, we propose and evaluate experimentally dynamic processor allocation policies that rely on determining job characteristics at runtime; in particular, we focus on measuring and using job efficiency and speedup.

Our work is intended to be a first step towards the eventual development of production schedulers that use runtime measured workload characteristics in making their decisions. The experimental results we present validate the following observations:

- Despite the inherent inaccuracies of runtime measurements and the added overhead of more frequent reallocations, schedulers that use runtime measurements of workload characteristics can significantly outperform schedulers that are oblivious to these characteristics.
- Runtime measurements are sufficient for schedulers to achieve performance surprisingly close to that possible when *a priori* efficiency and speedup information is available.
- The primary performance loss, relative to the use of *a priori* information, is due to the transient decisions of the schedulers as they acquire information on the running applications, rather than to measurement and reallocation overheads.

We consider both interactive environments, in which a response time directed scheduler is appropriate, and batch environments, in which maximizing useful instruction throughput is the primary goal. Our experiments are performed using prototype implementations running on a 50-node KSR-2 shared memory multiprocessor.

1 Introduction

We consider the use of runtime measured workload characteristics in parallel processor scheduling. Although many researchers have considered the use of application characteristics in this domain, most of this work has assumed that such information is available *a priori*. While it is useful to understand how to best schedule a set of jobs given *a priori*

This work was supported in part by the National Science Foundation (Grants CCR-9123308 and CCR-9200832) and the Washington Technology Center.

information on their behaviors, in practice, it can be difficult to obtain and accurately specify such information because of factors such as the sensitivity of job performance to the input data set and to the relative locations of allocated processors on the machine's interconnection network [1].

As an example, consider the speedup of MP3D, an application from the SPLASH [24] benchmark suite, when run on the KSR-2 multiprocessor. The KSR-2 has an interconnection network that is a hierarchy of rings. The basic communication time between two rings is roughly four times that for communication within any one [11]. Because of this, MP3D, which has poor locality, achieves optimal speedup at a number of processors that depends strongly on the location of allocated processors. In particular, if all allocated processors are located on the same ring, MP3D's speedup peaks at 12 processors. If allocated processors are split across two rings, speedup peaks at 24 processors. In both the cases where the user requests 12 processors, but the ones allocated are spread across two rings, and where the user requests 24 processors, but allocated processors are all on one ring, the achieved speedup is roughly 2/3 that of the actual optimum.

In this paper, we focus on gathering information about the current workload at runtime and using this information to make scheduling decisions; in particular, we measure and use job efficiency and speedup. While at first glance, it would appear that runtime measurements of job behaviors are clearly useful, the actual situation is considerably more complicated, especially in parallel systems. The value of runtime measurements to parallel processor allocation policies depends critically on the answers to the following questions:

- *How can speedup and efficiency be measured at runtime with acceptably high accuracy and low overhead?*
- *Do parallel applications have sufficiently stable characteristics that their recent past is a good indicator of the near future?*
- *How can the measures taken when an application is run on p processors be used to estimate its performance when run on q?*
- *Do the costs of the potentially many reallocations (which are inherent in this approach) required in the search to find appropriate final allocations outweigh the benefits?*

Our goal is to help answer these questions. Taken in this context, this paper describes work intended to address the way in which future realizable schedulers might make use of information gathered at runtime, focusing particularly on job efficiency and speedup.

We begin by presenting a scheme that allows the runtime measurement of efficiency and speedup at low overhead. We then examine two distinct scheduling scenarios: interactive systems, where minimizing response time is the goal, and batch systems, where maximizing the rate at which useful work is completed is the goal. Both kinds of computing already have significant roles on existing large scale parallel platforms [7].

---

[1] Of course, supercomputer users running the same application repeatedly on similar data sets are accustomed to providing this information. However, at the very least, this is an inconvenience. At the worst, apparently insignificant changes in the data set may in fact have a substantial effect on the optimum allocation, although this could go undetected by the user.

For the interactive environment, we propose a scheduler that uses measured speedups to adjust the processor allocation of each running job, attempting to maximize job speedup. For batch environments, we propose a scheduler that uses measured efficiencies to allocate processors in such a way as to *maximize system efficiency*.

We have implemented prototypes of both schedulers on a 50 node KSR-2. We evaluate the effectiveness of these prototypes using a number of workloads comprised of benchmarks from the SPLASH [24] and PERFECT Club [2] benchmark suites, the best applications available to us for this work. Our central result is that the use of runtime measurements can improve scheduler performance substantially, despite the inevitable noise in the gathered data and the overheads involved in its use, and that such schedulers can approach the performance attainable when accurate efficiency and speedup information is available *a priori*.

The remainder of the paper is organized as follows. In the next section, we discuss related work. Section 3 describes our technique for measuring job efficiency and speedup at runtime. Section 4 describes and evaluates a response-time oriented scheduler that makes use of these measurements. In Section 5, we turn to the problem of maximizing the completion rate of batch work, again proposing a policy that employs runtime measurements and evaluating its performance experimentally. Section 6 concludes our work.

2 Related Work

As previously mentioned, many researchers have studied the use of application character-istics by processor schedulers of multiprogrammed multiprocessor systems. Majumdar et. al. [13], Chiang et. al [3], Leutenegger and Vernon [12], Sevcik [22, 23], Ghosal et. al. [9], Rosti et. al. [21] and others have proposed using application characteristics such as speedup, average parallelism, and processor working set to improve the performance of static processor schedulers. More recently, Guha [10] has proposed that application characteristics such as efficiency and execution time can also be used profitably by dynamic processor schedulers. All of these studies, however, assume that accurate his-torical performance data is provided to the scheduler at job submission time. In contrast, we concentrate on using recently measured characteristics of running jobs to optimize performance for the specific workload in execution.

McCann et. al. [15] have proposed a dynamic scheduler that uses application-provided runtime idleness information to dynamically adjust processor allocations to improve processor utilization. This work differs from ours in two respects: (1) we consider all sources of inefficiency as opposed to just idleness, and (2) McCann et. al.'s scheduler attempts to reallocate processors at a much finer grain than does ours. Thus, the effectiveness of their scheduler is dependent on the existence of application idle periods that are long relative to processor reallocation overheads.

Feitelson and Rudolph [8] take a similar approach to ours, proposing to dynamically gather information about communicating sets of processes in an attempt to relax the constraints of co-scheduling. Sobalvarro and Weihl [25] also propose several ways to use runtime identification of sets of communicating processes to relax the constraints of co-scheduling.

3 Measuring Job Efficiency and Speedup at Runtime

3.1 Measuring Efficiency and Speedup

The basic parallel job characteristics we wish to exploit are efficiency and speedup. While these measures are normally applied to the complete execution of an application (for example, speedup on P processors is the job completion time when run on P processors divided by the job completion time when run on a single processor), we take a more short-term view in our work. In particular, we wish to measure efficiency and speedup over the fairly short-term past, with the intention of relying on it as a predictor of the near-term future. We therefore use the terms efficiency and speedup in this (more instantaneous) sense.

While efficiency and speedup are intimately related, in practice, efficiency is rather easily measured, whereas speedup is not. Thus, we only measure efficiency, or more precisely, we measure the inefficiencies due to overheads and subtract them from 1.0. Then, when necessary, we calculate speedup using:

$$Speedup(p) = Efficiency(p) * p \qquad (1)$$

It is well known that loss of efficiency in shared memory systems arises from a combination of *idleness* (e.g, load imbalances, synchronization constraints, and sequential portions of execution), *communication*, *system overhead* (e.g., system events such as page faults and clock interrupts), and *parallelization overhead* (e.g., per-processor initialization, work partitioning, and synchronization). Of these four sources of loss of efficiency, it is particularly difficult to measure parallelization overhead for hand-coded applications because initialization, work partitioning, and synchronization code are typically embedded directly in normal application code. Fortunately, our experience with a wide variety of benchmark programs shows that parallelization overhead is typically small [18]. Thus, we require only estimates of the first three components (idleness, communication, and system overhead) to accurately assess efficiency.

On the KSR-2, we rely on a combination of hardware and software support to measure inefficiencies. Each node in the KSR-2 has a hardware monitoring unit that maintains three critical user-readable hardware counters: elapsed wall-clock time, elapsed user-mode execution time, and accumulated processor stall[2]. Measuring communication and system overhead involves little more than periodically reading these counters. Measuring idleness is slightly more involved; we instrument all synchronization code in our runtime systems (KSR PRESTO [11] and CThreads [4]) to keep elapsed idle time using the wall-clock hardware counter. This idleness measurement scheme is relatively overhead free because idleness accounting is performed when the processor would otherwise not be doing any useful work. Of course, this approach assumes that all application synchronization takes place through calls to the PRESTO and CThreads libraries

---

[2] On shared memory systems such as the KSR-2, communication is required whenever data does not currently reside in the local cache, or is not in an appropriate state. Processors in many systems stall in this situation; that is, they execute no instructions until the remote data becomes available. Thus, processor stall corresponds to communication cost. On message passing machines, measuring performance loss due to communication would be even more straightforward, requiring only software support.

rather than through direct manipulation of shared variables. We did not, however, have to modify our applications to meet this assumption; none of our hand-coded programs violated this assumption while all synchronization in compiler-parallelized applications by definition takes place in the PRESTO runtime system.

3.2 Measurement Interval

As will be seen below, in order for our runtime measurements to be useful, it is essential that comparisons of efficiency and speedup measurements made at different processor allocations be meaningful. Since *instantaneous* speedup reflects the characteristic of only a small section of the full application code, performing such comparisons can be problematic. This difficulty could be resolved by measuring efficiencies and speedups over relatively long intervals of time. Unfortunately, this approach has two disadvantages: (1) it would be difficult to determine what constitutes a sufficiently long period for an arbitrary application; and (2) long measurement intervals increase the latency of the scheduler in responding to changes.

Thus, we instead exploit a characteristic shared by a large variety of scientific parallel applications. In particular, we currently consider only *iterative* parallel applications. An iterative application is one in which the majority of the execution is driven by a sequential loop (whose bodies may be entirely general, involving the execution of many parallel phases, subroutine calls, etc.)[3]. Empirical evidence shows that successive iterations tend to behave similarly, so that measurements taken for a particular iteration are good predictors of near future behavior [18]. Thus, for such applications, we equate a measurement interval to an application iteration, providing a basis by which to reasonably compare a job's performance as its processor allocation is varied. Note, however, that in general, our approach does not require applications to be iterative. At a minimum, what we do require is that there be some identifiable point in the application's execution where it can indicate that a unit of work has been completed. For example, in a fairly coarse grained application employing user-level threads as the basis of parallel execution, a work unit might be defined to be the work between the kernel thread's dequeuing and subsequent enqueuing (or termination) of a user-level thread.

4 Interactive Environments: Improving Response Time

In this section, we describe and evaluate a scheduling policy designed to improve response time in interactive environments through the use of runtime gathered job characteristics.

4.1 Policies

To evaluate whether runtime measurements can be used beneficially by a scheduler, we compare the multiprogramming performance of the following three policies:

---

[3] In [18], we found that five of the ten SPLASH applications and all seven of the Perfect Club applications we could compile were iterative.

EQUI: The basic scheduling policy on which we build is dynamic equipartition [26]. Under EQUI, each currently executing job is allocated an equal number of processors. Processor reallocations take place at job arrival and departure times. EQUI is representative of the space sharing approach to processor allocation that has been found to perform well for multiprogrammed shared-memory multiprocessors [26, 15].

ST-EQUI: At the highest level, the specific policy we propose to take advantage of runtime estimated speedup allocates an equal number of processors to each executing job, just as with EQUI. However, each time a reallocation takes place, each affected job engages in a *self-tuning* procedure [17] to estimate how many of its allocated processors should actually be used to maximize its current speedup. (We briefly describe self-tuning in Section 4.2.) It is well-known that many applications do not speed up monotonically with the number of allocated processors; instead, they slow down when executed on more processors than they can use efficiently. Thus, it is reasonable to expect such jobs to release excess processors because they have no incentive to keep them. Additionally, in any system that charges for resource use, there is a positive incentive to release excess resources. When one or more jobs release processors back to the system, the scheduler reallocates these processors as equally as possible among those jobs that can profitably make use of more than their fair share. A job that gives up processors can later ask for them back if its speedup changes.

AP-EQUI: AP-EQUI is similar to ST-EQUI, except that it uses *a priori* information on job speedup rather than runtime estimates. Given this information, AP-EQUI needs to reallocate processors only at job arrival and departure times. When reallocating processors, it gives each job no more processors than the number that maximizes job speedup.

It is intuitively clear that AP-EQUI should outperform ST-EQUI. Distinctions in performance between AP-EQUI and ST-EQUI serve to illustrate the impact of errors in our runtime measurements, as well as the overhead of more frequent reallocations and dynamic self-tuning.

The case is less clear for EQUI and ST-EQUI. ST-EQUI can outperform EQUI when one or more jobs determine that they are better off using fewer than their fair share of processors and release excess processors back to the system. On the other hand, EQUI can outperform ST-EQUI because ST-EQUI can be expected to reallocate processors much more frequently than EQUI, thereby incurring much greater reallocation overhead. Furthermore, under ST-EQUI, all jobs incur the cost of self-tuning, even when all jobs want their fair share of processors. To better understand this new source of overhead, we next present the self-tuning procedure in somewhat more detail.

4.2 Self-Tuning

In this section, we present a brief overview of self-tuning. Comprehensive details can be found in [17], which examines the use of this technique in a static (essentially uniprogramming) environment.

Self-tuning is an online search technique that allows a parallel job to: (a) dynamically measure its efficiencies at different allocations, (b) use these measurements to estimate speedups, and (c) automatically adjust its allocation to maximize its speedup. Our current implementation of self-tuning employs a heuristic-based optimization technique that is an adaptation of *the method of golden sections* (MGS) [16] to find the best allocation. MGS is a simple optimization procedure that finds the maximum of a unimodal function over a finite interval by iteratively computing and comparing function values and narrowing the interval in which the maximum may occur[4]. In our case, the function to be maximized is job speedup. A job that is self-tuning computes the function value at p by running a single iteration using p processors, measuring the resulting efficiency, and calculating speedup using equation 1 (Section 3.1).

There are two basic problems we must address in using MGS for self-tuning. The first is that speedup functions are not, in general, unimodal. We address this using a simple, greedy heuristic. When the results of speedup evaluations in the current interval of interest demonstrate that speedup is not unimodal, we reduce the interval of interest to the largest subinterval that contains the currently known maximum speedup and for which the known speedup values are conformal with a unimodal function. While this heuristic does not guarantee that self-tuning will always find the global maximum, the experiments in [17] show that this procedure works remarkably well, nearly always converging to a near optimal value.

The second problem we face is one of efficiency. Given an initial allocation of P processors, MGS normally starts searching within the the interval $[1, P]$. While MGS converges relatively quickly ($O(log(P))$ steps are required), the cost of individual probes can be quite large if the job has poor speedup at the probed number of processors. We address this by exploiting the fact that speedup cannot be super-linear[5]. In particular, we begin self-tuning by executing one application iteration using all P processors available to the application. This allows us to estimate $S(P)$, the job's speedup with P processors. Since speedups can never be super-linear, we know that the globally best number of processors must fall in $[S(P), P]$. Our search therefore starts in this interval instead of $[1, P]$. For applications with good speedup, the interval $[S(P), P]$ will typically be small, allowing self-tuning to be performed with little overhead. For applications with poor speedup but only modest slowdown, speedup will be similar at all points between $[1, P]$ and so, again, self-tuning can be carried out with little overhead. Only in the case where an application initially achieves good speedup but then slows down significantly as its allocation grows does self-tuning incur significant overhead. In this case, for large P, $S(P)$ is likely to be small, resulting in a large initial search interval $[S(P), P]$. Furthermore, measuring speedup can be expensive at large (close to P) and small (close to 1) allocations.

4.3 Workload

As explained in Section 1, we are interested in a diverse workload composed of both hand-coded parallel (SPLASH) and compiler-parallelized sequential (PERFECT Club) applications.

Our previous detailed study of these applications [18] suggests that they can be divided into three broad classes:

---

[4] For our purposes, a function $f(x)$ is unimodal over an interval $[a, b]$ if there is some $x^* \in [a, b]$ such that $f(x)$ is monotone non-decreasing in $[a, x^*]$ and monotone non-increasing in $[x^*, b]$.

[5] In our system, this property holds by definition since we estimate efficiency by measuring inefficiencies and subtracting them from 1.0.

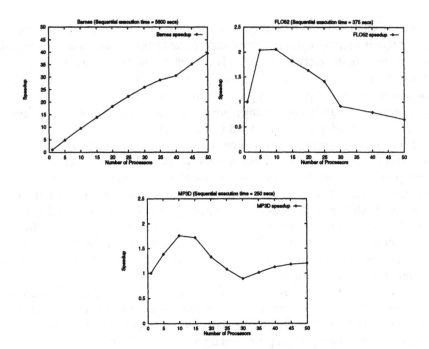

Fig. 1. *Speedup Characteristics of the Representative Jobs*

- *Good speedup.* Most of the hand-coded applications fall into this class, which is characterized by fairly good speedup that mostly rises monotonically as the job receives processors. Some of these applications exhibit modest slowdown beyond a certain number of allocated processors.
- *Poor speedup.* Almost all of the compiler-parallelized applications fall into this class, which is characterized by nearly negligible speedup at most processor values. Most of these applications exhibit significant slowdown beyond a certain number of allocated processors.
- *Erratic speedup.* This class consists of applications whose speedup is irregular, e.g., it varies over time or exhibits multiple local maxima. Such behavior can be observed in both hand-coded and compiler-parallelized applications [18].

Because it is infeasible to run experiments with all possible combinations from our benchmark suites, we instead use our taxonomy to reduce the number of jobs that must be considered, selecting a single representative application from each of the three classes. In particular, we chose the application exhibiting the best speedup from each class: Barnes from the SPLASH suite to exemplify good speedup, FLO52 from the PERFECT Club codes to exemplify poor speedup, and MP3D from the SPLASH suite to exemplify erratic speedup[6]. The measured speedup curves for these applications are given in Figure 1.

---

[6] We show in [17] that self-tuning is effective for a much larger number of applications than the 3 representative applications used in this study.

Next, we chose to set a maximum multiprogramming level of four, reasoning that (a) given our 50-processor machine, higher multiprogramming levels would increase processor demand to an extent that would render allocation decisions trivial, and (b) such a limit is prevalent in practice since memory constraints dictate that only a relatively small number of jobs can be allowed to run concurrently. This decision is supported by the measurements in [7], which indicate that multiprogramming levels of 2, 3, and 4 are the three most common during daytime hours in a production environment.

Note that in the work presented here, we do not address the question of which jobs should be activated when there are more jobs than the desired level of multiprogramming. Rather, we assume that some other mechanism, such as the feedback scheduling employed in sequential systems, is used for this purpose. (Parsons and Sevcik [19] present the design and evaluation of two such schemes, for example.) We consider the workload mixes we schedule to be the subset of a larger job mix chosen for current execution by such a mechanism.

4.4 Implementation

At the user-level, we implement *process control* to avoid loss of efficiency due to mismatches between threads and processors [26]. One limitation of our quick conversion of the benchmark programs, though, is that we have implemented application level dynamic scheduling only at iteration boundaries; the applications examine and adjust to the number of available processors each time they begin an iteration, but do not do so while executing any one iteration. It is clearly possible to do much more dynamic scheduling, e.g., [20, 1, 6, 14]; we did not do so because of the very large incremental implementation cost relative to our more restrictive change, and because we expect that ST-EQUI would perform even better when jobs are more responsive in responding to allocation changes. (Of the three policies, ST-EQUI reallocates processors most frequently, and is therefore most sensitive to the latency with which applications can respond to changing allocations.)

We have implemented the code required to perform self-tuning in the CThreads library. Thus, the self-tuning procedure is independent of the specific application to be run. Additionally, there is little code development overhead involved in using it; we merely depend on the application to call into our library at the beginning of each iteration.

4.5 Performance

Given the three representative applications and a maximum multiprogramming level of four, we constructed and evaluated all 31 of the possible static workload mixes containing more than a single job type. Figures 2–4 depict the performance of 16 representative samples of the 31 workload mixes under the EQUI and ST-EQUI policies for multiprogramming levels 2, 3, and 4 respectively. Response times under these two policies are shown normalized to those under AP-EQUI (the horizontal line on each graph). These results lead us to the following observations:

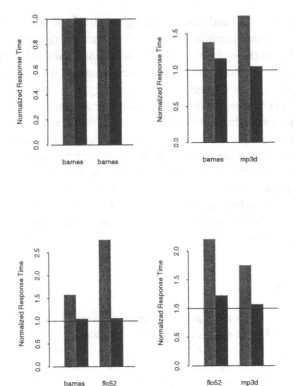

Fig. 2. *Response Time Results at Multiprogramming Level = 2. (Grey bars are results for EQUI; black bars are results for ST-EQUI. Results are normalized with respect to AP-EQUI.)*

- *The policy using runtime measurement (ST-EQUI) outperforms the similar policy that does not (EQUI).*

  This effect arises because all jobs can benefit by participating in cooperative processor allocation. In scenarios with high demand for processors (e.g., all jobs request their equipartition share), ST-EQUI behaves exactly as does EQUI, so its performance is no worse. However, in scenarios with more complex processor demands, ST-EQUI performs much better than does EQUI; jobs that start to slow down at allocations smaller than their EQUI-allocations run faster by shedding excess processors while jobs exhibiting good speedup gain these extra processors to run faster as well.

- *The policy using runtime measurements (ST-EQUI) performs nearly as well as the policy that uses* a priori *speedup information (AP-EQUI) in most cases.*

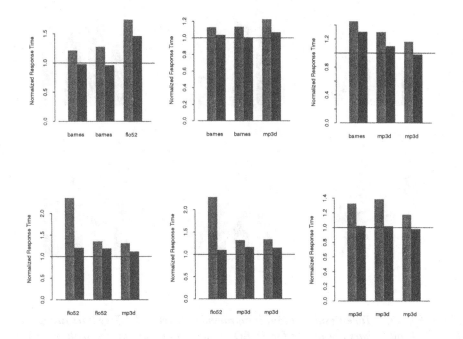

Fig. 3. *Response Time Results at Multiprogramming Level = 3. (Grey bars are results for EQUI; black bars are results for ST-EQUI. Results are normalized with respect to AP-EQUI.)*

While there are some noticeable distinctions in the performance obtained by individual applications under ST-EQUI and AP-EQUI, in general, the two achieve performance that is roughly equivalent. This is especially true when one considers the workload mix as a whole: while the two policies discriminate among the individual jobs somewhat differently, frequently worse performance for one application is offset by better performance for another.

– *The performance distinctions between the policy that uses runtime measurements (ST-EQUI) and the policy that uses* a priori *information (AP-EQUI) result from costs associated with transient allocations.*

Detailed examination of the decisions made by the two policies shows that ST-EQUI converges to a set of allocations with no or insignificant performance distinctions from those under AP-EQUI. This shows that, at least for the applications we examined, neither inaccuracies in the runtime measurements nor the inability of the search procedure to find appropriate allocations is a serious problem.

The primary cost of using runtime measurements in ST-EQUI relative to relying on perfect *a priori* information, as in AP-EQUI, is the penalty imposed by the sometimes poor allocations made during ST-EQUI's search. If the search procedure

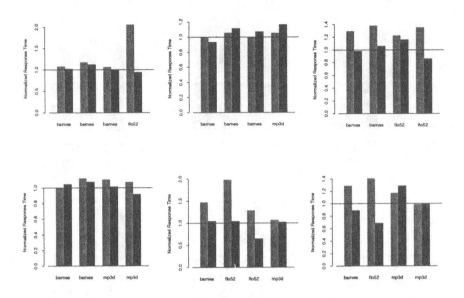

Fig. 4. *Response Time Results at Multiprogramming Level = 4. (Grey bars are results for EQUI; black bars are results for ST-EQUI. Results are normalized with respect to AP-EQUI.)*

allocates too many processors to an application that exhibits significant slowdown, that application is affected directly by the resulting long self-tuning time. Additionally, other applications may suffer an opportunity cost, since they do not have access to the excess processors until the application determines that it was allocated too many.

4.6 Summary

We have shown that ST-EQUI, a policy that gathers and uses runtime information on application performance, clearly outperforms EQUI, a similar policy that does not make use of runtime information. ST-EQUI is fair in the sense that it does not discriminate among job classes; it simply responds to jobs' requests to release/acquire processors, giving each job equal weight in its attempt to minimize response time. Because of this, ST-EQUI easily accommodates jobs that do not self-tune, since they receive allocations equivalent to those provided under EQUI.

In the next section, we explore schedulers that relax fairness in the interest of maximizing overall system efficiency for batch environments.

5 Batch Environments: Improving System Efficiency

In batch environments, such as are common for overnight runs of large parallel applications, the critical performance measure is not response time, but rather the rate at which useful work can be completed; the higher this rate, the larger the workload that can be processed in a fixed amount of time. In these environments, the goal of the scheduler is to maximize *system efficiency*, the sum of the efficiencies of all processors. In this section, we describe and evaluate a scheduling policy, EQUAL-EFF, that relaxes fairness in the interest of maximizing throughput.

5.1 The EQUAL-EFF Policy

The scheme we present below is motivated by consideration of how a scheduler designed to maximize system efficiency could be built in practice. It seems clear that any such allocation policy must reward applications exhibiting good efficiencies by allocating them many processors, and penalize those with bad efficiencies by allocating them only a few. An appealing structure for accomplishing this is to run all jobs for some quantum, measure their efficiencies, transfer processors from low efficiency to high efficiency applications, and then repeat the process. One advantage of this approach is its simplicity: it relies on only the recent efficiency measurements, which are easily and reliably obtainable, and so does not require knowledge of the full efficiency curves. Furthermore, we expect such a scheme to stabilize quickly to a set of reasonable allocations, and then to perform only a very modest rate of reallocations in the steady state.

Our early experiments with schedulers of this sort presented us with a set of problems that did not seem fundamentally difficult in the abstract, but which frustrated our attempts to build such a scheduler in practice. In particular, we needed a reliable way to decide whether or not the transfer of one or more processors from a low efficiency application to a high efficiency one was merited, and we needed a way to deal with the local irregularities found in real efficiency curves. While both these problems could be addressed by performing a thorough search of allocation choices, the transient poor allocations involved in such searches can make them quite expensive.

Instead of performing thorough searches of the allocation space, we choose another approach, which we present as a first step in understanding how to solve these problems. First, to address the local irregularities in the efficiency curve, we use an artificial curve extrapolated from the most recently measured efficiency alone. In particular, having just measured the efficiency of an application on p processors, we use the function $(1 + \beta)/(p + \beta)$, which is taken from [5], choosing β so that the function interpolates the most recent efficiency measurement.

Next, we determine allocations by following an *equal efficiency* rule; that is, we allocate processors in a way that causes all applications to have about equal efficiencies according to our extrapolated curves[7]. In particular, we compute allocations in a simple, greedy way: we initially assign a single processor to each application, and then

---

[7] Setting equal efficiency as a goal is a heuristic that is compatible with the scheduling structure described at the beginning of this subsection, a structure to which we plan to return. We address how well this heuristic does in achieving maximum system efficiency in the next subsection.

assign remaining processors one by one to the application with the currently highest (extrapolated) efficiency. The number of processors actually allocated to the jobs are then adjusted to match the newly computed allocation. We call this policy EQUAL-EFF.

In what follows, we present two sets of results. The first set is based on simulations, and is intended to show whether allocations based on equal-efficiency according to extrapolated efficiency curves come close to the goal of maximizing system efficiency. The second set of results is based on measurements of a prototype implementation, and so takes into account the inaccuracies inherent in the measurement process and the overheads involved in reallocating processors.

5.2 Evaluating the Inherent Effectiveness of EQUAL-EFF

Recall that our goal is to maximize system efficiency, but that we propose to do so by using extrapolated efficiency curves to determine allocations that result in nearly equal application efficiencies. In this subsection, we use simulations to determine whether such a procedure can come close to achieving our goal under the optimistic assumptions that measured efficiency information is perfectly reliable and that processor reallocation cost is negligible.

The inputs to the simulations are the measured application efficiency curves; the outputs are total system efficiencies. Given a set of jobs, our simulator begins by allocating available processors (nearly) equally. It then iteratively uses measured job efficiencies for the current allocation to derive extrapolated efficiency curves and follows EQUAL-EFF's allocation scheme to compute the next allocation. This process continues until successive allocations are identical. (It is not at all clear that this iterative process must always converge; however, in practice we did not encounter convergence problems.) This final allocation is used to compute system efficiency.

We compare the system efficiencies resulting from this process with the maximum possible system efficiencies. We compute the latter using a simple dynamic programming procedure that takes the full, measured speedup curves as its input. We call the policy that makes these allocations OPT-EFF.

Figure 5 plots the system efficiencies obtained by these simulations against the total number of processors in the system for a representative set of workload combinations, as well as the optimal system efficiencies computed for OPT-EFF. In all cases, the greedy scheme employed by EQUAL-EFF comes very close to the optimum, with the largest differences occurring only for very small numbers of processors. Furthermore, much of this difference is caused by local irregularities in actual speedup curves. Results from simulations that use smooth theoretical speedup curves show even smaller performance differences.

Based on the results of this simple model, we were motivated to continue to the prototype implementation of EQUAL-EFF. The results obtained from experiments with that prototype are presented next.

5.3 Experimental Performance Results

We evaluate the use of runtime measured job characteristics in improving scheduling in a batch environment by considering four related policies:

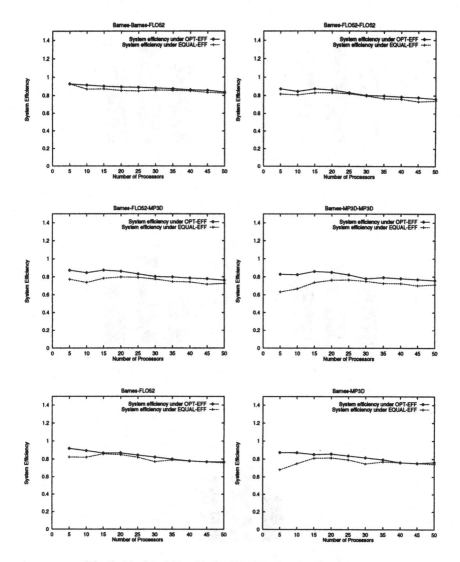

Fig. 5. *Modeled Results for EQUAL-EFF and OPT-EFF*

- EQUI. The basic dynamic equipartition policy (Section 4.1).
- EQUAL-EFF. The equal efficiency heuristic policy (Section 5.1).
- ST-EQUI. The self-tuned equipartition algorithm, which was designed to reduce response times (Section 4.1).
- ST-EQUAL-EFF. The EQUAL-EFF policy with the addition that each job also engages in self-tuning, releasing processors when it determines that it has been assigned more than it can profitably use.

The performance results under these policies are compared against those predicted by OPT-EFF. Because OPT-EFF is computed off-line, it does not capture any of the

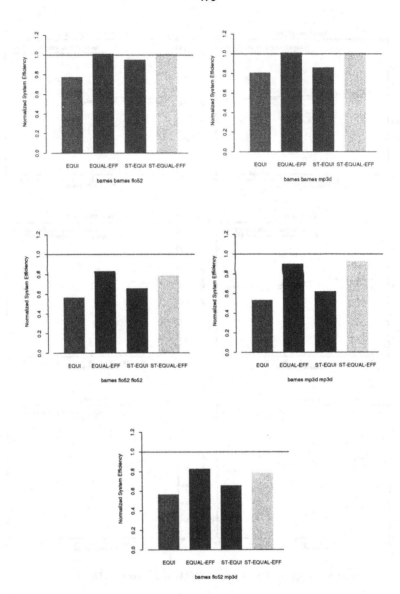

Fig. 6. *System Efficiency Results (Multiprogramming level = 3; results are normalized with respect to OPT-EFF).*

overheads that are inevitable in scheduling in practice, exaggerating its optimism.

We assessed performance with workloads composed of the same representative jobs as were used in Section 4. However, we used a single multiprogramming level of 3 in all experiments (a reduction from the maximum of 4 considered for the interactive environment) to reflect the likely larger size of jobs submitted for batch execution. (This change is supported by the measurements in [7].) Additionally, we present here results only for those workloads that include a Barnes job, the representative from the class of jobs having good speedup. Workloads without Barnes are relatively uninteresting, as there are 50/3 processors available to each job under simple equipartition, and this number exceeds the number that can be used profitably by the other two representative jobs in our mixes. For this reason, as well as space limitations, we omit these results in what follows.

Figure 6 presents the experimental results we obtained. From them, we draw conclusions similar to those in Section 4.5:

- *Policies using runtime measurements can greatly outperform those without access to such information.*
  This is supported by comparing the results for EQUAL-EFF, ST-EQUI, and ST-EQUAL-EFF scheduling to those for EQUI.
- *Equal-efficiency-based policies outperform Equipartition-based policies.*
  This is supported by comparing the results for EQUAL-EFF and ST-EQUAL-EFF to those for ST-EQUI.
- *Policies using runtime measurements can approach the performance of policies with access to a priori speedup information.*
  For all workloads, the performance of the equal efficiency policies is within 20% of those for the overly optimistic OPT-EFF.
- *The primary policy-induced loss of efficiency is the cost associated with the allocation search procedure.*
  In the cases where EQUAL-EFF and ST-EQUAL-EFF fail to approach closely the (theoretical) optimal performance of OPT-EFF, further examination revealed that it was because of the overhead associated with our search procedure, rather than because the search was settling on poor final allocation choices.

Because the EQUAL-EFF policy attempts to maximize throughput without regard to fairness, it is natural to wonder if jobs with poor speedup characteristics are starved under this discipline. Table 1 shows the job throughput rates (in jobs/minute) for each job class under our test workload mixes. If starvation were a problem in practice, we would expect to see sharp drops in throughput for FLO52 and MP3D when comparing an equal efficiency policy to an equipartition policy. The fact that this does not happen is a reflection of the equal efficiency policies' guarantee that every job be given at least one processor.

6 Conclusions

Our goal in this paper was to determine if parallel processor allocation policies could beneficially exploit runtime measurements of application performance. If so, such runtime

Load	Job	EQUI	EQUAL-EFF	ST-EQUI	ST-EQUAL-EFF
Barnes-Barnes-FLO52	Barnes	0.32	0.44	0.43	0.44
	FLO52	0.05	0.22	0.31	0.23
Barnes-Barnes-MP3D	Barnes	0.35	0.44	0.37	0.44
	MP3D	0.30	0.22	0.32	0.21
Barnes-FLO52-FLO52	Barnes	0.21	0.31	0.24	0.29
	FLO52	0.30	0.41	0.53	0.46
Barnes-MP3D-MP3D	Barnes	0.18	0.28	0.23	0.36
	MP3D	0.55	0.44	0.63	0.36
Barnes-FLO52-MP3D	Barnes	0.23	0.31	0.23	0.29
	FLO52	0.14	0.20	0.27	0.23
	MP3D	0.31	0.23	0.33	0.26

Table 1. *Job Throughput Rates (jobs/minute).*

characterization could replace a reliance on *a priori* specification of job characteristics, a time-consuming and possibly error-prone task, or could supplement the use of *a priori* information when available.

For a number of reasons, it was not obvious whether runtime measurements would be useful to parallel schedulers: it was not clear how to obtain such measurements, whether they would be sufficiently accurate to make reliable decisions, whether recent measurements would be good indicators of future behavior, how to interpret measures taken for an application with an allocation of p processors when considering changing its allocation to q processors, and whether the benefit of using runtime measurement would outweigh the additional overhead of more frequent reallocations.

We have formulated policies for both interactive and batch oriented environments that make use of information obtained by runtime measurement of application characteristics. Given the convenience of these policies for the users of the system, their resilience to changes in program behavior due to phase changes within a single run or to changes in datasets between runs, their good performance, and the evidence of our prototype that practical implementations are possible, we believe that the availability of runtime measurements is an important factor to be considered in parallel processor allocation policy design.

Acknowledgments

Mary Vernon provided insightful comments that helped with both the content and presentation of this work.

References

1. T. E. Anderson, B. N. Bershad, E. D. Lazowska, and H. M. Levy. Scheduler Activations: Effective Kernel Support for the User-Level Management of Parallelism. *ACM Transactions on Computer Systems*, 10(1):53–79, Feb. 1992.

2. M. Berry, D. Chen, P. Koss, D. Kuck, S. Lo, Y. Pang, L. Pointer, R. Roloff, A. Sameh, E. Clementi, S. Chin, D. Schneider, G. Fox, P. Messina, D. Walker, C. Hsiung, J. Scharzmeier, K. Lue, S. Orszag, F. Seidl, O. Johnson, R. Goodrum, and J. Martin. The PERFECT Club Benchmarks: Effective Performance Evaluation of Supercomputers. *The International Journal of Supercomputer Applications*, 3(3):5–40, 1989.

3. S.-H. Chiang, R. K. Mansharamani, and M. K. Vernon. Use of Application Characteristics and Limited Preemption for Run-To-Completion Parallel Processor Scheduling Policies. In *Proceedings of the ACM SIGMETRICS Conference*, pages 33–44, May 1994.

4. E. C. Cooper and R. P. Draves. C Threads. Technical Report CMU-CS-88-154, Department of Computer Science, Carnegie-Mellon University, June 1988.

5. L. Dowdy. On the Partitioning of Multiprocessor Systems. Technical report, Vanderbilt University, June 1988.

6. D. L. Eager and J. Zahorjan. Chores: Enhanced Run-Time Support for Shared-Memory Parallel Computing. *ACM Transactions on Computer Systems*, 11(1):1–32, Feb. 1993.

7. D. G. Feitelson and B. Nitzberg. Job Characteristics of a Production Parallel Scientific Workload on the NASA Ames iPSC/860. In *Proceedings of the IPPS'95 Workshop on Job Scheduling Strategies for Parallel Processing*, pages 337–360, Apr. 1995.

8. D. G. Feitelson and L. Rudolph. Coscheduling Based on Runtime Identification of Activity Working Sets. *International Journal of Parallel Programming*, 23(2):135–160, Apr. 1995.

9. D. Ghosal, G. Serazzi, and S. Tripathi. The Processor Working Set and Its Use in Scheduling Multiprocessor Systems. *IEEE Transactions on Software Engineering*, 17(5):443–453, May 1991.

10. K. Guha. Using Parallel Program Characteristics in Dynamic Processor Allocation Policies. Technical Report CS-95-03, Department of Computer Science, York University, May 1995.

11. Kendall Square Research Inc., 170 Tracer Lane, Waltham, MA 02154. *KSR/Series Principles of Operation*, 1994.

12. S. T. Leutenegger and M. K. Vernon. The Performance of Multiprogrammed Multiprocessor Scheduling Policies. In *Proceedings of the ACM SIGMETRICS Conference*, pages 226–236, May 1990.

13. S. Majumdar, D. L. Eager, and R. B. Bunt. Scheduling in Multiprogrammed Parallel Systems. In *Proceedings of the ACM SIGMETRICS Conference*, pages 104–113, May 1988.

14. E. P. Markatos and T. J. LeBlanc. Using Processor Affinity in Loop Scheduling on Shared-Memory Multiprocessors. *IEEE Transactions on Parallel and Distributed Systems*, pages 379–400, Apr. 1994.

15. C. McCann, R. Vaswani, and J. Zahorjan. A Dynamic Processor Allocation Policy for Multiprogrammed Shared-Memory Multiprocessors. *ACM Transactions on Computer Systems*, 11(2):146–178, May 1993.

16. G. P. McCormick. *Nonlinear Programming*. John Wiley & Sons, Inc., 1983.

17. T. D. Nguyen, R. Vaswani, and J. Zahorjan. Maximizing Speedup Through Self-Tuning of Processor Allocation. In *Proceedings of the 10th International Parallel Processing Symposium*, pages 463–468, Apr. 1996.

18. T. D. Nguyen, R. Vaswani, and J. Zahorjan. Parallel Application Characterization for Multiprocessor Scheduling Policy Design. In *Proceedings of the IPPS'96 Workshop on Job Scheduling Strategies for Parallel Processing*, Apr. 1996.

19. E. W. Parsons and K. C. Sevcik. Multiprocessor Scheduling for High-Variability Service Time Distribution. In *Proceedings of the IPPS'95 Workshop on Job Scheduling Strategies for Parallel Processing*, pages 127–145, Apr. 1995.

20. C. Polychronopoulos and D. Kuck. Guided Self-Scheduling: A Practical Scheduling Scheme for Parallel Supercomputers. *IEEE Transactions on Computers*, C-36(12):1425–1439, Dec. 1987.

21. E. Rosti, E. Smirni, L. W. Dowdy, G. Serazzi, and B. M. Carlson. Robust Partitioning Policies of Multiprocessor Systems. *Performance Evaluation*, 19:141–165, 1994.

22. K. C. Sevcik. Characterizations of Parallelism in Applications and their Use in Scheduling. In *Proceedings of the ACM SIGMETRICS Conference*, pages 171–180, May 1989.

23. K. C. Sevcik. Application Scheduling and Processor Allocation in Multiprogrammed Parallel Processing Systems. *Performance Evaluation*, 19(2/3):107–140, Mar. 1994.

24. J. P. Singh, W.-D. Weber, and A. Gupta. SPLASH: Stanford Parallel Applications for Shared-Memory. *Computer Architecture News*, 20(1):5–44, 1992.

25. P. B. Sobalvarro and W. E. Weihl. Demand-based Coscheduling of Parallel Jobs on Multi-programmed Multiprocessors. In *Proceedings of the IPPS'95 Workshop on Job Scheduling Strategies for Parallel Processing*, pages 106–126, Apr. 1995.

26. A. Tucker and A. Gupta. Process Control and Scheduling Issues for Multiprogrammed Shared-Memory Multiprocessors. In *Proceedings of the 12th ACM Symposium on Operating Systems Principles*, pages 159–166, Dec. 1989.

Parallel Application Characterization for Multiprocessor Scheduling Policy Design

Thu D. Nguyen, Raj Vaswani, and John Zahorjan

Department of Computer Science and Engineering, Box 352350
University of Washington, Seattle, WA 98195-2350 USA

Abstract. Much of the recent work on multiprocessor scheduling disciplines has used abstract workload models to explore the fundamental, high-level properties of the various alternatives. As continuing work on these policies increases their level of sophistication, however, it is clear that the choice of appropriate policies must be guided at least in part by the typical behavior of actual parallel applications. Our goal in this paper is to examine a variety of such applications, providing measurements of properties relevant to scheduling policy design. We give measurements for both hand-coded parallel programs (from the SPLASH benchmark suites) and compiler-parallelized programs (from the PERFECT Club suite) running on a KSR-2 shared-memory multiprocessor.

The measurements we present are intended primarily to address two aspects of multiprocessor scheduling policy design:

- In the spectrum between aggressively dynamic and static allocation policies, what is an appropriate choice for the rate at which reallocations should take place?
- Is it possible to take measurements of application speedup and efficiency at runtime that are sufficiently accurate to guide allocation decisions?

We address these questions through three sets of measurements:

- First, we examine application speedup, and the sources of speedup loss. Our results confirm that there is considerable variation in job speedup, and that the bulk of the speedup loss is due to communication and idleness.
- Next, we examine runtime measurement of speedup information. We begin by looking at how such information might be acquired accurately and at acceptable cost. We then investigate the extent to which recent measurements of speedup accurately predict the future, and so the extent to which such measurements might reasonably be expected to guide allocation decisions.
- Finally, we examine the durations of individual processor idle periods, and relate these to the cost of reallocating a processor at those times. These results shed light on the potential for aggressively dynamic policies to improve performance.

1 Introduction

A quantitative understanding of realistic workload characteristics is critical to the design of processor scheduling policies. Because such information has not been widely

This work was supported in part by the National Science Foundation (Grants CCR-9123308 and CCR-9200832) and the Washington Technology Center.

available, many scheduling studies have been performed using analytic or synthetic workload models [19, 17, 29, 5]. While such artificial workloads are a valuable tool, the increasing sophistication of the policies being studied requires a corresponding increase in the sophistication of the workload models. Our purpose in this paper is to identify and quantify workload characteristics that will help formulate and parameterize such models.

We address this issue in the context of multiprogrammed shared-memory multiprocessors through measurements of seventeen scientific applications when run on a 60 node KSR-2. The measurements we present are intended primarily to address two aspects of multiprocessor scheduling policy design:

- In the spectrum between aggressively dynamic and static allocation policies, what is an appropriate choice for the rate at which reallocations should take place?
- Is it possible to take measurements of application speedup and efficiency at runtime that are sufficiently accurate to guide allocation decisions?

We address these questions through three sets of measurements. First, we examine application speedup, and the sources of speedup loss. Our results confirm that there is considerable variation among jobs, and provide information that will support work on the use of speedup information in making scheduling decisions [13, 23].

Second, because it is at least burdensome, and perhaps impossible, to accurately collect and supply such information at job submission time, we look at the problem of estimating job speedup at runtime. We first demonstrate a technique for estimating "instantaneous speedup" at runtime that is both efficient and accurate. We next examine the extent to which recent measurements of application speedup accurately predict the near future. Clearly, for runtime measurements to be useful in scheduling, such predictions must be reliable. We find that this is a difficult problem, and propose what is at least a first step solution that engages the cooperation of the application in making measurements.

Finally, observing that idleness is a significant source of speedup loss, we examine the durations of individual processor idle periods, and relate these to the cost of reallocating a processor at those times. We find that while most idle periods are too short to justify reallocating a processor, there is still considerable idleness in those fewer periods of greater length. We examine how much processor time could be recovered by reallocation based on various conservative assumptions about the cost of doing so.

Because we believe that realistic workloads will be comprised of applications that are implemented using a variety of methodologies, our application suite consists of programs from two distinct development domains: (1) hand-coded parallel applications that implement sophisticated parallel algorithms and may include optimizations such as load balancing and careful data partitioning to minimize communication, and (2) compiler-parallelized sequential programs.

We use programs from the SPLASH and SPLASH-2 benchmark suites [30, 37] to represent hand-coded parallel applications, and programs from the PERFECT Club benchmark suite [3] and an industrial fluid dynamics program (obtained from Analytical Methods, Inc.) to represent compiler-parallelized sequential applications.

The remainder of the paper is organized as follows. Section 2 discusses related work. Section 3 documents our experimental platform. Section 4 looks at application speedup, and identifies and quantifies the major components of speedup loss. Section 5 examines the question of whether instantaneous speedup varies significantly during execution, and so sheds light on the extent to which recent measurements of application performance predict its future behavior. Section 6 reports measurements of the frequency and duration of processor idleness, characteristics important in deciding how aggressive schedulers should be in reallocating idle processors. Section 7 gives our conclusions.

2 Related Work

The PERFECT Club benchmark suite is one of several standard benchmark suites used to measure the capability of parallelizing compilers [3]. As such, many studies have characterized the behavior of a number of these PERFECT Club programs, e.g., [7, 11, 26]. However, these studies have typically focused on properties of the code that affect a compiler's ability to parallelize them, and not, as we do, on properties of their execution that affect a scheduler's ability to best schedule parallelized versions of the programs.

For the SPLASH and SPLASH-2 benchmark suites, Singh et al. [30] and Woo et al. [37] provide significant information, including speedup, cache behavior, and synchronization wait time. Our measurements supplement their reports by quantifying sources of speedup loss, as well as more fine-grained application behaviors such as frequency and duration of idle periods. Furthermore, we contrast the behaviors of these applications with those of compiler-parallelized applications, and consider the implications of their differences to the design of parallel processor scheduling policies.

Feitelson and Nitzberg [12] report a variety of statistics on the parallel workloads of an iPSC/860 located at NASA Ames. They discuss what we call submitted workload mix characteristics, such as the ratio of sequential to parallel jobs, resource usage patterns (e.g., the correlation between total resource requirement and the degree of parallelism), job submission rates, and system utilization. In contrast, we characterize fine-grained behaviors of individual applications in order to answer questions such as *"how often do applications idle one or more of their allocated processors?"* and *"are idle periods long enough with respect to reallocation cost such that reallocation in response to application idleness can improve system utilization?"*.

Cypher et al. [8] report measurements for a number of applications running on message-passing multiprocessor systems in a manner similar to ours. However, because they were attempting to address architectural issues, they concentrate on different measures (e.g., memory and I/O requirements) than those presented here. Similarly, many other researchers (e.g., [9, 1, 27]) report results from studies of application memory behavior.

3 The Experimental Environment

3.1 Hardware and Software Platform

All measurements were done on a Kendall Square Research KSR-2 COMA shared-memory multiprocessor. Our machine consists of 60 40-MHz dual-issue proprietary processors, partitioned into two clusters of 30. Each processor is connected to a 256-KByte data cache, 256-KByte instruction cache, and a 32-MByte attraction memory. Processors in each cluster, and the clusters themselves, are connected by separate 1 GB/s. slotted ring networks[1]. The attraction memories cooperate to implement a sequentially consistent, globally-shared address space. The unit of transfer and sharing between attraction memories is 128 bytes.

Each node in the KSR-2 contains a hardware monitoring unit called the *Event Monitor* that compiles information such as cache misses and processor stall (communication) time. This information is made available to the system and user jobs through a set of read-only registers.

The KSR-2 runs a variant of the OSF/1 UNIX operating system. We use CThreads [6], an efficient user-level threads package, as the vehicle of parallelism. We instrumented CThreads using the event monitors to collect the data presented in the remainder of this paper.

SPLASH and SPLASH-2 programs run directly on CThreads. We use both the KSR KAP [16] and Stanford SUIF compilers [36] to parallelize sequential programs. We use both systems because they represent different tradeoffs in technology and product maturity. KSR KAP is a commercial product that has been adapted specifically to the KSR architecture and optimized through productization. SUIF, on the other hand, is a research vehicle. As such, SUIF implements many state-of-the-art parallelization techniques not present in KAP, but has been less concerned with standard optimizations and has not been tuned to the KSR architecture.

3.2 Applications

Tables 1 and 2 list the applications that we measured, and give brief descriptions of each as well as their execution time when run on a single processor[2]. This single-processor time represents the execution of a parallel version of the program running on a single processor, not of a sequential version of the program. We use these as the base times in computing speedup, rather than the times for true sequential versions, because our interest is in schedulers; the performance gap between the sequential version and parallel version executing on a single processor highlights the weakness of the program or compiler, but does not present an opportunity exploitable by the scheduler.

For reasons of space, in what follows, we show results for only a representative sample of our seventeen applications. We refer the reader to [24] for an expanded version of this paper containing more comprehensive data.

---

[1] Note, however, that Dongarra and Dunigan have measured a peak bandwidth of only 8 MB/s on a KSR-1, which has 20-MHz processors connected by the same network as in the KSR-2 [10].

[2] All applications were measured while running default data sets that came with the benchmark suites, except that the number of iterations for QCD were reduced from 100 to 2 to shorten execution times in our experiments.

Application	Exec. time (secs)	Description
Barnes †	1159.14	Barnes-Hut N-body simulation.
Fft †	6.12	Fast Fourier transform.
Fmm †	602.98	Fast Multipole Method N-body simulation.
LocusRoute	78.56	VLSI standard cell router.
MP3D	25.02	Simulation of rarefied hypersonic flow.
Ocean †	1663.02	Model currents in ocean basin.
Pverify	52.30	Logical verification.
Raytrace †	271.90	Rendering of 3-dimensional scene.
Radix †	199.50	Integer radix sorting.
Water †	300.00	N-body molecular dynamics problem.

Table 1. *Hand-coded applications. († from SPLASH-2, remainder from SPLASH.)*

Application	KAP Exec. time (secs)	SUIF Exec. time (secs)	Description
ADM	364.12	–	Hydrodynamic simulation using mesoscale hydrodynamic model.
ARC2D	904.14	1699.48	Analysis of fluid flow problems using Euler equations.
DYFESM	175.94	327.48	Analysis of symmetric anisotropic structures.
FLO52	374.36	406.66	Analysis of transonic inciscid flow past an airfoil using unsteady Euler equations.
QCD	157.16	230.38	Simulation of gauge theory using a Monte Carlo-based algorithm.
TRACK	412.38	–	Tracking of moving targets based on sensor inputs.
USAero	3240.16	–	CFD computation.

Table 2. *Compiler-parallelized sequential applications. (All except USAero from PER-FECT Club suite.)*

4 Speedup and Sources of Speedup Loss

4.1 Application Speedup

In this section, we examine the speedup characteristics of the jobs in our workload. We begin by giving the speedup functions for all jobs, both to better document the workload and to support previous work by others asserting that schedulers should take individual job speedups into consideration in making allocation decisions. We then identify and

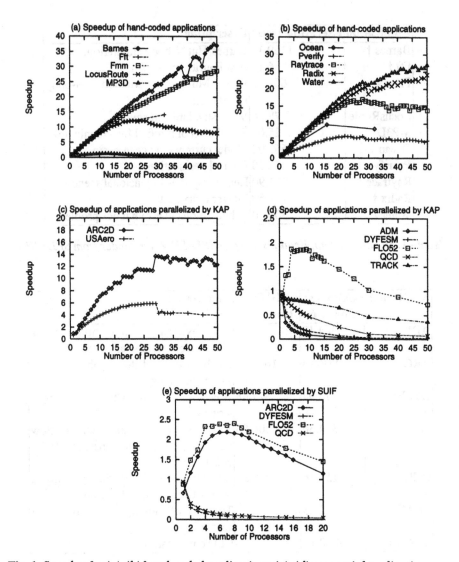

Fig. 1. *Speedup for (a), (b) hand-coded applications, (c), (d) sequential applications parallelized by KAP, and (e) sequential applications parallelized by SUIF. (Note: Different Y-axis scales are used for legibility.)*

quantify the sources of speedup loss as a prelude to an investigation of how speedup might be characterized through runtime measurement.

Figure 1 plots speedup against the number of processors. (The experiments for the applications parallelized by SUIF were terminated at 20 processors because the slowdown they experienced caused running times to be excessive. Also, not all applications could be run successfully with SUIF: either the compiler itself or the parallelized application failed during execution.) We observe that:

- Speedups vary greatly, even among applications in the same class (hand-coded or compiler-parallelized).
- Speedup is typically much worse for compiler-parallelized applications than for hand-coded applications.
- Most speedup curves are relatively smooth and roughly convex-shaped. This implies that speedup values for a relatively few allocations might allow reasonably accurate extrapolation to other allocations. (See [23] for an application of this idea to scheduling.)
- For most hand-coded applications, there is an allocation beyond which they slow down gradually. With the exception of ARC2D when parallelized by KAP, all compiler-parallelized jobs slow down significantly after achieving their peak speedups.
- Hand-coded applications seem to tolerate crossing the cluster boundary fairly well, whereas the two compiler-parallelized applications that were still speeding up at 30 processors (USAero and ARC2D), slow down when they are spread across clusters.

We now turn our attention to quantifying and characterizing factors contributing to speedup loss as applications are executed on larger processor allocations.

4.2 Loss of Speedup

We have two goals in this subsection. One immediate goal is to document the sources of speedup loss in our applications as part of our workload characterization. A second, longer term objective, is to work towards an accurate and efficient scheme for measuring speedup at runtime.

It is well-known that loss of speedup in shared-memory systems arise from the following factors [21, 28]:

1. **Idleness:** at times, parallel programs must idle allocated processors because of insufficient parallelism or load imbalance.
2. **Communication:** in shared-memory machines such as the KSR-2, communication takes place when the executing thread refers to data that either does not currently reside in its cache or is not in the appropriate state. In the case of the KSR-2, this can occur for both the processor cache and the attraction memory (which itself is a cache). KSR-2 processors stall while waiting for the data to be fetched from a remote node. Thus, on the KSR-2, communication overheads appear as processor stall.
3. **System overhead:** even sequential programs incur system overhead because of events such as page faults, clock interrupts, etc. Such overhead can be more significant for highly parallel programs, however, because these events typically occur on every processor (and so must occur more often for a program running on more processors). Furthermore, the asynchronous nature of these events can degrade the performance of tightly-coupled parallel programs.
4. **Parallelization overhead:** parallel programs typically must incur computational overheads that are not present in sequential programs, such as per-processor initialization, work partitioning, and locking and unlocking on entry and exit of a critical section.

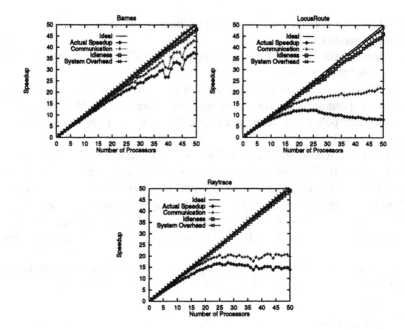

Fig. 2. *Loss of speedup for hand-coded applications. (The distance from each curve to the curve below it represents the speedup loss due to that factor.)*

Of the four sources, it is particularly difficult to measure parallelization overhead for hand-coded applications because initialization, work partitioning, and synchronization code are typically scattered throughout the application code. Thus, in what follows, we measure only idleness, communication, and system overhead, and infer parallelization cost from the remaining speedup loss.

Figures 2 and 3 plot speedup and speedup loss due to idleness, communication, and system overhead for a number of applications that achieve modest to good speedup. In each graph, the lowest curve represents actual measured speedup. Each curve above the speedup function represents what speedup would have been had a single source of speedup loss been eliminated. In order from bottom to top, we consider communication, idleness, system overhead, and parallelization overhead. (We also plot ideal (linear) speedup.) The graphs are cumulative; e.g., the curve for which idleness overhead has been set to 0 also has communication cost set to 0. Thus, the distance between each pair of curves in the figure indicates the magnitude of speedup loss due to the overhead associated with the higher curve. (Parallelization overhead is the difference between the ideal and system overhead curves.)

We observe that parallelization overhead is negligible, and that system overhead is typically very small compared to idleness and communication cost. On average, parallelization overhead accounts for less than 1% of application processor time while system overhead accounts for less than 3%. We note, though, that production workloads stressing the capacity of main memory could exhibit considerably more system overhead due to paging than we observe using these benchmark suites.

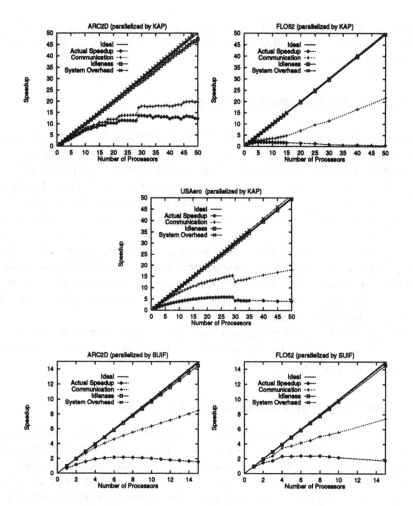

Fig. 3. *Loss of speedup for compiler-parallelized applications. (The distance from each curve to the curve below it represents the speedup loss due to that factor.)*

On the other hand, both hand-coded and compiler-parallelized applications can contain significant idleness, although compiler-parallelized applications tend to exhibit more. Among all the hand-coded applications we studied, idleness can be as high as 60% of processor time; even Barnes, the application showing the best overall speedup in our application suite, can contain as much as 20% idleness. KAP-parallelized applications can contain up to 83% idleness, while SUIF-parallelized applications can contain up to 50% idleness.

Similarly, both hand-coded and compiler-parallelized applications can contain significant communication overhead. Hand-coded applications seem to be divided into two classes, those that slow down and those that continue to speed up with increasing allocation size up to the maximum number of processors available. Interestingly, almost all those that slow down exhibit considerably worse communication losses than those that do not (e.g., up to 94% of MP3D execution time can be attributed to communication overhead). Applications parallelized by either KAP or SUIF can contain up to 50% communication overhead.

5 Runtime Measurement of Speedup

In the previous section we observed that there is considerable variation in speedup behavior among jobs, encouraging the development of policies that use speedup information in making allocation decisions. Most speedup-sensitive policies that have been proposed to date have been static, and so require *a priori* specification of each job's speedup function. In this section we investigate a different approach that would be of use to dynamic policies, the acquisition of speedup characterizations at runtime through measurement. The attraction of using runtime measurements is both its convenience (since it relieves the user of the burden of providing this information) and its potentially greater accuracy (since applications whose speedup are sensitive to their input data or the relative locations of their allocated processors cannot be characterized *a priori*). Of course, runtime measurements can also be used to complement *a priori* information when such information is available.

We begin by looking at how accurate runtime speedup measurements can be made at reasonable overhead. We then examine the extent to which recent measurements of speedup predict future behavior.

5.1 Estimating Speedup Through Runtime Measurement

In the previous section we found that the majority of speedup loss is due to idleness and communication. In fact, Figures 2 and 3 show that there are very small differences between ideal speedup and the sum of actual speedup, idleness loss, and communication loss. As noted, however, system overhead can be more significant for programs with large memory requirements, where paging becomes a more significant source of overhead. These observations suggest that reasonably accurate measurements of speedup for scheduling purposes can be made at runtime by monitoring these three components of speedup loss.

We have implemented this approach to runtime measurement on our KSR-2. To measure communication cost and system overhead, we rely on hardware support. The per-node event monitors available on the KSR-2 (see Section 3.1) maintain three critical hardware counters: elapsed wall-clock time, elapsed user-mode execution time, and accumulated processor stall (communication). Dividing stall time by wall-clock time gives us the efficiency loss due to communication, from which we can infer the corresponding speedup loss. Dividing the difference between wall-clock time and user-mode time by wall-clock time gives us the efficiency loss due to system activities.

This method of computing communication cost and system overhead is quite efficient. If the scheduler is implemented in the operating system kernel, then accessing these counters is simply a matter of reading the appropriate hardware registers. If the scheduler is implemented as a user-level server, the hardware registers would need to be mapped to shared-memory or the server would have to make use of low-level messaging services to read the remote registers. Note that in order for such a user-level server to read the remote registers, it would need to interrupt the running thread. If sample intervals are not too small, however, this is unlikely to be a significant source of overhead.

To measure idleness, we need to depend on the application itself. If applications are built using runtime systems such as Cthreads, then idleness measurements can be made without requiring explicit programmer effort by placing the measurement code in the thread package. Currently, we instrument the Cthreads synchronization code to keep running counts of processor idleness, and make this information available to the system via a piece of system-designated shared-memory. This approach is relatively overhead-free because idleness accounting is performed when the processor would otherwise not be doing any useful work. Of course, this approach assumes that all application synchronization takes place through calls to the CThreads libraries rather than through direct manipulation of shared variables. We did not, however, have to modify our applications to meet this assumption; none of our hand-coded programs violated this assumption, while all synchronization in compiler-parallelized applications by definition takes place in the thread package.

Note that while we have relied on the specific hardware counters on the KSR-2 processor, many modern processors include similar functionality. For example, both the DEC Alpha and the Intel Pentium processors contain counters for various sorts of cache misses, which could be translated into estimates of communication cost [31, 4].

5.2 Using Speedup Measurements to Predict Future Behavior

For runtime speedup measurements to be of practical use to schedulers, application speedups must be *predictable*. By predictable we mean that if an application's speedup is measured over some interval, the application will continue to execute at roughly that speedup for some time to come. In the remainder of this section we consider the question of application speedup predictability. To facilitate comparisons of prediction errors for different allocations of processors, we normalize our results. Specifically, we measure prediction errors in terms of efficiency, rather than speedup itself.

The simplest approach to predicting future speedup is to use quantum-based measurements of current speedup and to guess that the future will look like the past. Intuitively, we expect longer quantum lengths to result in more accurate predictions.

We evaluate this approach to speedup prediction through trace-based simulation. We first create traces for each of our applications. Each trace contains measured efficiencies for each $100ms$ of execution. Given these traces, we can compare the efficiency measured during each proposed *measurement quantum, $Q > 100ms$*, to the efficiency observed during the next quantum[3].

To evaluate the error of the efficiency predictions, we need to choose an appropriate measure. (For example, a natural choice might be mean absolute error.) Because we are interested in how useful these predictions will be to schedulers, choosing an appropriate

---

[3] Predicting that efficiency in the next quantum will be equal to efficiency in the just completed quantum is, of course, only one possible choice. We also investigated another natural choice, the use of exponentially decaying histories of all past observations. We found this technique to be generally less accurate, however.

measure is a difficult problem. On the one hand, the measure should reflect the average difference between the predicted and actual future efficiencies. On the other hand, the average difference alone is not sufficient information: it understates the error because occasional very incorrect predictions might induce a scheduler to make unfortunate allocation choices that can degrade performance much more than proportional to the error in the predictions (see, for example [22]). At the other extreme, looking at the maximum single-prediction error probably overestimates error, since errors of that magnitude may be exceedingly rare.

Because of the conflicting demands on the error measure to reflect both the common and the worst cases, we use a measure that can be parameterized to flow smoothly from one extreme to the other. In particular, let $M(Q)_i$ be the measured efficiency during the ith quantum of length Q, and let the complete execution consist of $N(Q)$ quanta. The measure of prediction error we use is

$$Error = \sqrt[C]{\frac{1}{N(Q)-1} \sum_{i=1}^{N(Q)-1} (|M(Q)_{i+1} - M(Q)_i|)^C} \qquad (1)$$

For $C = 1$, this is the mean absolute error; as $C \to \infty$, the measure increasingly reflects the maximum absolute error.

Figures 4 and 5 graph our error measure for a selected subset of our applications. In each graph, the X-axis represents the measurement quantum length, Q, in ms, and the Y-axis the error measure. The distinct curves on each graph correspond to different values of C, the parameter of our measure.

We make three observations based on this data. First, for some applications, even quite long measurement intervals are not sufficient to obtain good accuracy, while for others much shorter intervals suffice. This makes choosing a system measurement interval difficult: long intervals are needed for some jobs, but shorter intervals are more advantageous to the scheduler (since they allow more frequent opportunities to correct inappropriate allocations).

Second, for all applications, the accuracy at a fixed measurement interval improves as the application is allocated more processors. This is simply a reflection of a changing time scale: the job is able to execute a larger fragment of its code in a fixed time period such that the time period becomes more representative of overall behavior.

Finally, many of the applications exhibit mild periodic behavior in accuracy as a function of quantum length.

All of these observations have a common explanation: there is little reason to expect the next measurement interval to look like the previous one unless the application is executing substantially similar code in both. Stated differently, we expect efficiency measurements to be most accurate in predicting future behavior when the measurement interval corresponds to the execution of some section of code that will be repeated.

In related work [22, 23], we have made use of this observation, exploiting a particularly simple (but also quite common) program structure: an outer sequential loop that drives the execution. In those works we show that schedulers that use measurements taken over intervals corresponding to executions of the outer loop can significantly improve application as well as system performance.

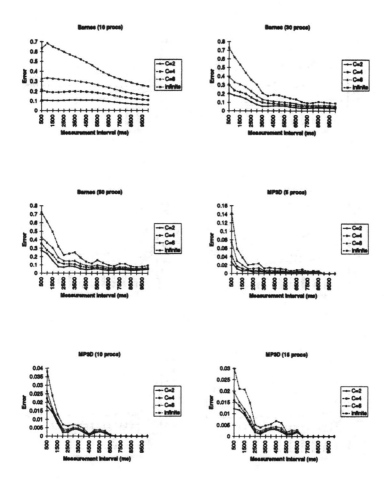

Fig. 4. *Prediction Error Versus Measurement Quantum Length (Q). (Note: Different Y-axis scales are used for legibility.)*

Of course, having to rely on a particular program structure (as well as the cooperation of the application to indicate when it has reached the beginning of an iteration) is not ideal. It remains to be seen whether it is possible to design schedulers that can accurately predict speedup without having to depend on application cooperation. Our data suggests that such a scheduler would have to dynamically "learn" the appropriate quantum for individual applications.

6 Processor Idle Periods

Multiprocessor scheduling disciplines can be broadly characterized as being static (the allocation made to a job is kept fixed for its entire execution), quasi-dynamic (realloca-

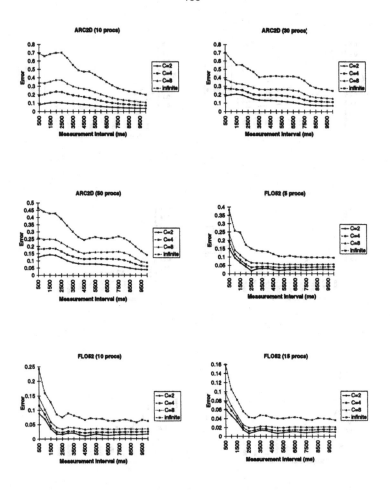

Fig. 5. *Prediction Error Versus Measurement Quantum Length (Q). (Note: Different Y-axis scales are used for legibility.)*

tions are performed at job arrival and departure moments, but not otherwise), or dynamic (reallocations may be performed at any time). In this section we focus on application characteristics that reflect on the opportunity to improve performance through dynamic reallocations.

The primary potential advantage of dynamic policies over quasi-dynamic ones is their ability to exploit the processor idleness that occurs during execution due to such things as sequential portions of execution, load imbalance, and contention for critical sections. The speedup results given in Section 4 show that there is considerable idleness in typical applications. To take advantage of this idleness, however, the duration of individual idle periods must exceed the cost associated with reallocating the processor. In the next subsection, we examine the reallocation cost on our machine. In succeed-

From	Fill Time
local attraction memory	1.28ms
within cluster	8.96ms
outside cluster	30.72ms

Table 3. *Time required to completely refill the KSR-2's 256KB processor cache.*

ing subsections we present measurements providing indications of whether processor idleness can be exploited through dynamic reallocation.

6.1 Processor Reallocation Cost

There are two components to processor reallocation cost: *system path length* and *cache penalty*. System path length is the time required to execute operating system code for reassigning a processor from one job to another, i.e., to perform a context switch. Measurements on our KSR-2 shows path length context switch costs in the range of 3 to 5ms. However, the KSR-2 processor reallocation mechanism was designed for ease of implementation, and uses a simple but very inefficient approach. In contrast, measurements of a Sequent Symmetry, an older shared-memory multiprocessor with much slower processors, indicate path length costs for context switching of about 750μs [20]. Based on this somewhat conflicting information, it appears that context switch path length costs below 1ms are easily possible on modern multiprocessors. However, it is unlikely that designers of production systems will invest the effort to optimize context switching until it becomes clear that there is a tangible payoff. For this reason, a conservative estimate of 1-2ms context switch times may be a reasonable reflection of typical systems.

The cache penalty component of reallocation cost reflects the fact that dynamic movement of processors can adversely affect program cache behavior, and therefore performance. The importance of cache performance to modern processor speed has motivated the recent work on cache-affinity scheduling [33, 32, 14, 35].

To evaluate the cache related cost of dynamic reallocation, we look at the worst-case times on the KSR-2. Recall that each processor in the KSR-2 has two caches, a 256 KByte processor cache and a 32 MB attraction memory. In what follows we focus on the processor cache, as we believe it will be the major source of cache interference over the reallocation intervals we are considering. A miss in the processor cache can be filled by three levels in the memory hierarchy: the local attraction memory, the attraction memory of another processor on the same cluster, and the attraction memory of a processor on another cluster. Table 3 gives the times required to completely fill the 256 KByte processor cache from these three levels of machine memory.

6.2 Idle Period Length Distribution

We consider first the distribution of the length of processor idle periods. Figure 6 gives results for five applications that achieves moderate to good speedup. For each number

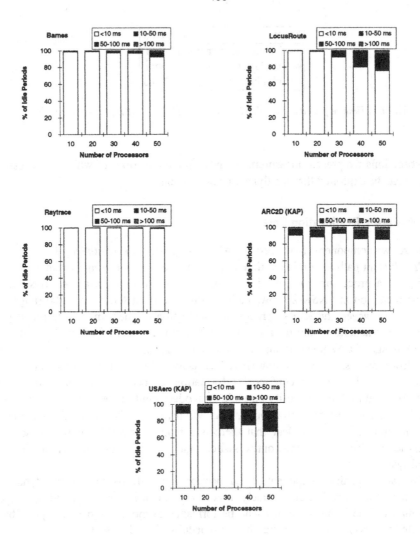

Fig. 6. *Distribution of idle period lengths. (Each component of the bars is the fraction of the total number of idle periods whose lengths fall in the intervals given in the legend.)*

of processors we show the percentage of all idle periods with durations that fall into four intervals: (0-10*ms*), [10-50*ms*), [50-100*ms*), and >100*ms*.

These graphs show that an overwhelming number of idle periods are short – less than 10*ms*. Furthermore, more detailed examination of the data shows that the average length of these short idle periods is typically well below 1*ms*. This suggests that aggressive dynamic reallocation (e.g., reallocating at the beginning of every idle period) may be ineffective or even detrimental to system performance for both application classes,

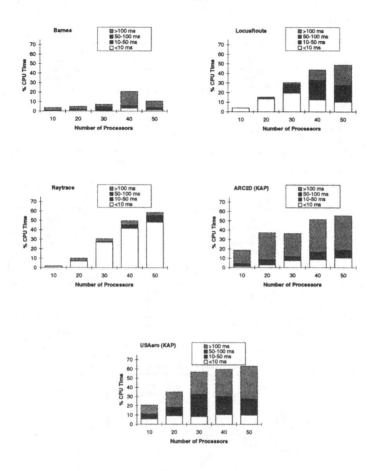

Fig. 7. *Distribution of idle time. (Each component of the bars is the fraction of processor time represented by idle periods whose lengths fall in the intervals given in the legend.)*

since estimated reallocation cost (Section 6.1) is longer than the length of the typical idle period for either class. This set of results for compiler-parallelized applications were particularly surprising, suggesting that sequential portions typically run for only short periods of time.

6.3 Idle Period Time Distribution

One approach to dealing with short idle periods is to filter them by waiting a short time before context switching. Ousterhout [25], Lo and Gligor [18], and Karlin et al. [15] take this approach in the context of implementing locks for mutual exclusion, where such filtering is called "two-phase blocking" or "spin-then-block." McCann et. al. [20] have proposed a delayed reallocation scheme as part of a dynamic scheduling policy.

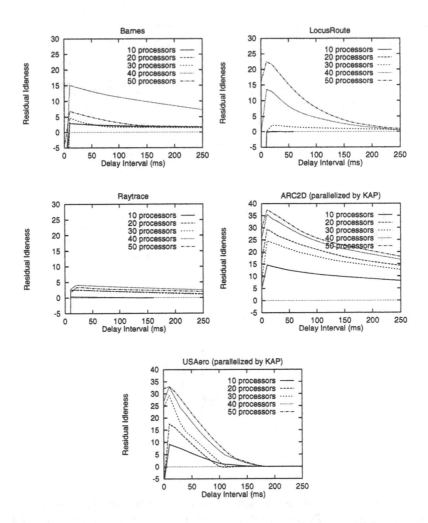

Fig. 8. *Residual idleness as a percentage of processor time assuming a 10ms total reallocation cost.*

A natural question to ask is how much idleness exists whose duration exceeds the context switch delay time. We address this question in Figure 7. Each bar shows the percent of total processor time represented by idle periods with durations in (0-10ms), [10-50ms), [50-100ms), and >100ms. This figure shows that long idle periods, although few in numbers, can account for a large fraction of total processor time, providing evidence that delayed reallocation may be profitable, at least for many applications.

6.4 Residual Idleness After Filtering

A delay-based reallocation scheme can improve performance only if application *residual idleness* – idleness remaining after the delay interval has elapsed – exceeds the cost of

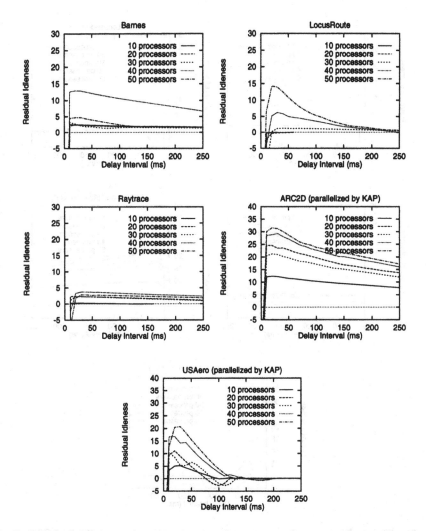

Fig. 9. *Residual idleness as a percentage of processor time assuming a 30ms total reallocation cost.*

reallocating the processor. Thus, we now consider residual idleness.

In what follows, we compute residual idleness by subtracting the sum of the delay time and the reallocation time from the total duration of each idle period greater than the delay time. The reallocation time includes two reallocation path length costs and two cache fill times. Because the latter depends strongly on both the workload (because of the footprints of the original and replacing applications) and on the system (because data placement decisions affect cache refill time), we use a number of different assumptions about the total cost to reflect different possible scenarios. We use 10ms as a conservative estimate for the case that either footprints are small or else the cache can be refilled from the local attraction memory. We use 70ms as an estimate for the case of very large footprints that must be filled from memories not on the local cluster. Finally, we

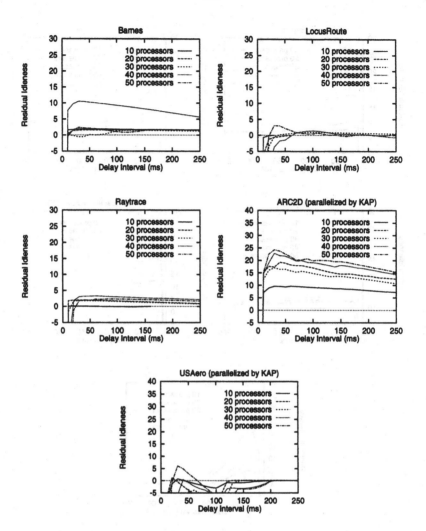

Fig. 10. *Residual idleness as a percentage of processor time assuming a 70ms total reallocation cost.*

use 30*ms* as a compromise between these extremes, representing perhaps a more likely cost.

Figures 8 and 9 plot residual idleness as a function of the delay before reallocation, assuming a total reallocation cost of 10*ms* and 30*ms* respectively. The Y-axis value of each point on each curve shows residual idleness as a fraction of total job processor time. The initial rise in the curves represents the benefit of a short delay – uselessly short idle periods are filtered out. The gradual decrease in the curves for longer delays represents the lost opportunity to use the processor as the delay to reallocate increases.

These figures show that delays from 10*ms* to about 20*ms* can result in significant recovery of processing power in many applications, while for the rest there is little or no loss. We also note that the appropriate delay time depends only weakly on the reallocation

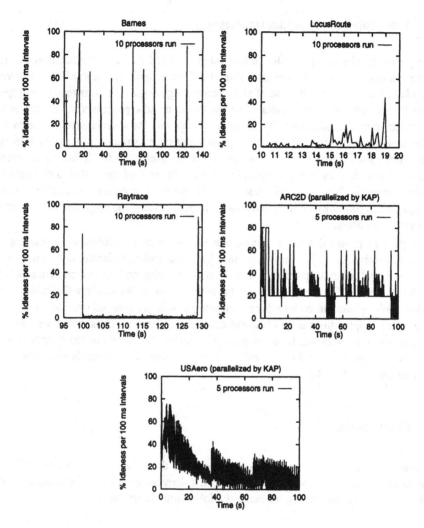

Fig. 11. *Idleness (measured over 100ms intervals) versus time.*

cost, indicating that it is more strongly tied to characteristics of the applications (i.e., the distribution of idle period lengths) than to reallocation times. At these reallocation costs, the distinctions in distributions among the applications are remarkably small; all give acceptable results for similar delay times.

Figure 10 plots normalized residual idleness assuming a reallocation cost of $70ms$. At this cost, dynamic reallocation becomes less attractive. The previously productive delay range (10-$20ms$) can seriously degrade performance for some applications, although dynamic reallocation continues to recover significant processing power for others.

6.5 Using Idle Periods to Run Interactive Jobs

The previous subsection has shown that idleness-based dynamic reallocation can improve system performance, especially if incurred cache penalties are small and receiving threads can effectively make use of short processing periods. For this reason, we speculate that it may be more profitable to reallocate an idle processor to an interactive job rather than a parallel one. While current proposals for space-sharing systems that address support of interactive work typically partition available processors into two pools, one to run interactive jobs and one to run parallel jobs [34, 2], taking advantage of processors idled by parallel jobs could reduce the size of the partition dedicated to interactive work. Of interest to such schemes is whether idle periods occur often enough to support the running of interactive jobs without degrading the response time observed by interactive users.

Figure 11 plots idleness timelines, that is, "instantaneous idleness" against application execution time. We show timelines for hand-coded applications running on 10 processors and compiler-parallelized applications running on 5 processors. Timelines for different number of processors are similar to those shown. We observe that while hand-coded applications can contain long compute periods between idle periods, compiler-parallelized applications display almost continuous idleness. Thus, while we have not yet pursued this proposal, it seems plausible that at least some of the support for interactive computing could be provided by making use of temporarily idle processors allocated to parallel jobs.

7 Conclusions

In this paper, we have presented measurements of the behavior of two distinct implementation classes of scientific applications on a shared-memory multiprocessor system. Based on our measurements, we make the following observations:

- Significant differences exist in the speedup behavior of applications, supporting the importance of work on scheduling policies that use speedup information to guide scheduling decisions.
- For systems where *a priori* speedup information is not available, in many cases, it is possible to characterize general application behavior using runtime measurements of idleness, communication, and system overhead.
- On shared-memory systems, in order to reliably predict application speedups at runtime, the scheduler must rely on information provided by the runtime system.
- Although most idle periods are too short to merit reallocation of the processor, for some applications, long idle periods represent a significant fraction of execution time. We have shown that, for these applications, imposing a short delay before reallocating a processor when it goes idle is effective in filtering out the short idle periods and recovering much of this idleness.

Acknowledgments

Mary Vernon provided insightful comments that helped with both the content and presentation of this work. We thank Analytical Methods, Inc. for providing the USAero CFD application.

References

1. A. Agarwal and A. Gupta. Memory-Reference Characteristics of Multiprocessor Applications under MACH. In *Proceedings of the ACM SIGMETRICS Conference*, pages 215–225, May 1988.
2. I. Ashok and J. Zahorjan. Scheduling a Mixed Interactive and Batch Workload on a Parallel, Shared Memory Supercomputer. In *Supercomputing '92*, pages 616–625, Nov. 1992.
3. M. Berry, D. Chen, P. Koss, D. Kuck, S. Lo, Y. Pang, L. Pointer, R. Roloff, A. Sameh, E. Clementi, S. Chin, D. Schneider, G. Fox, P. Messina, D. Walker, C. Hsiung, J. Scharzmeier, K. Lue, S. Orszag, F. Seidl, O. Johnson, R. Goodrum, and J. Martin. The PERFECT Club Benchmarks: Effective Performance Evaluation of Supercomputers. *The International Journal of Supercomputer Applications*, 3(3):5–40, 1989.
4. J. Chen, Y. Endo, K. Chan, D. Mazieres, A. Dias, M. Seltzer, and M. Smith. The Measured Performance of Personal Computer Operating Systems. In *Proceedings of the 15th ACM Symposium on Operating system Principles*, pages 299–313, Dec. 1995.
5. S.-H. Chiang, R. K. Mansharamani, and M. K. Vernon. Use of Application Characteristics and Limited Preemption for Run-To-Completion Parallel Processor Scheduling Policies. In *Proceedings of the ACM SIGMETRICS Conference*, pages 33–44, May 1994.
6. E. C. Cooper and R. P. Draves. C Threads. Technical Report CMU-CS-88-154, Department of Computer Science, Carnegie-Mellon University, June 1988.
7. G. Cybenko, L. Kipp, L. Pointer, and D. Kuck. Supercomputer Performance Evaluation and the Perfect Benchmarks. In *Proceedings of the 1990 International Conference on Supercomputing, ACM SIGARCH Computer Architecture News*, pages 254–266, Sept. 1990.
8. R. Cypher, A. Ho, S. Konstantinidou, and P. Messina. Architectural Requirements of Parallel Scientific Applications with Explicit Communication. In *Proceedings of the 20th Annual International Symposium on Computer Architecture*, pages 2–13, May 1993.
9. F. Darema-Rogers, G. Pfister, and K. So. Memory Access Patterns of Parallel Scientific Programs. In *Proceedings of the ACM SIGMETRICS Conference*, pages 46–58, May 1987.
10. J. J. Dongarra and T. Dunigan. Message-Passing Performance of Various Computers. Technical Report CS-95-299, University of Tennessee, July 1995.
11. R. Eigenmann, J. Hoeflinger, Z. Li, and D. Padua. Experience in the Parallelization of Four Perfect-Benchmark Programs. Technical Report 1193, Center for Supercomputing Research and Development, Aug. 1991.
12. D. G. Feitelson and B. Nitzberg. Job Characteristics of a Production Parallel Scientific Workload on the NASA Ames iPSC/860. In *Proceedings of the IPPS'95 Workshop on Job Scheduling Strategies for Parallel Processing*, pages 337–360, Apr. 1995.
13. K. Guha. Using Parallel Program Characteristics in Dynamic Processor Allocation Policies. Technical Report CS-95-03, Department of Computer Science, York University, May 1995.
14. A. Gupta, A. Tucker, and S. Urushibara. The Impact of Operating System Scheduling Policies and Synchronization Methods on the Performance of Parallel Applications. In *Proceedings of the ACM SIGMETRICS Conference*, pages 120–133, May 1991.

15. A. Karlin, K. Li, M. S. Manasse, and S. Owicki. Empirical Studies of Competitive Spinning for a Shared-Memory Multiprocessor. In *Proceedings of the 13th ACM Symposium on Operating Systems Principles*, pages 41–55, Oct. 1991.

16. Kendall Square Research Inc., 170 Tracer Lane, Waltham, MA 02154. *KSR Fortran Programming*, 1993.

17. S. T. Leutenegger and M. K. Vernon. The Performance of Multiprogrammed Multiprocessor Scheduling Policies. In *Proceedings of the ACM SIGMETRICS Conference*, pages 226–236, May 1990.

18. S.-P. Lo and V. Gligor. A Comparative Analysis of Multiprocessor Scheduling Algorithms. In *Proceedings of the 7th International Conference on Distributed Computing Systems*, pages 356–63, Sept. 1987.

19. S. Majumdar, D. L. Eager, and R. B. Bunt. Scheduling in Multiprogrammed Parallel Systems. In *Proceedings of the ACM SIGMETRICS Conference*, pages 104–113, May 1988.

20. C. McCann, R. Vaswani, and J. Zahorjan. A Dynamic Processor Allocation Policy for Multiprogrammed Shared-Memory Multiprocessors. *ACM Transactions on Computer Systems*, 11(2):146–178, May 1993.

21. A. J. Musciano and T. L. Sterling. Efficient Dynamic Scheduling of Medium-Grained Tasks for General Purpose Parallel Processing. In *Proceedings of the International Conference on Parallel Processing*, pages 166–175, Aug. 1988.

22. T. D. Nguyen, R. Vaswani, and J. Zahorjan. Maximizing Speedup Through Self-Tuning of Processor Allocation. In *Proceedings of the 10th International Parallel Processing Symposium*, pages 463–468, Apr. 1996.

23. T. D. Nguyen, R. Vaswani, and J. Zahorjan. Using Runtime Measured Workload Characteristics in Parallel Processor Scheduling. In *Proceedings of the IPPS'96 Workshop on Job Scheduling Strategies for Parallel Processing*, Apr. 1996.

24. T. D. Nguyen, R. Vaswani, and J. Zahorjan. Parallel Application Characterization for Multiprocessor Scheduling Policy Design. Technical report, Department of Computer Science and Engineering, University of Washington, In preparation.

25. J. K. Ousterhout. Scheduling Techniques for Concurrent Systems. In *Proceedings of 3rd International Conference on Distributed Computing Systems*, pages 22–30, Oct. 1982.

26. P. Petersen and D. Padua. Machine-Independent Evaluation of Parallelizing Compilers. Technical Report 1173, Center for Supercomputing Research and Development, 1992.

27. E. Rothberg, J. P. Singh, and A. Gupta. Working Sets, Cache Sizes, and Node Granularity Issues for Large-Scale Multiprocessors. In *Proceedings of the 20th Annual International Symposium on Computer Architecture*, pages 14–25, May 1993.

28. K. C. Sevcik. Characterizations of Parallelism in Applications and their Use in Scheduling. In *Proceedings of the ACM SIGMETRICS Conference*, pages 171–180, May 1989.

29. K. C. Sevcik. Application Scheduling and Processor Allocation in Multiprogrammed Parallel Processing Systems. *Performance Evaluation*, 19(2/3):107–140, Mar. 1994.

30. J. P. Singh, W.-D. Weber, and A. Gupta. SPLASH: Stanford Parallel Applications for Shared-Memory. *Computer Architecture News*, 20(1):5–44, 1992.

31. R. L. Sites, editor. *Alpha Architecture Reference Manual*. Digital Press, 1992.

32. M. Squillante and E. Lazowska. Using Processor-Cache Affinity Information in Shared-Memory Multiprocessor Scheduling. *IEEE Transactions on Parallel and Distributed Systems*, 4(2):131–143, February 1993.

33. D. Thiebaut and H. S. Stone. Footprints in the Cache. *ACM Transactions on Computer Systems*, 5(4):305–329, Nov. 1987.

34. A. Tucker and A. Gupta. Process Control and Scheduling Issues for Multiprogrammed Shared-Memory Multiprocessors. In *Proceedings of the 12th ACM Symposium on Operating Systems Principles*, pages 159–166, Dec. 1989.

35. R. Vaswani and J. Zahorjan. The Implications of Cache Affinity on Processor Scheduling for Multiprogrammed, Shared Memory Multiprocessors. In *Proceedings of the 13th ACM Symposium on Operating Systems Principles*, pages 26–40, Dec. 1991.

36. R. P. Wilson, R. S. French, C. S. Wilson, S. P. Amarasinghe, J. M. Anderson, S. W. K. Tjiang, S.-W. Liao, C.-W. Tseng, M. W. Hall, M. S. Lam, and J. L. Hennessy. SUIF: An Infrastructure for Research on Parallelizing and Optimizing Comilers. Technical report, Computer Systems Laboratory, Stanford Univeristy.

37. S. C. Woo, M. Ohara, E. Torrie, J. P. Singh, , and A. Gupta. The SPLASH-2 Programs: Characterization and Methodological Considerations. In *Proceedings 22nd Annual International Symposium on Computer Architecture*, pages 24–36, June 1995.

Dynamic vs. Static Quantum-Based Parallel Processor Allocation*

Su-Hui Chiang   and   Mary K. Vernon
suhui@cs.wisc.edu   *vernon@cs.wisc.edu*

Computer Sciences Department
University of Wisconsin
Madison, WI 53706 USA

Abstract. This paper improves upon previous synthetic workload models and compares the performance of dynamic spatial equipartitioning (EQS) and the semi-static quantum-based FB-PWS processor allocation defined in [23], under synthetic workloads that have not previously been considered. These new workloads include realistic repartitioning overheads and job characteristics that are consistent with system measurement, anticipated trends, and experience. The overall conclusion from the results is that the EQS policy is generally superior to the FB-PWS policy *even under realistic repartitioning overheads*. We find cases where the EQS system saturates earlier than the FB-PWS system, and vice versa. This leads to the definition of a modified EQS policy, called EQS-PWS, which has performance equal to or better than EQS and FB-PWS for all workloads examined in this paper.

1   Introduction

In static quantum-based parallel processor allocation policies, each job is configured for a static number of processors and timesharing is used to share the processors among the jobs. Ousterhout's coscheduling policies [21] are examples of this class of policies. Semi-static quantum-based policies allow limited changes in processor allocations as system load changes. Such policies greatly reduce the frequency of job reconfiguration (which can involve significant data repartitioning overheads) as compared with dynamic policies such as the spatial equipartitioning (EQS) policy.

In a recent paper [23] Parsons and Sevcik have proposed a new semi-static quantum-based parallel processor allocation policy, FB-PWS, that has the following characteristics:

load-adaptability: the number of processors allocated to a newly arriving job decreases as the number of jobs in the system increases,

processor working set (pws): as load increases, the allocation for a newly arriving job is proportional to it's *pws* measure [9], where *pws* is the num-

---

*This research was partially supported by the National Science Foundation under grants CCR-9024144, CDA-9024618, and GER-9550429.

ber of processors that permit the job to run at approximately the knee of its execution-time vs efficiency profile [15][1],

Multilevel-Feedback (FB): in each quantum, priority is given to the jobs that have so far received least service,

infrequent repartitioning: In each quantum, at most one job runs on a smaller number processors than it's initial allocation (and those processors would otherwise be idle).

They also define another semi-static quantum-based policy called FB-ASP that is similar to FB-PWS but does not use the *pws* measure.

Parsons and Sevcik show that, under particular workloads with job characteristics that have been observed in practice, the FB-PWS policy is competitive with EQS *even when repartitioning is assumed to have zero cost.* This is an impressive result since FB-PWS commits to a processor allocation at job arrival time. Previous static allocation policies have generally not been competitive with dynamic policies such as EQS under zero repartitioning cost [13, 29, 19, 4]. They also show that FB-PWS and FB-ASP can substantially outperform EQS under an ad hoc model of repartitioning costs that is intended to illustrate the possible impact of repartitioning overheads on relative policy performance.

In this paper, we further investigate the relative performance of EQS and FB-PWS. First, we examine how idealized EQS and FB-PWS compare for synthetic workloads that are not considered in [23], but that are designed to represent parallel workloads encountered in practice. An improved approach to representing application speedup characteristics is developed as part of this effort (see section 3). Second, we assess whether specific features of the FB-PWS policy might be incorporated in the EQS policy to improve performance. In particular, we consider a specific use of the *pws* measure to modify the processor allocations computed by the EQS policy, leading to a new policy called EQS-PWS. Finally, we consider how processor repartitioning might be handled in a practical implementation of EQS or EQS-PWS. We compare the EQS, EQS-PWS, and FB-PWS policies under workload models and repartitioning overheads that are based on recent system measurements ([8, 6, 7, 1, 10]) extrapolated to future production parallel systems.

We are primarily interested in evaluating relative policy performance for daytime workloads, and thus the principal measure of interest is mean job turnaround time. We note that results in the previous literature suggest that the EQS and FB policies provide good performance for small ("interactive") jobs. For example, the EQS policy like the *processor sharing* policy for uniprocessor systems, has the key property that expected response time is *proportional to* the job's service requirement. This property is called "fairness" in [12]. We also note that the FB-PWS policy has reduced potential for starvation of large jobs as compared with the FB policy for uniprocessor systems, due to it's load-adaptive space-sharing property. Further investigation of these and other more detailed measures is left for future work.

---

[1]Specifically, *pws* is the minimum number of processors that maximizes the ratio of speedup, $S(n)$, to the cost function $n/S(n)$.

The synthetic workloads that are used to evaluate the processor allocation policies in this paper are based on measured characteristics of parallel workloads, but do not include memory and I/O resource requirements. In fact, neither the FB-PWS nor the EQS policy can be directly applied to real workloads in which memory or I/O requirements are significant. For example, in the case of memory requirements, each policy must be modified to ensure that jobs are allocated enough memory to execute reasonably efficiently, resulting in reduced space-sharing and greater time-sharing of the processing power. The degree to which the performance of each policy will change depends on the specific memory requirements in a workload of interest. The goal of the policy evaluations in the absence of memory and I/O requirements is to provide a baseline of policy performance comparisons, as well as some understanding of the relative policy strengths and weaknesses that may usefully guide the design and evaluation of more complex high performance policies for real workloads.

The remainder of this paper is organized as follows. Section 2 provides definitions of the FB-PWS, FB-ASP, and EQS policies. Section 3 defines our system assumptions and synthetic workload models, including a revised method for modeling application speedups. Section 4 provides the policy comparisons for both the idealized case (where repartitioning cost is assumed to be zero) and for repartitioning overheads that are estimated from system measurement. Section 5 contains the conclusions of this work.

2 Policy Definitions

The FB-PWS, FB-ASP, and EQS policies considered initially in this paper are each defined below.

2.1 FB-PWS and FB-ASP

The FB-PWS policy is proposed and clearly defined in [23]. The brief definition is repeated here for the sake of reader convenience.

An arriving job, j, is configured for the following partition size:

$$min\left\{ N_j, \frac{min(pws_j, P)}{S + min(pws_j, P)} \times P \right\},$$

where N_j is the job's maximum parallelism, pws_j is the *processor working set* measure for the job (defined in section 1), S is the sum of the processor allocations for all jobs currently in the system, and P is the number of processors in the system. At the start of each time slice, jobs are examined in order of least acquired processing time, where acquired processing time is the number of processor-seconds so far allocated to the job. Each job in turn is scheduled to run on the number of processors it is configured for, until there are fewer processors left than any of the remaining jobs' configurations. In this case the scheduler runs the highest priority unscheduled job on the remaining processors.

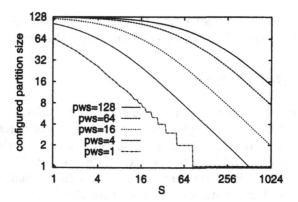

Figure 1: Configured partition size vs. S for FB-PWS
$N_j \geq P; P = 128$

Thus, only the last job scheduled for execution in each quantum may run on a different number of processors than its initial configuration.

The FB-ASP policy is identical to the FB-PWS policy, except that an arriving job is configured for $min(N_j, P/J)$ processors, where J is the number of jobs in the system including the new arrival.

Note that processor allocations decrease as system load (S) increases. For the FB-PWS policy, Figure 1 illustrates the relationship between allocation size and S for several values of pws_j, assuming $P = 128$ and $N_j \geq P$ for each job j. Note that the allocations approach being proportional to pws as S increases, and the allocations are generous unless pws is small and S is large. Even when S is quite large (e.g., greater than 128), the allocation for a newly arriving job with $pws = P$ is still a significant fraction of P. This allows efficient jobs with long service times to execute on a reasonable number of processors after shorter jobs have departed.

2.2 EQS

The spatial equipartitioning policy, EQS, was initially proposed by Tucker and Gupta in [27] and has been evaluated and/or refined in many subsequent studies (e.g., [13, 18, 16]). When a job arrival or departure occurs, the processors are dynamically reallocated so that each job has an equal fraction of the processors unless a job has smaller maximum parallelism than the equipartition value. In the latter case, each such job is allocated a number of processors equal to its maximum parallelism, and the equipartition value is recursively computed for the remaining processors and jobs. The precise processor allocations may differ from the equipartition value by small adjustments to avoid non-integer allocations. In this paper, we adjust up for jobs that have less acquired processing time, and adjust down for jobs that have more acquired processing time.

Note that for the EQS policy as defined above, repartitioning can occur quite frequently. In section 4 we examine the impact of realistic repartitioning overheads and we consider a "practical implementation" of the EQS policy in which full repartitioning only occurs once every 500 seconds.

3 Model Definition

In this section we define the system and synthetic workloads that will be simulated to evaluate scheduling policies in section 4. To date, traces of production parallel workloads do not include job speedup functions, which are needed to evaluate the EQS and FB-PWS policies. Thus, we formulate a synthetic workload model that mimics the variation in job parallelism and service demands in the traces, and can represent a variety of speedup behaviors that are observed in practice.

3.1 System Assumptions

The system is assumed to contain P processing nodes, each functionally and performance-equivalent with respect to applications in the workload. Communication costs are represented in the synthetic workload model; otherwise, details of the interconnection network and memory system are left unspecified.

We assume that jobs are capable of adapting to changes in the number of processors that are allocated to them. Adaptive programming techniques and runtime support for program restructuring are active areas of research and appear to be feasible for both shared memory and message passing systems (e.g., [27, 20, 6]). Although job reconfiguration can involve substantial cost, particularly if massive data movement is required, the results in [6, 11] show that the benefit of better processor scheduling can outweigh the associated cost. This key issue is explored further for EQS and FB-PWS in section 4.

We assume that the system knows the maximum number of processing nodes that each job can make productive use of, either because this information is specified when the job is submitted or because the system is capable of determining this information at runtime using methods such as the self-tuning approach recently proposed by Nguyen et. al. [20]. Similarly, for the FB-PWS policy (or the EQS-PWS policy yet to be defined), we assume that the system is capable of knowing the pws measure for each job, perhaps from runtime estimation techniques similar to those described in [20].

In the remainder of the paper we assume the set of processing nodes are dedicated to servicing a parallel workload. One might also imagine that the nodes are a set of currently idle nodes in a non-dedicated network of workstations (NOW) that is available for serving large (parallel) jobs. Such a system requires an effective policy for recruiting idle nodes as well as efficient mechanisms for migrating the processes of parallel jobs away from nodes that are preempted by a higher priority user [2, 30, 1]. Although we do not consider the impact of node interruptions nor particular policy customizations that might be needed, we consider synthetic workloads and repartitioning overheads that are relevant to such environments. Repartitioning overheads are discussed further in section 4.

3.2 Synthetic Workload Model

Job arrivals occur at rate λ, and are modeled as a Poisson process except in one set of experiments where we investigate whether higher variability in inter-arrival times changes the impact of repartitioning overhead on relative policy performance.

The set of characteristics that define each job are:

W_j - the work (total cpu service requirement) that the job must perform,

N_j - the maximum number of nodes that the job can productively use,

and a yet-to-be-specified set of parameters that correspond to the communication and other execution overheads in a particular model of job speedup. These job characteristics are discussed below. Section 3.2.1 develops a model of job execution overheads suitable for the goals of this study. We then describe the characterization of job parallelism (section 3.2.2), job service requirement (section 3.2.3), and correlation among the various model parameters (section 3.2.4). The workload model is summarized in section 3.2.5.

3.2.1 Job Execution Overheads

One possible functional form for job execution time, proposed in [26], is defined as follows:

$$T_j(n) = \frac{\phi W_j}{n} + \alpha + n\beta, \qquad \phi \geq 1, \quad \alpha, \beta \geq 0, \tag{1}$$

where

- n is the number of processors allocated to the job,
- ϕ is an inflation factor that models load imbalance in the computation,
- α represents fixed overheads such as per-processor initialization, and
- β represents communication overhead, which increases with n.

The speedup function, $\frac{W_j}{T_j(n)}$, for the above execution time function is:

$$S_j(n) = \frac{1}{\frac{\phi}{n} + \frac{\alpha}{W_j} + \frac{n\beta}{W_j}}, \qquad \phi \geq 1, \quad \alpha, \beta \geq 0, \tag{2}$$

and the point at which this speedup function is maximized, M_j, is:

$$M_j = \begin{cases} \sqrt{\frac{W_j \phi}{\beta}} & \text{if } \beta > 0 \\ \infty & \text{if } \beta = 0. \end{cases} \tag{3}$$

The parameters of equation (1) correspond to overheads that are observed in practice, and the equation has been shown to match well with measured speedup functions if ϕ, α, and β are adjusted to yield best fit [28]. Below we propose a few modifications to the equation that improve its intuitive appeal and are needed for our study. We then point out some important characteristics of the revised speedup function.

To derive the new speedup function, we first observe that one minor deficiency in equation (1) is that load imbalance and communication overhead costs are incurred even for $n = 1$. Another minor deficiency is that ϕ, the inflation factor that represents total idle time due to load imbalance, is independent of n, whereas in practice load imbalance generally increases as n increases. We further observe that for any given job it is equally valid to define a new communication overhead parameter, β', such that $\beta = \beta' W_j$. That is, for the given job, the communication overhead is expressed as a fraction of W_j; of course, this fraction may vary among different jobs. With these motivations in mind, we make the following small modifications to equation (1):

$$T_j'(n) = \frac{(1+(n-1)\phi')W_j}{n} + \alpha + (n-1)\beta'W_j,$$
$$\alpha \geq 0, \quad 0 \leq \phi', \beta' \leq 1. \tag{4}$$

Note that the above *linear* increase in load imbalance with n may overestimate the increases that are typically observed in real workloads. However, with suitable controls and/or conservative estimates for ϕ', defined later in this paper, the simple linear dependence is adequate for the present purposes.

As will be discussed further in section 3.2.2, equation (2) cannot represent particular workloads of interest because the speedup depends directly on W_j. We fix this problem in the speedup function corresponding to equation (4) by assuming the fixed overhead, α, is negligible.[2] We justify this approximation as follows. First, typically only the jobs with small processing requirement have non-negligible fixed overhead, and these jobs tend to account for negligible amounts of total processor usage in parallel systems [8]. Second, the approximation will be imperceptible even for these jobs if the other parallelism overheads are non-negligible. Finally, due to the assumed linear increase in load imbalance with n in equation (4), α has approximately the same impact on the shape of the speedup function as does ϕ'. For these reasons, the approximation that $\alpha = 0$ shouldn't affect the policy comparisons in this paper. Making this change in equation (4), yields the following speedup function:

$$S_j'(n) = \frac{1}{\frac{1}{n}+\frac{(n-1)\phi'}{n}+(n-1)\beta'},$$
$$\alpha = 0, \quad 0 \leq \phi', \beta' \leq 1, \tag{5}$$

that has the following maximum, M_j':

$$M_j' = \begin{cases} \sqrt{\frac{1-\phi'}{\beta'}} & \text{if } \beta' > 0 \\ \infty & \text{if } \beta' = 0. \end{cases} \tag{6}$$

The revised speedup function has two parameters: ϕ' and β'. The impact of varying ϕ' and β' on the shape of the speedup curve is shown in Figures 2(a) and (b), respectively. For each curve, the value of *pws* is shown, as is $M \equiv M_j'$

---

[2]In this case, the speedup could still be correlated with W_j if we specify a correlation between any of the execution overhead parameters and W_j, as discussed in section 3.2.4.

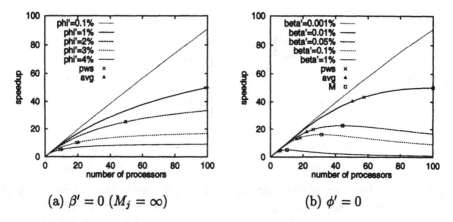

(a) $\beta' = 0$ $(M_j = \infty)$

(b) $\phi' = 0$

Figure 2: Curves generated by the modified speedup function (equation 5)

if $M'_j \leq P$ (see figure 2(b). Note that the increase in speedup between $n = pws$ and $n = \min(M'_j, P)$ is small. This is the motivation for allocating processors in proportion to pws at high load, as in the FB-PWS policy. Also note that the new speedup function is capable of representing a variety of curves that match those that are observed in practice, similar to the speedup function in equation (2).

If execution efficiency on N_j processors, $S_j(N_j)/N_j$, is equal to c, it is straightforward to show from equation (5) that

$$(N_j - 1)\phi' + N_j(N_j - 1)\beta' = \frac{1}{c} - 1. \qquad (7)$$

We will use the above equation to define particular overhead characteristics in the experiments in section 4.3.

Finally, we consider an alternate speedup model [5, 16], that has been used widely in studies of scheduling policy performance [13, 17, 4, 20]:

$$S_j(n) = \frac{(\delta + 1)n}{\delta + n}. \qquad (8)$$

We note that this function is a special case of equation (5) in which $\beta' = 0$ and

$$\phi' = \frac{1}{1 + \delta}. \qquad (9)$$

Thus, the curves in Figure 2(a) are also examples of the speedup function in equation (8). Furthermore, $pws = \delta$ for this speedup function; thus several of the curves are labeled with the determining parameter δ. Since efficiency *increases* as δ increases, we will find it convenient to produce a positive correlation between efficiency and W_j in some of the synthetic workloads by setting $\beta' = 0$ and specifying a distribution for δ that is positively correlated with W_j. For $\delta \geq P$ (i.e., $\phi' \leq \frac{1}{P+1}$), note that the efficiency on $n \leq P$ processors is greater than or equal to 50%, as shown in equation (8) and illustrated in Figure 2(a).

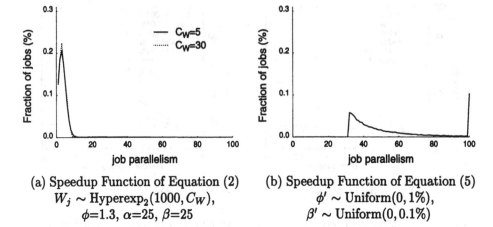

(a) Speedup Function of Equation (2)
$W_j \sim \text{Hyperexp}_2(1000, C_W)$,
$\phi=1.3$, $\alpha=25$, $\beta=25$

(b) Speedup Function of Equation (5)
$\phi' \sim \text{Uniform}(0, 1\%)$,
$\beta' \sim \text{Uniform}(0, 0.1\%)$

Figure 3: Distributions of $N_j = M_j$ (P=100)

3.2.2 Job Parallelism

One approach to generating a synthetic workload [23] is to specify the distributions of the parameters that characterize the job speedups, and then to let job parallelism, N_j, be equal to the point at which the speedup function is maximized, M_j. This can be done using either the speedup function in equation (2) or equation (5). Below we discuss the disadvantages of this approach and then define the approach and distributions of N_j that will be used in our policy performance comparisons.

One drawback of setting $N_j = M_j$ is that the complex relationship between M_j and the parameters of the speedup function may lead to an unanticipated or undesirable distribution of job parallelism. For example, Figures 3(a) and (b), give the distributions of $N_j = M_j$ for the speedup functions in equation (2) and equation (5), respectively. In each case, the speedup parameters are set at particular (reasonable) values. In Figure 3(a), M_j depends directly on W_j (see equation (3)); thus the hyperexponential distribution of W_j, or any other realistic distributions of W_j, leads to a skewed distribution toward very low job parallelism. This distribution or the distribution in Figure 3(b) may not be the desired parallelism distribution for the synthetic workload.

The approach of setting $N_j = M_j$ also limits the types of correlations that can be specified among work, parallelism, and execution efficiency. For example, one cannot model both high correlation between work and job parallelism (as observed in [8]) but weak correlation between work and efficiency. This may be desirable because, for example, both small program development runs of highly efficient parallel codes, as well as large jobs with moderate communication overheads may be expected in a parallel system of interest.

We solve these problems by taking a different approach. First, we explicitly specify the distribution of job parallelism. Next, we explicitly specify the distributions of W_j, ϕ', and β', and possibly correlations among these parameters, subject only to the following constraint:

$$\beta' \leq \frac{1-\phi'}{N_j^2}. \tag{10}$$

This constraint guarantees $N_j \leq M_j$ for the speedup function in equation (5).[3] Note that if $\beta' = 0$ then equation (10) is trivially satisfied due to the practical restriction that $0 \leq \phi' \leq 1$.

The distributions of job parallelism that will be used to compare policy performance are illustrated in Figure 4. These distributions are motivated by the variation in job parallelism reported for daytime user jobs on the iPSC/860 machine at NASA Ames [8], and also on the SP/2 machine at the Cornell Theory Center [10]. The distributions in Figure 4 were generated from a parameterized *bounded geometric distribution* of job parallelism that is adapted from prior work [13, 17] and has the following four parameters:

N_{max} - the maximum value for job parallelism,

$P_{N_{max}}$ - the probability that an arriving job has parallelism equal to N_{max},

p - the parameter of the bounded geometric distribution of parallelism for all other jobs, and

$N^* \leq N_{max}$ - the value of parallelism whose probability will increase by the probability for parallelism greater than N_{max} in the geometric distribution.

An arriving job has parallelism N_{max} with probability $P_{N_{max}}$. Otherwise, the parallelism of the job is chosen from a geometric distribution with parameter p. If the selected parallelism is larger than N_{max}, the job is assigned parallelism N^*.

One rationale for the bounded geometric distribution is that one can expect a significant number of highly parallel jobs; i.e., all of the production jobs that can run fairly efficiently on as many processors or nearly as many processors as are available in the system. Another rationale is that there is another class of jobs made up of program-development runs and codes that cannot run efficiently on P or close to P processors. In this class of jobs, one can perhaps expect the probability to decrease as the parallelism increases. We note that one discrepancy between this model and the data in [8] is that parallelism equal to two has lower probability in the measured system than suggested by the bounded geometric. This type of discrepancy shouldn't have great impact on the relative policy performance comparisons in this paper. Finally, the parameter N^* is included to model the preferred parallelism equal to 32 in the measured iPSC/860 and SP/2 workloads [8, 10].

---

[3]Note that the restriction $N_j \leq M_j$ assumes that either users are sophisticated enough not to request more than M_j processors (because the job execution time will be longer), or self-tuning [20] is used to achieve same result. Allowing $M_j > N_j$ assumes that users sometimes configure their jobs to run on at most $N_j < M_j$ processors, for convenience or because the speedup model doesn't accurately reflect a sharp decline in the actual speedup function beyond N_j.

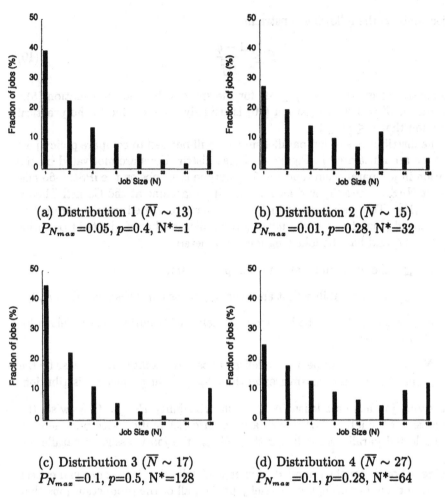

(a) Distribution 1 ($\overline{N} \sim 13$)
$P_{N_{max}}$=0.05, p=0.4, N*=1

(b) Distribution 2 ($\overline{N} \sim 15$)
$P_{N_{max}}$=0.01, p=0.28, N*=32

(c) Distribution 3 ($\overline{N} \sim 17$)
$P_{N_{max}}$=0.1, p=0.5, N*=128

(d) Distribution 4 ($\overline{N} \sim 27$)
$P_{N_{max}}$=0.1, p=0.28, N*=64

Figure 4: Example Bounded-Geometric Distributions for Job Parallelism
$N_{max} = 128$

3.2.3 Job Service Requirement

In some workloads, we model job service requirement, W_j, by a two-stage hyperexponential distribution with mean $\overline{W}$ and coefficient of variation, C_W. We use the notation $W_j \sim \text{Hyperexp}_2(\overline{W}, C_W)$ to denote this distribution.

For most experiments, mean job service requirement will be proportional to either job parallelism or the square of job parallelism. Let $\overline{N}$ represent mean job parallelism and $\overline{W}$ represent the overall mean job service requirement. Also let $W_{j|n}$ be the service requirement for a given job, j, that has parallelism $N_j = n$. To specify mean service requirement proportional to job parallelism, $W_{j|n}$ has a two-stage hyperexponential distribution with mean $\frac{n}{N}\overline{W}$, and coefficient of variation called $C_{W|n}$; *i.e.*,

$$W_{j|n} \sim \text{Hyperexp}_2(\frac{n}{N}\overline{W}, C_{W|n}).$$ (11)

This model was proposed in [14] and formalized in [16]. If mean service requirement is correlated with the square of job parallelism, then the multiplier for $\overline{W}$ is replaced by $\frac{n^2}{N^2}$. The reported measures of $W_{j|n}$ vs. n for the iPSC/860 workloads at NASA Ames [8] lie between these two cases.

3.2.4 Correlation Between Workload Parameters

In some experiments, we will assume that execution overheads are on average lower for jobs with larger total service requirement. In these cases, we will use the same notation as in equation (11). For example,

$$\delta_{j|w} \sim \text{uniform}(\frac{w}{\overline{W}}100, \frac{w}{\overline{W}}200)$$ (12)

specifies that the values of δ are selected from a uniform distribution with a lower bound and upper bound that are each proportional to the job service requirement ($W_j = w$), with overall mean value for δ equal to 150.

3.2.5 Workload Model Summary

In summary, the synthetic workloads used to evaluate relative policy performance in this paper have four parameters: N_j (job parallelism), W_j (total service requirement), ϕ' (load imbalance), and β'(communication overhead, as a fraction of total work). These parameters have the following characteristics: (1) a bounded geometric distribution of job parallelism (N_j) as illustrated in Figure 4, (2) a two-stage hyperexponential distribution of W_j, in most cases with mean proportional to N_j or N_j^2 as defined in section 3.2.3, and (3) load imbalance overhead ($\phi' = \frac{1}{1+\delta}$) and communication overhead (β') that are either fixed values or are selected from a specified distribution. In some experiments, the *average* execution overhead will be inversely proportional to service requirement, as defined in section 3.2.4. The execution overhead parameters must also satisfy the constraint in equation (10), which guarantees that the job's speedup function is non-decreasing up to N_j processors. This workload model is very similar to the previous workload model in [17]. The new features are the communication overhead parameter, β', the N^* parameter in the bounded geometric distribution for N_j, and the distributions for the execution overhead that will be specified in the next section.

4 Policy Comparisons

In this section we present the results of policy comparison experiments that are based on simulations with a variety of synthetic workloads. The discussion is focussed on comparisons between the FB-PWS, EQS, and EQS-PWS policies, although results for the FB-ASP policy [23] are also provided in the figures for the sake of completeness.

The four parameters that characterize each job in the synthetic workloads are summarized in section 3.2.5. The distribution of job parallelism, N_j, will be one of the four distributions depicted and numbered in Figure 4, depending on the experiment. The distributions for the execution overhead parameters will be explained as each experiment is introduced; these distributions are motivated by comparisons with earlier results [23] or by speedups that are encountered in practice (e.g., [24, 22]). Arrivals are assumed to be Poisson unless otherwise specified, and the system size (P) is 128 processing nodes in all experiments.

The simulations were performed using the batch means method of generating confidence intervals, with batch size ranging from 100,000 to 200,000 job departures, depending on the particular experiment. Except as noted, reported results have 90% confidence intervals that are within 5% or less of the given value.

Section 4.1 compares the EQS and FB-PWS policies for several workloads, assuming zero repartitioning cost for both policies and zero swapping cost for FB-PWS. Section 4.2 introduces the EQS-PWS policy and compares this policy against EQS and FB-PWS, again assuming zero cost for swapping and repartitioning. Finally, Section 4.3 compares the three policies under a case of realistic partitioning overheads.

4.1   Comparisons under Zero Repartitioning Cost

We first compare the EQS and FB-PWS under a workload that is nearly identical to Workload 2 in [23]. That is, we use the speedup function in equation 5, set the overhead parameters and distribution of W_j as given in Figure 5, and let $N_j = M_j$. Note that because we have modified the execution time function so that load imbalance increases linearly in the processor allocation, we have chosen $\phi' = 0.003$ such that the load imbalance on 100 processors is the same as the fixed overhead in Workload 2.

Figure 5 gives the ratio of mean response time for the FB-PWS policy to the mean response time of EQS, as a function of offered load, $\rho = \lambda \overline{W}/P$, for both $C_W = 5$ and $C_W = 30$. When $\rho = 0.9$, system utilization for FB-PWS or EQS is in the range of 92% - 99%. The response time ratio for FB-ASP is also given for completeness, as noted above. Similar to the results reported in [23], these results show that FB-PWS is competitive with EQS throughout the range of offered load, and also that the system with the EQS policy saturates at a slightly earlier point than the FB-PWS system.[4]

The workload in Figure 5 has a distribution for N_j that is very similar to the distribution in Figure 3(a). Thus, nearly all of the jobs have parallelism < 10, and a negligible fraction of jobs have parallelism greater than 50. Furthermore, in this workload, larger W_j implies larger pws and larger pws implies higher effi-

---

[4]We also reproduced several of the graphs in [23], not shown in this paper, to validate that we have correctly implemented the policy simulations.

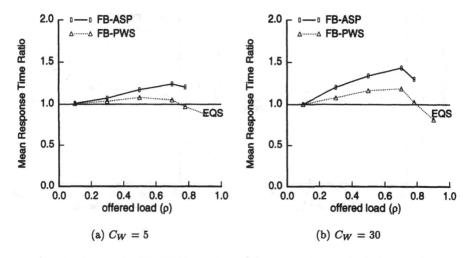

Figure 5: FB-PWS vs. EQS under workload 2 in [23]
$W_j \sim \text{Hyperexp}_2(1000, C_W), \; N_j = M_j, \; \phi' = 0.003, \alpha = 25, \beta = 25$

ciency on any given processor allocation. This workload thus might be favorable for the FB-PWS policy that uses the *pws* measure to determine allocations.

Figure 6 shows relative policy performance for two workloads that have the following characteristics that differ from Figure 5:

- Distribution of job parallelism that is more consistent with observed workloads; i.e., Distribution 1 in Figure 4.
- Moderate sublinearity in the speedups of large jobs. ϕ' is fixed and β' is *inversely proportional* to N_j^2.[5] Thus, larger N_j implies higher *pws* and higher *pws* implies higher efficiency on any given processor allocation. Also, W_j has *mean* proportional to N_j^2 and coefficient of variation approximately equal to 36. However, *larger W_j does not necessarily imply larger pws or higher efficiency.*

Due to the correlation between mean service requirement and N_j^2, jobs with $N_j \geq 32$ account for 98% of the system resource usage by this workload, in agreement with system measurements in [8].

For the workload in Figure 6(a) ($\phi' = 0$), FB-PWS is comparable to the EQS policy throughout the entire range of offered load. When load imbalance is more significant (i.e., $\phi' = 0.01$, which implies that efficiency loss due to load imbalance is 50% on 100 processors), FB-PWS saturates sooner than EQS. The reason FB-PWS does less well for this workload is that jobs with large N_j (and large *pws* due to low communication overhead) will, on average, experience less space-sharing under FB-PWS than under EQS (see Figure 1). Since these jobs dominate system resource usage and have modest speedups due to load imbalance, the FB-PWS system saturates sooner. We note that the results in

---

[5] In fact, β' is defined such that N_j is the point where the speedup curve is maximized.

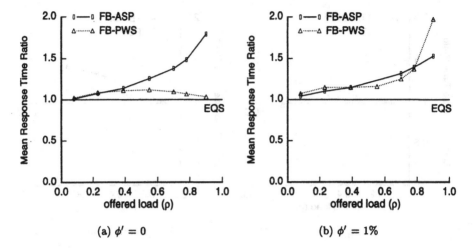

(a) $\phi' = 0$ (b) $\phi' = 1\%$

Figure 6: The impact of large jobs with moderate execution overhead
$N_j \sim$ Distribution 1, $\;W_{j|n} \sim$ Hyperexp$_2(\frac{n^2}{N^2}1000, 10)$, $\;\; \beta' = \frac{1-\phi'}{N^2}$
$$(C_W = 36)$$

Figure 6(a) and (b) are largely the same if the workloads are changed to have $C_{W|n} = 2$ ($C_W = 6.6$), except that the FB-ASP policy has better performance at high load in the case that $\phi' = 0$.

As a final set of comparisons of FB-PWS and EQS under zero repartitioning cost, Figure 7 shows relative policy performance for workloads with similar parallelism (Distribution 3 in Figure 4) and the same distribution of W_j as in Figure 6. However, the communication overhead (β') is assumed to be zero and the overhead due to load imbalance ($\phi' = \frac{1}{1+\delta}$) is selected from a *uniform distribution* for δ. Recall that $pws = \delta$, and that Figure 2 shows that if $\delta > 100$ the job will have efficiency greater than approximately 50% on any processor allocation. Since δ is nondeterministic, large N_j does not imply large pws nor high efficiency on a given feasible processor allocation.

In Figure 7(a), efficiency is positively correlated with W_j; in Figure 7(b), efficiency is independent of W_j. The results are very similar to the results in Figure 6(a) and (b), respectively. Thus, in these cases, the weaker correlation between N_j and efficiency has not affected the relative performance of the policies.

4.2 The EQS-PWS Policy

Recall the four characteristics of FB-PWS that are possibly beneficial to policy performance from section 1. The load adaptive property is also a characteristic of the EQS, and repartitioning issues will be considered in section 4.3. Furthermore, we have seen that multilevel feedback can lead to earlier system saturation (Figures 6-7) if a significant fraction of the jobs with large W_j and large parallelism have only moderate speedups. On the other hand, the EQS

215

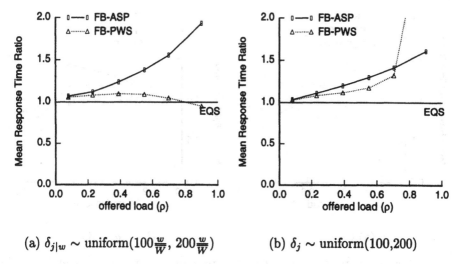

(a) $\delta_{j|w} \sim$ uniform$(100\frac{w}{W}, 200\frac{w}{W})$ (b) $\delta_j \sim$ uniform$(100,200)$

Figure 7: Policy comparison with variable load imbalance overhead
$N_j \sim$ Distribution 3, $W_{j|n} \sim$ Hyperexp$_2(\frac{n^2}{N^2}1000, 2)$, $\beta' = 0$
$(C_W = 6.6)$

policy saturates earlier than the FB-PWS policy in Figure 5, perhaps indicating that the EQS policy could be improved by using the *pws* measure to adjust processor allocations for this (and possibly other) workloads. This motivates the following new policy that we call EQS-PWS.

In the EQS-PWS policy, processor allocation proceeds in two phases. In the first phase processors are assigned to jobs as in the EQS policy, except that each job's processor allocation is bounded by min(pws_j, N_j) instead of N_j. If there are idle processors left after phase one, the idle processors are equipartitioned among the jobs, using $N_j - \min(pws_j, N_j)$ as the upper bound on the additional processors given to job j.

The EQS-PWS policy is identical to the EQS-AVG policy defined in [4], except that the *pws* measure is used in place of average parallelism (*avg*). In [4], the EQS-AVG was found to have approximately the same performance as EQS, but new workload parameters are considered in this paper. Furthermore, figure 2(b) shows that eliminating the allocations above *pws* processors at high load may be more favorable than eliminating allocations above *avg* processors.

For the workloads in Figures 6-7, EQS-PWS has *identical performance* to EQS, indicating that there is not much benefit to using the *pws* measure for those workloads. Note that this is another reason why FB-PWS doesn't perform as well at high loads in figures 6(b) and 7(b).

Figures 8 and 9 show the relative performance of the EQS-PWS policy for the workload in Figure 5 and a new workload, respectively. The workload in Figure 9 is similar to the workload in Figure 7, except that the execution overhead parameter, $\delta = pws$, has a hyperexponential distribution instead of a uniform distribution, leading to much greater speedup sublinearity, and perhaps

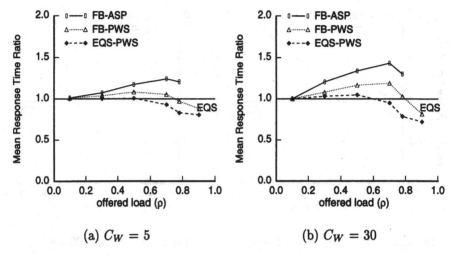

(a) $C_W = 5$ (b) $C_W = 30$

Figure 8: Performance of EQS-PWS under workload 2 in [23]
$W_j \sim \text{Hyperexp}_2(1000, C_W)$, $N_j = M_j$, $\phi' = 0.003, \alpha = 25, \beta = 25$

unrealistically poor speedups for the majority of the jobs. However, in this case there is more potential for the EQS-PWS and FB-PWS policies to outperform EQS.

In Figures 8 and 9, EQS-PWS has performance equal to or better than EQS and FB-PWS over the entire range of offered load. In particular, the EQS-PWS policy does not saturate earlier than FB-PWS in Figure 8 or Figure 9(a). Results for EQS-AVG, not given in the figures, show that for the workloads in figures 5 through 9, EQS-AVG has very nearly the same performance as EQS-PWS.

4.3 Comparisons with Repartitioning Overheads

Our final set of experiments are aimed at determining the impact of realistic repartitioning overhead on the relative performance of the EQS, EQS-PWS, and FB-PWS policies. In this case we use a new synthetic workload – one that corresponds closely with the workload measurement data in [8]. Below we explain the workload, the repartitioning overheads, and the results.

The key features of the workload are:

- Distribution 4 of Figure 4 is used for job parallelism. This was derived from the measured distribution in [8], by shifting some of the probability mass for $n = 32$ to higher values of parallelism. The shift corrects for the incentives in the measured system for parallelism equal to 32 during the daytime. In a system with EQS or FB-PWS scheduling, such incentives would not be necessary.
- The service requirement is determined by a set of values for $\overline{W_{j|n}}$ and $C_{W|n}$, $n = 1, 2, 4, 8, ..., 128$, that are computed from Table 2 in [8]. Specifically, $\overline{W_{j|n}}$ is initially set to $n\times$ the average runtime for job size n, and $C_{W|n}$ is

217

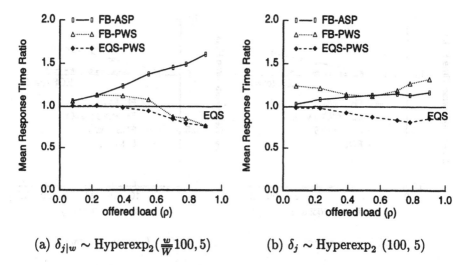

(a) $\delta_{j|w} \sim \text{Hyperexp}_2(\frac{w}{\overline{W}}100, 5)$ (b) $\delta_j \sim \text{Hyperexp}_2 (100, 5)$

Figure 9: Policy comparison for workloads with very sublinear speedup
$N_j \sim$ Distribution 1, $W_{j|n} \sim \text{Hyperexp}_2(\frac{n^2}{N^2}1000, 10)$, $\beta' = 0$
$(C_W = 36)$

set to the coefficient of variation in runtime for n, and then the mean values
were adjusted proportionately downward (to remove execution overhead)
to get the measured system load.[6] Note the large value of average total
service requirement ($\overline{W}$ = 10566 seconds, or approximately 2.9 node-
hours) for this measured iPSC/860 workload. The measured average node-
hours of running time per application (with overhead), is approximately
double that value.

- For the parallelism overheads, we let

$$\phi' \sim \text{uniform}(0, \frac{1/c_1 - 1}{N_j - 1}) \tag{13}$$

and then

$$\beta' \sim \text{uniform}(0, \min(\frac{1/c_2 - 1}{N_j(N_j - 1)} - \frac{\phi'}{N_j}, \frac{1 - \phi'}{N^2})), \tag{14}$$

where $c_1 = 0.75$ and $c_2 = 0.5$ (see equation (7)). For this workload, these
distributions yield first an execution efficiency on N_j processors, E, that
is approximately uniformly distributed between 75% and 100%, and then
an efficiency on N_j processors that is approximately uniformly distributed
between 50% and E. This is a somewhat arbitrary, but well-specified model
of the spread of execution efficiencies that are encountered in practice. In

---

[6]These calculations are necessarily approximate since runtime includes execution overhead
whereas total processing requirement does not. Processing requirements (without overhead)
are not given in the measured data. However, we anticipate that the computed values give
approximately the correct relative magnitudes of the average work as a function of job parallelism, and this is more important than quantitative accuracy of the individual values.

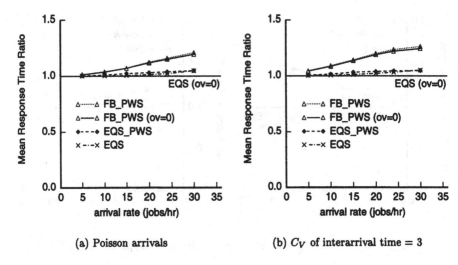

(a) Poisson arrivals   (b) C_V of interarrival time = 3

Figure 10: Policy Comparison with Repartitioning Overhead
$N_j \sim$ Distribution 4, $\overline{W} = 10566$ seconds, $C_W = 4.26$,
$c_1 = 0.75, c_2 = 0.5$

the absence of data in the literature, we have relied on a variety of informal information about parallel job speedups in developing this model.

The workload defined above provides one more context for comparing policy performance, irrespective of repartitioning overhead. Note also that the overall mean $\overline{W}$ for the measured system is larger than assumed in the synthetic workloads for our previous experiments.

For repartitioning overhead, we assume that *each time* the processor allocation changes for a job, the *entire job will stall* for 5 seconds. This estimate was arrived at by computing the time to fetch 32 megabytes of data from a remote memory, either in a network of workstations that runs the GMS global memory management system [7] or in the KSR or DASH memory systems [20, 3]. In GMS, each remote fetch of an 8-kilobyte page requires 2 milliseconds. In KSR, it takes 30 milliseconds to fill a 256KB cache from remote memory [20]. In DASH, each remote fetch of a 16-byte cache block requires approximately 170 cycles on a 33 MHz processor. Thus, the transfer of 32 megabytes requires approximately 4-10 seconds in these systems. Anticipating continued improvements in network latencies, we conservatively select 5 seconds for the repartitioning overhead.

Figure 10(a) shows the mean response time ratios of FB-PWS, EQS-PWS and EQS with repartitioning overhead with respect to an EQS system with zero repartitioning cost. The ratio for FB-PWS with zero repartitioning overhead is also given. Job arrival rate is varied up to 30 jobs/hour, which is higher than observed on the NASA Ames iPSC/860 (Figure 12 of [8]) or the Cornell Theory Center SP/2 [10]. The system utilization at arrival rate of 30 jobs/hour is 82%-85%.

The results in Figure 10(a) show that relative policy performance is un-

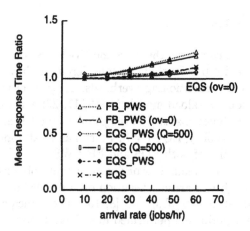

Figure 11: Policy Comparison with Repartitioning Overhead
Poisson arrivals, $N_j \sim$ Distribution 4, $\overline{W} = 5283$ seconds, $C_W = 4.25$,
$c_1 = 0.75, c_2 = 0.5$

changed for the given workload, with or without repartitioning overhead, even though processor repartitioning occurs on every arrival and departure in the EQS system. Figure 10(b) shows that this result holds even if the coefficient of variation of interarrival times is increased to three by using a two-stage hyperexponential distribution of interarrival times, reflecting the measured coefficient of variation in [8].

To see what would happen if arrival rate is doubled to 60/hour, we halved each of the values of $\overline{W_{j|n}}$ and re-ran the experiment. The results are shown in Figure 11. For the EQS and EQS-PWS policies, we include a new case where the system performs full repartitioning at most once per every 500 second quantum. In this case, the system gives immediate service to an arriving job by judiciously stealing processors from a job that is already executing; jobs with largest service so far received, or with allocations greater than the equipartition value, have highest priority for relinquishing some of their processors to a newly arriving job. Repartitioning overhead is charged for each job reconfiguration that occurs between or at quantum boundaries.

The relative policy performance is unchanged for the higher arrival rates in Figure 11, but the EQS and EQS-PWS policies that only perform full repartitioning at the beginning of every 500 sec quantum have perceptibly better performance at high load than the policies that do repartitioning at every job arrival or departure..

Overall, the experiments in this section provide evidence that EQS or EQS-PWS provides superior performance *even when realistic data repartitioning overheads are considered*, yet the FB-PWS policy is still a remarkably competitive alternative over a wide range of workloads.

5 Conclusions

In this paper, we have compared the EQS and FB-PWS policies under synthetic workloads that have not previously been considered, yet have realistic job characteristics [8, 10] and repartitioning overheads. As part of this effort, we have improved the previous workload models in [13, 17, 23] and we have shown how the different speedup functions used in the previous models are related. Finally, we have defined a new policy, EQS-PWS, which has what appear to be the most promising characteristics of both EQS and FB-PWS.

A key feature of our realistic workloads is that job service requirements are substantial enough to warrant execution on a parallel system, and thus job arrival rate is at most 30−60 jobs/hour [8, 10]. The principal conclusions that we reach from the experiments performed in section 4, are:

- The EQS policy is generally superior to the FB-PWS policy *even when realistic repartitioning overheads are considered.*
- If a reasonable fraction of the jobs with large parallelism and large total service requirement have moderate execution overheads (e.g., 50% - 75% efficiency on P processors), then a system with FB-PWS scheduling saturates before a system with EQS scheduling (Figures 6(b), 7(b)), due to less effective space sharing.
- If a large fraction of the jobs are very inefficient; that is, they have pws significantly smaller than their maximum parallelism, then EQS saturates before FB-PWS (Figures 8, 9(a)).
- For the workloads examined, EQS-PWS always performs as well as or better than EQS and FB-PWS. In particular, EQS-PWS avoids the early saturation of EQS in systems with a large fraction of very inefficient jobs.
- Although the above differences are worthy of consideration in future policy design, the overall differences in performance among the EQS, EQS-PWS, and FB-PWS policies are perhaps surprisingly small.

Given the results in this paper, we would argue that the simple EQS policy, which does not require knowledge of the pws measure for each job, may be the preferred policy. However, the ultimate choice of policy will also depend on at least two factors: (1) the significance of the cases where EQS-PWS outperforms EQS, and (2) how well the pws measure can be estimated in practice. Fruitful areas for further investigation include: (1) quantifying the workload characteristics that lead to differences in relative mean response times of the policies, (2) examination of more detailed measures such as expected response time conditioned on job service requirement, (3) how well the pws measure can be estimated at runtime using techniques similar to those in [20], and (4) suitable modifications to the policies to support jobs with large memory requirements.

Acknowledgements

The authors gratefully acknowledge comments and suggestions by Thu Nguyen, John Zahorjan, other workshop participants, and the anonymous reviewers, which helped to improve this paper.

References

[1] R. H. Arpaci, A. C. Dusseau, A. M. Vahdat, L. T. Liu, T. E. Anderson, D. A. Patterson, The Interactions of Parallel and Sequential Workloads on a Network of Workstations. *Proc. 1995 ACM Sigmetrics Joint Int'l. Conf. on Measurement and Modeling of Computer Systems*, Ottawa, pp. 267-278, May 1995.

[2] A. Bricker, M. Litzkow, M. Livny, Condor Technical Summary. Technical Report TR 1069, Computer Sciences Dept., University of Wisconsin, Madison, WI, January 1992.

[3] R. Chandra, S. Devine, B. Verghese, A. Gupta, M. Rosenblum, Scheduling and Page Migration for Multiprocessor Compute Servers. *Proc. 6th Int'l. Conf. on Architectural Support for Programming Languages and Operating Systems (ASPLOS-VI)*, San Jose, CA, pp. 12-24, October 1994.

[4] S.-H. Chiang, R. K. Mansharamani, M. K. Vernon, Use of Application Characteristics and Limited Preemption for Run-to-Completion Parallel Processor Scheduling Policies. *Proc. 1994 ACM Sigmetrics Conference on Measurement and Modeling of Computer Systems*, Nashville, TN, pp. 33-44, June 1994.

[5] L. W. Dowdy, On the Partitioning of Multiprocessor Systems. Technical Report, Vanderbilt University, July 1988.

[6] G. Edjlali, G. Agrawal, A. Sussman, J. Saltz, Data Parallel Programming in an Adaptive Environment. *Proc. 9th Int'l. Parallel Processing Symposium* Santa Barbara, CA, April 1995.

[7] M. J. Feeley, W. E. Morgan, F. H. Pighin, A. R. Karlin, H. M. Levy, C. A. Thekkath, Implementing Global Memory Management in a Workstation Cluster. *Proc. Symp. on Operating Systems Principles*, Copper Mountain, CO, pp. 201-212, December, 1995.

[8] D. G. Feitelson, B. Nitzberg, Job Characteristics of a Production Parallel Scientific Workload on the NASA Ames iPSC/860. *Proc. IPPS '95 Workshop on Job Scheduling Strategies for Parallel Systems*, Santa Barbara, CA, pp. 337-360, April 1995.

[9] D. Ghosal, G. Serazzi, S. Tripathi, The Processor Working Set and Its Use in Scheduling Multiprocessor Systems. *IEEE Trans. on Software Engineering*, Vol. 17, No. 5, pp. 443-453, May 1991.

[10] S. Hotovy, Workload Evolution on the Cornell Theory Center IBM SP2. *Proc. IPPS '96 Workshop on Job Scheduling Strategies for Parallel Systems*, Honolulu, Hawaii, April 1996.

[11] N. Islam, A. Prodromidis, M. S. Squillante, Dynamic Partitioning in Different Distributed-Memory Environments. *Proc. IPPS '96 Workshop on Job Scheduling Strategies for Parallel Systems*, Honolulu, Hawaii, April 1996.

[12] L. Kleinrock. *Queueing Systems, Vol II: Applications*. John Wiley & Sons, 1976.

[13] S. T. Leutenegger, M. K. Vernon, The Performance of Multiprogrammed Multiprocessor Scheduling Policies. *Proceedings of the ACM SIGMETRICS Conference on Measurement & Modeling of Computer Systems*, Boulder, CO, pp. 226-236, May 1990.

[14] S. Majumdar, D. L. Eager, R. B. Bunt, Scheduling in Multiprogrammed Parallel Systems. *Proc. 1988 ACM Sigmetrics Conference on Measurement and Modeling of Computer Systems*, Santa Fe, NM, pp. 104-113, May 1988.

[15] S. Majumdar, D. Eager, and R. Bunt. Characterisation of programs for scheduling in multiprogrammed parallel systems. *Performance Evaluation*, Vol. 13, pp. 109-130, 1991.

[16] R. Mansharamani. Efficient Analysis of Parallel Processor Scheduling Policies. Ph.D. Thesis, Computer Sciences Dept., University of Wisconsin, Madison, WI, November 1993.

[17] R. K. Mansharamani, M. K. Vernon, Properties of the EQS Parallel Processor Allocation Policy. Technical Report #1192, Univ. of Wisconsin - Madison Computer Sciences Dept., November 1993.

[18] C. McCann, R. Vaswani, J. Zahorjan, A Dynamic Processor Allocation Policy for Multiprogrammed, Shared Memory Multiprocessors. *ACM Transactions on Computer Systems*, Vol. 11, No. 2, pp. 146–178, May 1993.

[19] V.Naik, S. Setia, and M. Squillante. Performance Analysis of Job Scheduling Policies in Parallel Supercomputing Environments. *Proceedings of Supercomputing'93*, November 1993.

[20] T. D. Nguyen, R. Vaswani, J. Zahorjan, Using Runtime Measured Workload Characteristics in Parallel Processor Scheduling. *Proc. IPPS '96 Workshop on Job Scheduling Strategies for Parallel Systems*, Honolulu, Hawaii, April 1996.

[21] J. K. Ousterhout, Scheduling Techniques for Concurrent Systems, *Proc. 3rd Int'l. Conf. on Distributed Computing Systems.* pp. 22-30, October 1982.

[22] J. D. Padhye, L. W. Dowdy, Dynamic versus Adaptive Processor Allocation Policies for Message Passing Parallel Computers: An Empirical Comparison. *Proc. IPPS '96 Workshop on Job Scheduling Strategies for Parallel Systems*, Honolulu, Hawaii, April 1996.

[23] E. W. Parsons, K. C. Sevcik, Multiprocessor Scheduling for High-Variability Service Time Distributions. *Proc. IPPS '95 Workshop on Job Scheduling Strategies for Parallel Systems* Santa Barbara, CA, pp. 127-145, April 1995.

[24] V. G. J. Peris, M. S. Squillante, V. K. Naik, Analysis of the Impact of Memory in Distributed Parallel Processing Systems. *Proc. 1994 ACM Sigmetrics Conference on Measurement and Modeling of Computer Systems*, Nashville, TN, pp. 5-18, June 1994.

[25] K. C. Sevcik, Characterizations of Parallelism in Applications and Their Use in Scheduling. *Proc. 1989 ACM SIGMETRICS/Performance '89 Int'l. Conf. on Measurement and Modeling of Computer Systems*, Berkeley, CA, pp. 171-180, May 1989.

[26] K. C. Sevcik, Application Scheduling and Processor Allocation in Multiprogrammed Parallel Processing Systems. *Performance Evaluation*, Vol. 19, No. 2/3, pp. 107-140, March 1994.

[27] A. Tucker, A. Gupta, Process Control and Scheduling Issues for Multiprogrammed Shared-Memory Multiprocessors. *Proceedings of the 12th ACM Symposium on Operating System Principles*, pp. 159-166, December 1989.

[28] C.-S. Wu, Processor Scheduling in Multiprogrammed Shared Memory NUMA Multiprocessors, Master's thesis, University of Toronto, 1993.

[29] J. Zahorjan, C. McCann, Processor Scheduling in Shared Memory Multiprocessors. *Proc. 1990 ACM Sigmetrics Conference on Measurement and Modeling of Computer Systems*, Boulder, CO, pp. 214-225, May 1990.

[30] S. Zhou, J. Wang, X. Zheng, P. Delisle, Utopia: A Load Sharing Facility for Large Heterogeneous Distributed Computing Systems. Technical Report, University of Toronto, 1992.

Dynamic versus Adaptive Processor Allocation Policies for Message Passing Parallel Computers: An Empirical Comparison *

Jitendra Padhye[1] and Lawrence Dowdy[2]

[1] Department of Computer Science, University of Massachusetts at Amherst, ***
Amherst, MA 01003.
[2] Department of Computer Science, Vanderbilt University,
Nashville, TN 37235.

Abstract. When a job arrives at a space-sharing multiprocessor system, a decision has to be made regarding the number and the specific identities of the processors to be allocated to it. An adaptive policy may consider the state of the system at arrival time but it does not allow preemption of any of the running jobs. A dynamic partitioning policy may preempt one or more of the currently running jobs to accommodate the new arrival. In this paper performance of dynamic and adaptive policies is investigated experimentally on a message passing architecture (Intel Paragon). The workload model is based on matrix computation applications commonly found on large systems used for scientific programming. Results are reported for single and multiclass cases. A sensitivity analysis with respect to workload speedup characteristics is presented. Our results show that if the preemption overheads are kept low, dynamic polices result in noticeable improvement in overall performance of the system.

1 Introduction

Multiprogramming is a common way of improving performance of large multiprocessor systems. Most common parallel applications have sublinear speedup curves and hence can not take full advantage of all system processors. For a heavily used system it is not uncommon to have several parallel jobs waiting to use the multiprocessor. In such cases, performance can be improved by sharing the multiprocessor among all or some of the waiting jobs. This can be achieved via either space sharing [SRSDS94] or time sharing [GTU91].

Under space sharing scheduling polices, an incoming job is assigned to a subset of the total available processors. Thus, multiple jobs can be active within the multiprocessor at the same time. Space sharing policies can either be dynamic or adaptive. Several issues such as application speedup characteristics, underlying multiprocessor architecture, and special requirements of certain application

---

* Supported in part under sub-contract 19X-SL131V administered through the Mathematical Sciences Section of Oak Ridge National Laboratory.
*** This work was done at Vanderbilt University.

workloads are among the factors affecting performance of processor allocation strategies for multiprogramming parallel systems. In this paper, effects of some of these factors on the performance of dynamic and adaptive space sharing policies are investigated empirically.

Several dynamic and adaptive processor allocation policies have been discussed in the literature [MEB88, TG89, PD89, LV90, DCDP90, ZM90, GTU91, ZB91, MVZ93, SST93, RSDSC94, SEV94, CMV94, MZ94]. Performance analysis of dynamic space sharing scheduling policies has been largely based on simulation studies and Markovian analysis of small systems. For a simulation study to be accurate and realistic, detailed knowledge of various parameters of the system under consideration is necessary. Also, validation of the simulation models is difficult. Detailed Markovian analysis of complex scheduling policies to verify simulation models is possible only for small systems (e.g. less than 10 processors) [SRSDS94, DCDP90, MEB88]. For larger systems, simplifying assumptions have to be made, resulting in a loss of accuracy.

Experimental studies on dynamic processor partitioning policies have been done mainly for shared memory architectures [GTU91, TG89]. In this paper, experimental analysis of dynamic processor partitioning policies for a message passing architecture is presented. To this end, two dynamic processor partitioning policies based on those discussed in [MZ94] and one adaptive policy presented in [RSDSC94] are implemented on the Intel Paragon. Two workload programs are used to compare behavior of the implemented scheduling policies. One is a synthetic workload program designed to emulate various speedup curves and other characteristics of common scientific applications. The flexibility of the synthetic workload allows easy emulation of a wide variety of load conditions for comparing the scheduling policies. The other workload program is based on a parallel, preemptible, distributed memory version of a matrix conjugate gradient program. This program is representative of typical scientific workloads and has been used for similar purposes in the past [BMSD95]. Our results show that if the preemption overheads are kept low, dynamic polices result in noticeable improvement in the performance of the system. This result is not surprising theoretically, however, experimental validation studies have been lacking. This study is an effort to fill that gap.

The rest of the paper is organized as follows. Section 2 describes the dynamic and adaptive scheduling policies and the two workload programs used for this study. A brief description of the Intel Paragon architecture is also presented. The results of the study are presented in Section 3. Section 4 presents the conclusions and directions for future work.

2   Policies and Workloads

This section briefly describes the three scheduling policies studied in this paper, the two workload programs used for comparisons, and the architecture of the Intel Paragon. Due to space constraints, this section provides only a brief overview of the actual implementation. More details may be found in [P96].

2.1 The Intel Paragon

The Intel Paragon supercomputer consists of several nodes connected in a mesh configuration. The computer used for this study has 66 nodes connected in a 11x6 matrix. Several nodes are dedicated to special tasks such as disk and network control. Each node consists of two Intel i860 processors sharing 16 MB of memory. One of the processors runs the application program while the other acts as a communication co-processor. To route messages between the nodes, a wormhole routing protocol is used. The operating system conforms to OSF/1 standards. Although the machine is capable of supporting MIMD (or MPMD) computing model, most applications use the SPMD model for computing. The workloads for this study use the SPMD model. A detailed description of the Paragon architecture may be found in [INT93].

2.2 The Adaptive Scheduling Policy

The adaptive scheduling policy chosen for this study is the Robust Adaptive (RA) scheduling policy described in [RSDSC94]. This policy has been shown to have better performance than several other non-preemptive scheduling policies. The RA scheme actually represents a suite of scheduling policies rather than a single scheduling algorithm. The version chosen here is a representative one and has been used in subsequent studies [SRSDS94]. The main feature of the RA policy is that it adapts to load changes over a period of time. Two identical jobs may be allocated different sized partitions, depending upon the system state when each job arrives. When a new job arrives in the system, it is placed at the end of a queue of jobs awaiting service. The scheduler calculates a "target" partition size using the following formula:

$$max\left(1, \left\lfloor \frac{\text{Total number of processors in the system}}{\text{Number of jobs waiting in the queue}} \right\rfloor \right)$$

The scheduler does not schedule any jobs until at least "target" number of processors are free. It then starts allocating "target" number of processors to each job in the queue. If the processors can be allocated, then the job is started immediately. The target is not recomputed during this time. When no more jobs can be scheduled, either due to an empty queue or due to a lack of sufficient free processors, the scheduler stops scheduling new jobs and recomputes a new target. The target recalculation allows RA to adapt to changes in the load condition. A higher load results in a longer queue, which results in a smaller target which in turn means that more jobs are scheduled.

2.3 Dynamic Partitioning Policies

Dynamic partitioning policies can interrupt currently executing jobs in order to redistribute processors among the jobs because of job arrivals and/or departures. Thus, dynamic scheduling policies can quickly adapt to transient changes in the workload flow. The two dynamic processor partitioning policies considered in this study are based on policies discussed in [MZ94]. Implementing preemption on a message passing architecture is a non-trivial task. The steps taken to ensure "safe" preemption of jobs while keeping the preemption overhead low, are briefly described in Section 2.4.

Equipartitioning. This policy tries to equally allocate the available processors among all jobs that are present in the system. On each new arrival or departure, all the currently executing jobs are preempted. The new partition size for each job is calculated using the following formula:

$$max \left(1, \left\lfloor \frac{\text{Total number of processors in the system}}{\text{Number of ready jobs}} \right\rfloor \right)$$

The number of ready jobs includes the new arrivals and the jobs that have been preempted. Since at least one processor has to be allocated to each job, it may not be possible to restart all the ready jobs. However, the scheduler always restarts all the preempted jobs.

The policy suffers from two major disadvantages. First, a job can be preempted several times [4] under this policy. Even when individual preemptions are not very costly, the total cost can be prohibitive. Secondly, this policy suffers from *synchronization delays*. Since some of the currently running jobs may finish during the process of repartitioning, [5] the scheduler has to wait until all the processors in the partition are released before calculating the new partition size for each job. A job that has been preempted is forced to wait until all the remaining running jobs free their partitions. This synchronization delay may be a source of significant overhead.

Folding. This policy preempts at most one of the currently running jobs as a result of an arrival or a departure. Hence, the policy does not suffer from excessive synchronization delays. At each new arrival, the scheduler checks to see if there are free processors. If there are free processors in the system, the new job is started on all of them. No preemptions take place in this case. If there are no free processors then the scheduler checks the size of largest partition currently allocated to a job. If this size is greater than 1, then the job running on the largest partition is preempted and half of the processors are given to the incoming job. This is called *folding*. If there are multiple candidates for folding then the implementation can select any one of them. The implementation used for this study preempts the most recently arrived job in the event of such a tie. At any time, if the system has any idle processors, and no jobs are waiting in the ready queue, then the job executing on the smallest partition is preempted and the idle processors are merged with the job's old partition and the job is restarted on the new partition thus formed. This is called *unfolding*. If there

---

[4] Theoretically, once per every subsequent job arrival and job departure.

[5] These are the jobs that finish *after* the scheduler has sent out preemption requests. The scheduler will not restart these jobs.

are several candidates for unfolding, the implementation may choose any one of them. The implementation used for this study unfolds the most recently arrived job in the system.

2.4 Minimizing the Cost of Preemption

A parallel job may not be preempted "safely" [6] at any arbitrary time during its execution. This may happen due to several reasons (e.g. the job might be executing a piece of non-reentrant code). At other times, it might be safe to preempt the job, but the cost of preemption might be high. This may happen when the job is in the middle of a distributed computation and preemption requires realignment of data. It is difficult for the scheduler to determine when it is easy (i.e. safe as well as cheap) to preempt a job. Hence, this implementation requires that all the jobs have certain *break points*, where it is safe to preempt the job and the preemption overheads can be kept low. A job responds to a preemption request by the scheduler only when it is at a breakpoint.

The processor allocation routines of all the dynamic schedulers implemented for this study observe the *subset* restriction to minimize any data redistribution overhead that the job might incur as a result of preemption. The *subset* restriction is defined as follows. If P_1 and P_2 represent the sets of processors in two successive partitions allotted to a job then:

$$P_1 \cap P_2 = P_1 \text{ if } |P_1| \le |P_2|$$
$$= P_2 \quad \text{otherwise}$$

This restriction helps to minimize the data transfers required during redistribution. In addition, the routine tries to allocate contiguous partitions. The preemption process is carried out in four steps.

1. The scheduler sends preempt requests to all the jobs it wishes to preempt. Whenever each job reaches its next breakpoint, it informs the scheduler that it is ready to be preempted.
2. Once the scheduler receives such replies from all the jobs to whom such requests are sent[7], it calculates the new processor allocations. All the jobs that will be preempted are informed of their new partitions.
3. Depending on the size of the new partition, the job executes one of the following two steps.
   (a) If the size of the new partition is smaller than the size of the previous partition, then the job is termed as *LOSER*. A *LOSER* job determines the subset of its old partition that forms the new partition. The data is redistributed so that all the application data is stored on the processors in this subset.
   (b) If the size of the new partition is larger than the old one, then the job is termed a *WINNER*. A *WINNER* job has to wait until the extra processors are allocated to it to do its data redistribution.

---

[6] In this context, *safety* essentially implies ensuring *correctness*.

[7] Or, if the job terminates.

4. Once the data redistribution is finished, the jobs release their processors and the scheduler restarts the jobs on their new partition after it finishes its internal bookkeeping operations. After the restart, the *WINNER* jobs redistribute their data and start execution. The *LOSER* jobs, on the other hand, having already finished their data redistribution, resume execution immediately.

The entire preemption sequence is implemented as a series of calls to a set of library routines. These routines are independent of the nature of the application program and the scheduling policy.

2.5 Workload Description

This section describes the two workloads used for the experimental study. The first is a synthetic workload, designed to have enough flexibility to emulate various speedup curves. Number of computations, amount of communication and preemption overheads are all easily adjustable. The second workload is based on the Conjugate Gradient method for matrices. The program is a representative example of the scientific workload and has been used for similar purposes in other studies [BMSD95]. [8]

The Synthetic Workload. The synthetic workload is designed to be flexible enough to generate various speedup curves by varying workload parameters. The workload is capable of spawning as many tasks as the number of allocated processors. When the workload is started on a given partition, the lowest numbered node in the partition is selected as the co-ordinator. The workload operates in phases. Each phase consists of three subphases, namely, the *broadcast communication subphase*, the *compute subphase*, and the *collect communication subphase*. In the broadcast communication subphase, the co-ordinator broadcasts a message to each node in the partition. This message contains initialization parameters for that phase and other problem related data. In the compute subphase, each node in the partition does a certain amount of computation. There is no communication among the nodes during this subphase. During the collect communication subphase, each node in the partition sends back a message to the co-ordinator node. This message contains partial results and other synchronization data. At the end of each phase the nodes undergo a barrier synchronization. After the barrier synchronization, the job is in a safe state for preemption. At this point the co-ordinator checks to see if a preemption request has arrived from the scheduler. If such a request is present, the preemption sequence is executed and the job preempts. Otherwise, the next phase of the communicate-compute-communicate cycle is started. The amount of computation and communication during each subphase can be specified individually for each phase. The amount

---

[8] Other models of large, parallel, scientific workloads and arrival processes exist, and it will be interesting to study the effectiveness of dynamic partitioning policies for various workload models.

of data redistribution to be done in the event of preemption can also be specified. Changing the amount of computation or communication done in each phase yields workloads with different speedup curves. The preemption cost can be varied by changing the data redistribution required in the event of preemption or by changing the number or the length of the phases. Note that the cost of a preemption is reflected in the waiting time of the jobs that are waiting in the arrival queue and synchronization delay for the jobs that have already been preempted. The speedup curves generated by the synthetic workload having 50 phases appear in Figure 1. For each curve, the number of *total* computations done per phase is indicated in the legend. For all curves the message size during broadcast as well as in the collect communication phase is 32 bytes.

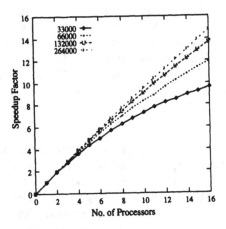

Fig. 1. Speedup Curves for the Synthetic Workload

Conjugate Gradient Workload. The program implements the conjugate gradient method for matrices. The task graph of the program is similar to many scientific and engineering applications found on large multiprocessor systems. More details about the program can be found in [BMSD95]. The program executes a specified number of iterations or until a user specified accuracy is achieved. For test purposes, the accuracy testing feature is disabled and the program continues for a specified number of iterations. During each iteration several distributed computations are carried out, requiring significant communication among processors belonging to the job. At the end of each iteration, all the processors undergo barrier synchronization. After the synchronization, the job is in a safe state to be preempted and the co-ordinator (lowest numbered processor) checks for preemption request. Data redistribution involves redistributing data contained in five different arrays or matrices. Thus, the preemption overhead involved can be high. The speedup curves for the CG workload are shown in the Figure 2. The

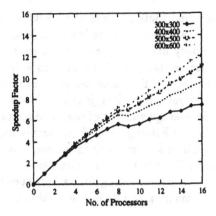

Fig. 2. Speedup Curves for the Conjugate Gradient Workload

different speedup curves are generated by using different matrix sizes. For each curve, the legend indicates the number of rows and columns of the matrix used as the data set for the program. Each CG program performs 250 iterations on the data matrix.

3 Results

This section is organized as follows. In Section 3.1, the performance of the Equipartitioning policy is compared against that of the Folding policy. In Section 3.2, sensitivity analysis results of the relative performance of RA and Folding policies are presented. Factors considered include constant versus exponential demand, speedup curves, and multiclass workloads. In Section 3.3, the performance of the RA and the Folding policies is compared on a larger multiprocessor to show that the results are scalable. For all policies, the smallest possible partition size is one processor. For the dynamic policies, the number of times a job may be preempted is bounded only by the number of "safe" preemption points in the job. Experimental results indicate that the performance of the restricted version of the dynamic scheduling policies (where the number of preemptions of a job and/or the minimum partition size are bounded by anything other than the base limits described above) depends strongly on the speedup characteristics of the workload. Hence only the comparisons between the base versions of the policies are presented.

3.1 Equipartitioning versus Folding

Figure 3 compares the performance of the Equipartitioning and the Folding scheduling policies. The workload used is the CG program with a 500x500 matrix. Each preemption requires redistribution of approximately 2 megabytes of data. The speedup curve of the program is shown in Figure 2. The interarrival times are exponentially distributed, while the workload demand is constant, (i.e. each program in the workload stream is identical to all others). It may be seen that the Folding policy exhibits a better response time than the Equipartitioning policy at all arrival rates, and the difference between them increases with increasing arrival rates. Folding allocates more processors to each job than Equipartitioning at all arrival rates. Thus, jobs have lower execution times under Folding. In addition, the average number of preemptions per job is higher under Equipartitioning than under Folding. Also, Equipartitioning suffers from higher synchronization delays. These factors result in increased waiting time (and hence increased response times) for jobs under Equipartitioning. Folding continues to significantly outperform Equipartitioning for various speedup curves and workload mixes. Hence, the remaining results in this section compare only RA versus Folding.

3.2   RA versus Folding

Constant versus Exponential Workload Demands. The synthetic workload is used to compare the performance of the policies under constant and exponential workload demands, instead of the CG program, since it is easier to vary the demand imposed by the synthetic workload on the multiprocessor by varying the number of computations done in each phase. Figure 4 compares the performance of the RA and the Folding scheduling policies using the synthetic workload. The workload performs 66000 floating point multiplications per phase. When preempted, 0.5 megabytes of data require redistribution. The speedup curve of the workload is shown in Figure 1. The interarrival times are exponentially distributed, while the workload demand is constant.

It can be seen that the Folding gives a better response time than RA at all arrival rates. The maximum difference in the response times is approximately 17%, achieved at higher arrival rates. The better performance of the Folding policy can be attributed to the reduction in the waiting time of the jobs under Folding. The Folding policy schedules a newly arrived job as soon as it can preempt one of the running jobs. If there are idle processors, then the arriving job does not have to wait at all. RA makes a newly arrived job wait until it can allocate a partition of current target size [9]. Except at very low arrival rates, the target partition size usually can not be allocated until at least one of the currently executing jobs finishes execution. Thus the jobs experience higher waiting time under RA. Folding is able to allocate more processors to each job than RA at higher arrival rates. However, job execution times are higher under Folding than under RA. This is due to preemption overheads the jobs experience under Folding. This can be seen from two graphs in Figure 4: 1) when execution time is plotted as a function of average number of processors per job and 2) when execution time is plotted as a function of the arrival rate. The maximum increase in the execution time is approximately 17%. It should also be noted that

---

[9] In other words, Folding is work-conservative, while RA is not.

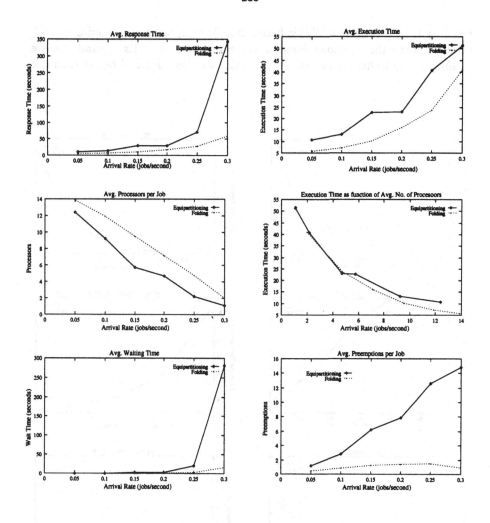

Fig. 3. Equipartitioning versus Folding

these preemption overheads are the result of a relatively small number of preemptions. On average, fewer than 1.5 preemptions per job occur at any arrival rate. It is important to note that the preemption overheads also depends upon the sizes of partitions before and after the preemptions. These sizes determine *how many* processors will participate in the preemption and, hence, affects the data redistribution overhead.

Figure 5 compares the performance of the RA and the Folding scheduling policies when the workload demand is exponentially distributed. The synthetic workload program is used for this comparison as well. All the workload parameters are the same as in the previous comparisons, except that the workload demand is exponentially distributed. It is noted that the improvement in the response time (maximum 25%) is better than the improvement (maximum 17%) achieved when the workload demand was constant. Due to its dynamic nature, Folding is able to handle the variations in the workload demand better than RA.

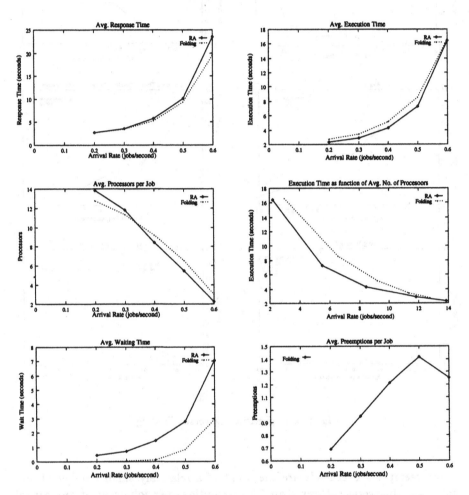

Fig. 4. RA versus Folding: Synthetic Workload with Constant Demand

Performance under Different Speedup Curves. Figure 6 compares the performance of the RA and the Folding policies when scheduling a CG workload with a 300x300 matrix. When preempted, approximately 0.72 megabytes of data require redistribution. The speedup curve of the workload is shown in Figure 2. The interarrival times are exponentially distributed, while the workload demand is constant.

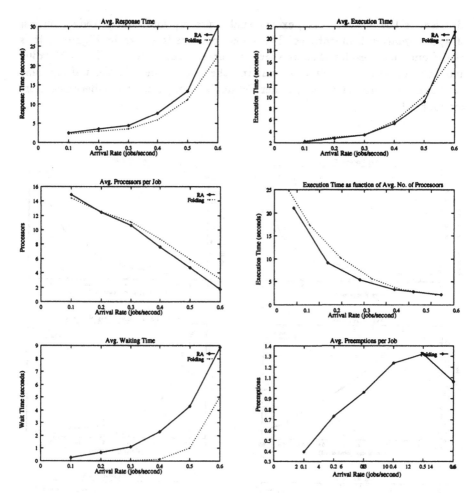

Fig. 5. RA versus Folding: Synthetic Workload with Exponential Demand

Once again, the Folding policy exhibits a better response time than RA for all arrival rates. The maximum improvement in the response time is approximately 19%. As in the case of synthetic workload, the execution time is better under RA policy than under Folding for all arrival rates. The maximum difference is approximately 20%. The average number of preemptions per job is small at both lower as well as higher arrival rates, while it peaks in the middle of the range. At lower arrival rates, an executing job is less likely to be preempted during its execution, since new jobs arrive at a slower rate. At higher arrival rates, several of the currently executing jobs are likely to have partitions consisting of single processors, and these can not be preempted for further folding. Thus, the average number of preemptions goes down at both higher and lower arrival rates.

Figure 7 shows the performance of the RA and the Folding policies when scheduling a CG workload with a 500x500 matrix. All other parameters are identical to the 300x300 case, except that a preemption requires redistribution of approximately 2 megabytes. The speedup curve is shown in Figure 2. It is seen from these results that as speedup curve becomes flatter (i.e. a 300x300 matrix as opposed to a 500x500 matrix), the improvement in the waiting time (and hence the response time) under Folding as compared to RA becomes more pronounced.

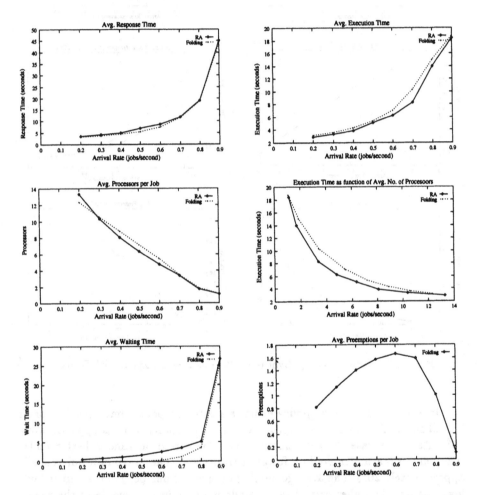

Fig. 6. RA versus Folding: Conjugate Gradient Workload with a 300x300 Matrix

Performance under Multiclass Workloads. Figure 8 compares the performance of the RA and the Folding policies when scheduling a two-class workload. Each class constitutes approximately 50% of the total workload. The first class (class A) consists of a CG program with a matrix size of 300x300, while the

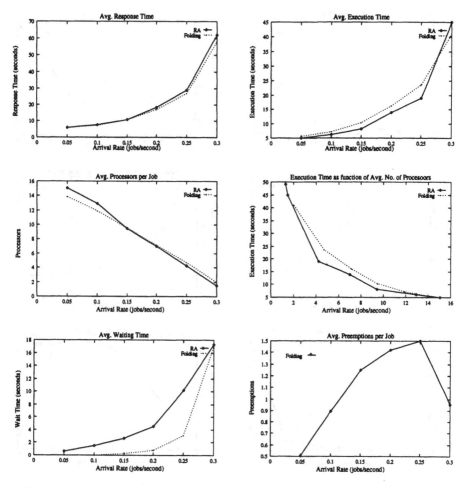

Fig. 7. RA versus Folding: Conjugate Gradient Workload with a 500x500 Matrix

second class (class B) has a matrix size of 500x500. Folding performs better than RA while scheduling a multiclass workload. Being a dynamic policy, Folding can adapt to transient changes in the workload flow better than RA. This behavior, as seen previously, is also observed when the workload demands are exponentially distributed rather than being constant. The maximum improvement in the response time is approximately 19%, achieved at relatively high arrival rates. Figure 9 compares the performance of the two policies when 20% of the programs are from class A while 80% come from class B. Since the workload now has less diversity, the difference between the performance of the two policies is narrowed. Specifically, the maximum improvement in the response time under Folding is approximately 9%, as opposed to 19% in the previous case.

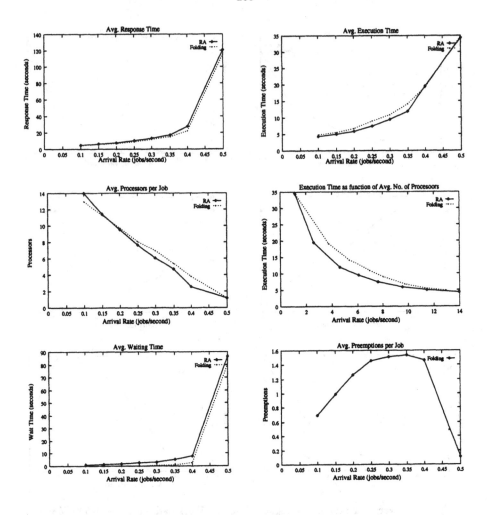

Fig. 8. RA versus Folding: Multiclass Workload 1

3.3 Comparison under Higher Numbers of Processors

The general behavior observed in the previous sections remains consistent as
the number of processors in the multiprocessor increases. Figure 10 presents a
comparison of the RA and the Folding policies with 500x500 CG workload. The
workload demand is constant while the interarrival times have a negative exponential distribution. All the other parameters are the same as in the previous
analysis (e.g. Section 3.2.2). It can be seen that better response times are obtained under Folding than under RA for most arrival rates. As the number of
processors in a multiprocessor increases, good workload speedup characteristics
are necessary to take advantage of dynamic scheduling provided under Folding.
It is possible that under Folding for a job to be unfolded to run on the entire

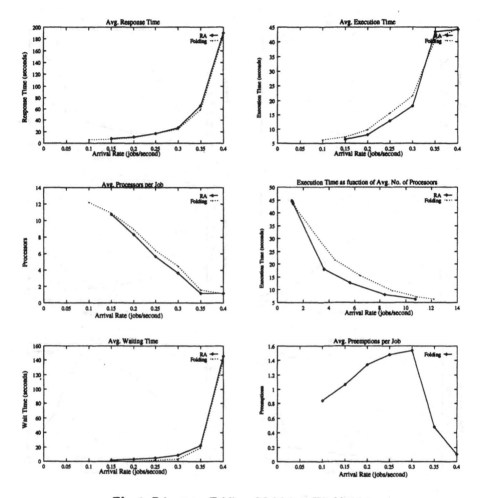

Fig. 9. RA versus Folding: Multiclass Workload 2

multiprocessor. If the job has poor speedup characteristics, or if the job has negative speedup (possible when allocated a very large number of processors), unfolding may prove detrimental to the overall performance.

4   Conclusions

This paper presents an experimental comparison between an adaptive scheduling policy (RA) and a dynamic scheduling policy (Folding). Both policies are implemented on a parallel computer with a message passing architecture. An open system model of the workload flow is implemented. The observed response time is the primary metric used for comparison. The results indicate that it is possible to achieve improved average response time using the dynamic Folding

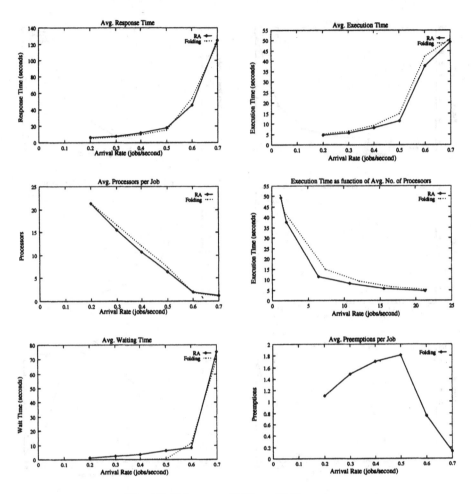

Fig. 10. RA versus Folding: 32 Processors

policy instead of an adaptive policy in many workload environments. In addition, the following conclusions can be drawn from the observed results:

- In most cases, the improvement in the response time is a direct result of the reduction in the time a job spends waiting in the ready queue.
- As jobs become less scalable, the advantages of using a dynamic scheduling policy like Folding become more apparent. The Folding policy is able to dynamically preempt processors from a currently executing job (where they are not providing any significant improvement in the execution time) and allocate them to a new job to take advantage of the efficient use of a few processors allocated to a newly arrived job. The adaptive policy may require the new arrivals to wait until at least one of the executing jobs completes.

- As the workload flow becomes more *random* (e.g. exponential demand as opposed to constant), Folding performs better than RA. The dynamic nature of the Folding policy allows it to adapt more quickly to transient changes common under exponentially distributed workload demands. The same is true in case of a multiclass workload.

- The overhead incurred by a workload while executing under a dynamic policy (e.g, Folding) can be relatively high. Careful implementation of the workload-scheduler interface and implementation of a conservative processor allocation policy can help reduce this overhead.

- Although dynamic policies can improve performance, excessive use of pre-emptions to reallocate processors can prove detrimental.

It is somewhat interesting to note that Folding and RA exhibit similar overall performance, typically within 10-15% of each other. The overall conclusion is that that a dynamic policy like Folding should be used to schedule jobs on a multiprocessor if the workload speedup characteristics are non-linear or if the demand is not constant (i.e, either exponentially distributed or multi-class workload) and if repartitioning overhead is low. An adaptive policy like RA should be used if the workload demand is constant, the workload is single-class, and has good speedup characteristics. An example is shown in Figure 11. The workload used for this comparison is similar to the synthetic workload described in Section 2, except that it has 15 phases instead of 250. This lowers the execution time relative to the scheduling overhead. In this case, RA outperforms Folding. It may also be possible for Equipartitioning to perform better than Folding under certain circumstances. Some pertinent results are presented in [IPS96]. Mary Vernon has suggested [V96] that on parallel systems of the future, the job arrival rates would be very low (30 jobs/hour) and at such low arrival rates, Folding and Equipartitioning may have similar performance.

Areas for future study include validating the results on a larger multiprocessor and comparing the policies under various distributions of arrival rates and workload demands. The experiments can be repeated on other machines using different processor interconnection networks and/or different message routing algorithms. The data from these experiments can be used to create better analytical and simulation models.

5 Acknowledgments

Evgenia Smirni, Emilia Rosti, Manish Madhukar and Jürgen Brehm provided invaluable help and suggestions throughout this study. We also wish to thank the staff members of the Center for Computational Sciences at the Oak Ridge National Labs for the use of the Intel Paragon. We also thank the referees for their helpful comments.

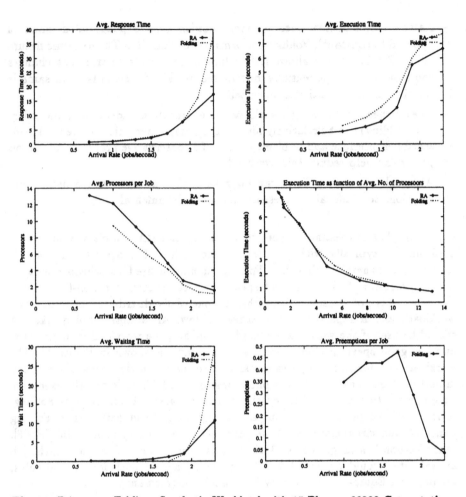

Fig. 11. RA versus Folding: Synthetic Workload with 15 Phases, 66000 Computations per Phase

References

[BMSD95]   J. Brehm, M. Madhukar, E. Smirni, L. W. Dowdy, "PerPreT - A performance prediction tool for massively parallel systems," *Int. Conf. on Modeling Techniques and Tools for Computer Performance Evaluation*, September 1995.

[CMV94]   S.-H. Chiang, R.K. Mansharamani, M.K. Vernon, "Use of application characteristics and limited preemption for run-to-completion parallel processor scheduling policies," *Proc. ACM SIGMETRICS*, 1994, pp. 33-44.

[DCDP90]   K. Dussa, B.M. Carlson, L.W. Dowdy, K.-H. Park, "Dynamic partitioning in a transputer environment," *Proc. ACM SIGMETRICS*, 1990, pp. 203-213.

[GTU91]   A. Gupta, A. Tucker, S. Urushibara, "The impact of operating system scheduling policies and synchronization methods on the performance of parallel applications," *Proc. ACM SIGMETRICS*, 1991, pp. 120-132.

[INT93]   Intel Corporation, **Paragon OSF/1 User's Guide**, 1993.

[IPS96]   N. Islam, A. Prodormidis and M. Squillante, "Dynamic Partitioning in Different Distributed-Memory Environments," *In this volume.*

[LV90]   S.T. Leutenegger, M.K. Vernon, "The performance of multiprogrammed multiprocessor scheduling policies," *Proc. ACM SIGMETRICS*, 1990, pp. 226-236.

[MEB88]   S. Majumdar, D.L. Eager, R.B. Bunt, "Scheduling in multiprogrammed parallel systems," *Proc. ACM SIGMETRICS*, 1988, pp. 104-113.

[MVZ93]   C. McCann, R. Vaswani, J. Zahorjan, "A dynamic processor allocation policy for multiprogrammed shared memory multiprocessors," *ACM Transactions on Computer Systems*, Vol 11(2), February 1993, pp. 146-178.

[MZ94]   C. McCann, J. Zahorjan, "Processor allocation policies for message-passing parallel computers," *Proc. ACM SIGMETRICS*, 1994, pp. 19-32.

[P96]   J. Padhye, "Preemptive versus non-preemptive processor allocation policies: an empirical comparison", Technical Report, Department of Computer Science, Vanderbilt University, 1996.

[PD89]   K.-H. Park, L.W. Dowdy, "Dynamic partitioning of multiprocessor systems," *International Journal of Parallel Programming*, Vol 18(2), 1989, pp. 91-120.

[RSDSC94]   E. Rosti, E. Smirni, L.W. Dowdy, G. Serazzi, B.M. Carlson, "Robust partitioning policies for multiprocessor systems," *Performance Evaluation*, Vol 19(2-3), March 1994, pp. 141-165.

[SEV94]   K.C. Sevcik, "Application scheduling and processor allocation in multiprogrammed multiprocessors," *Performance Evaluation*, Vol 19(2-3), March 1994, pp. 107-140.

[SRSDS94]   E. Smirni, E. Rosti, G. Serazzi, L. W. Dowdy, K. C. Sevcik "Performance gains from leaving idle processors in multiprocessor systems" *Proc. International Conference on Parallel Processing*, 1995.

[SST93]   S.K. Setia, M.S. Squillante, S.K. Tripathi, "Processor scheduling in multiprogrammed, distributed memory parallel computers," *Proc. ACM SIGMETRICS*, 1993, pp. 158-170.

[TG89]   A. Tucker, A. Gupta, "Process control and scheduling issues for multiprogrammed shared-memory multiprocessors," *Proc. of the 12th ACM Symposium on Operating Systems Principles*, 1989, pp. 159-166.

[V96]   Mary Vernon, Personal Communication.

[ZB91]   S. Zhou, T. Brecht, "Processor pool-based scheduling for large-scale NUMA multiprocessors," *Proc. ACM SIGMETRICS*, 1991, pp. 133-142.

[ZM90]   J. Zahorjan, C. McCann, "Processor scheduling in shared memory multiprocessors," *Proc. ACM SIGMETRICS*, 1990, pp. 214-225.

Dynamic Partitioning in Different Distributed-Memory Environments

Nayeem Islam[1], Andreas Prodromidis[2], Mark S. Squillante[1]

[1] IBM T. J. Watson Research Center, Yorktown Heights NY 10598, USA
[2] Columbia University, New York NY 10027, USA

Abstract. In this paper we present a detailed analysis of dynamic partitioning in different distributed-memory parallel environments based on experimental and analytical methods. We develop an experimental testbed for the IBM SP2 and a network of workstations, and we apply a general analytic model of dynamic partitioning. This experimental and analytical framework is then used to explore a number of fundamental performance issues and tradeoffs concerning dynamic partitioning in different distributed-memory computing environments. Our results demonstrate and quantify how the performance benefits of dynamic partitioning are heavily dependent upon several system variables, including workload characteristics, system architecture, and system load.

1 Introduction

Parallel computer systems, consisting of numerous tightly- or loosely-coupled nodes, represent an increasingly important class of high-performance computing environments that make it possible to solve large and complex problems. Fundamental to realizing these performance benefits is the design of scheduling policies which allocate nodes among the parallel jobs submitted for execution in a manner that tends to minimize job response time and maximize system throughput. A number of scheduling strategies have been proposed for such parallel environments, each differing in the way nodes are shared among the jobs. One particularly important class of scheduling policies is based on *space sharing* where the nodes are partitioned among different parallel jobs.

There are three basic types of space-sharing policies. The *static partitioning* of the nodes into a fixed number of disjoint sets, each of which are allocated to individual jobs, is a space-sharing strategy that has often been employed in a number of commercial systems. This is due in part to its low system overhead and its simplicity from both the system and application viewpoints. The static scheduling approach, however, can lead to relatively low system throughputs and resource utilizations under nonuniform workloads [33, 26, 27, 30, 34], which can be common in scientific and engineering computing environments. *Adaptive partitioning* policies, where the number of nodes allocated to a job is determined when jobs enter and leave based on the current system state, have also been considered in a number of research studies [21, 38, 16, 26, 27, 32, 7, 30]. This approach tends to outperform its static counterparts by adapting partition sizes to the current load. On the other hand, the performance benefits of adaptive partitioning can be limited due to its inability to adjust scheduling decisions in response to subsequent workload changes. These potential problems are alleviated under *dynamic partitioning*, where the size of the partition allocated to a job can be modified during its execution, at the expense of increased overhead [37, 9, 21, 38, 17, 23, 26, 27, 34].

The relative runtime costs of a dynamic partitioning policy are heavily dependent upon the parallel architecture and application workload. In uniform-access, shared-memory systems, these overheads tend to be relatively small and thus the benefits of dynamic partitioning outweigh its associated costs. A number of research studies have made this quite clear, showing that dynamic partitioning outperforms all other space-sharing strategies in such environments [37, 21, 38, 17, 23]. In more distributed parallel environments, however, the overheads of a dynamic partitioning policy can be significant due to factors such as data/job migration, node preemption/coordination and, in some cases, reconfiguration of the application [9, 26, 27, 31].

There are several fundamental issues that must be considered in order to effectively exploit dynamic partitioning in distributed computing environments. First, the applications must be capable of executing on variable numbers of nodes and must be capable of reconfiguring the number of nodes on which it executes. In this paper we develop a system approach to provide this functionality for an important class of parallel applications. Moreover, our approach provides the system structure to extend this functionality to applications beyond those considered herein.

Another important issue concerns the overheads of dynamic partitioning in distributed computing environments, where a better understanding of these fundamental scheduling costs is needed to determine the manner in which such policies can be effectively employed in different distributed-memory systems. To complement and extend previous studies of repartitioning overheads for certain distributed-memory environments [26, 27, 31], we conduct a detailed measurement-based analysis of dynamic partitioning overheads in computing environments based on the IBM SP2 and a network of workstations. An experimental testbed is developed on both system architectures, which we use to obtain measurement data for distinct workloads composed of an important class of parallel applications. In our analysis we identify two different types of overheads: one is due to the system, such as process management, and the other is attributable to application reconfiguration.

We also use our experimental testbed together with an analytic model to analyze the impact of these overheads on the system performance characteristics of dynamic partitioning strategies in various distributed-memory environments. System measurements are used to parameterize, validate and complement the model, whereas the computational efficiency of the model allows us to examine a large design space. Our detailed analysis of dynamic partitioning and its associated overheads combine these experimental and analytical methods to yield fundamental insights into the performance characteristics of real parallel systems. Such coupling of experimental and analytical work is rare, and we believe it has proven to be an effective tool for parallel system design and analysis.

Our results show that the benefits of dynamic partitioning in distributed computing environments depend heavily upon the application workload as well as the reconfiguration overhead. We show that dynamic partitioning provides significant improvements in performance over other forms of space sharing under many workloads when the costs of repartitioning are fairly small relative to the workload execution requirements, and our results quantify these considerable performance gains. Under certain workload conditions, however, the costs associated with dynamic partitioning tend to outweigh its benefits, particularly at light to moderate system loads for the class of parallel applications considered.

In Section 2 we describe the scheduling policies considered. Section 3 presents various aspects of the experimental testbed used in this study, including the system hardware and software architectures, and the parallel application workload. We then briefly describe the analytic models used in this study. Sections 5 and 6 present some of the results of our experiments and quantitative analysis. Our concluding remarks are presented in Section 7.

2   Scheduling Policies

We now define the two main policies considered in this paper: a dynamic equi-partitioning (DEP) scheme and a static partitioning (SP) policy. Throughout this paper, we use P to denote the number of nodes in the system and we use M to denote the minimum number of nodes allocated to any job (i.e., the nodes are allocated in units of M). The maximum number of node partitions under each policy is therefore given by $N \equiv P/M$. Jobs that have not been allocated nodes wait in a first-come first-served (FCFS) *system queue*.

2.1   Dynamic Equi-Partitioning

A DEP policy basically attempts to equally divide the nodes among the jobs in the system, up to a maximum of the first N jobs. If a job arrives to the system when $i - 1$ jobs are being executed, $1 \leq i \leq N$, then the nodes are repartitioned among the i jobs such that each job is allocated (on average) P/i nodes. A job arrival that finds $i \geq N$ jobs in the system is placed in the FCFS system queue to wait until a node partition becomes available. When one of the $i + 1$ jobs in execution departs, $0 \leq i < N$, the system reconfigures the nodes allocations so that each job receives (on average) P/i nodes. A job departure when $i > N$ simply causes the job at the head of the system queue to be allocated the available partition, and no repartitioning is performed.

We consider a particular form of DEP in which the number of applications repartitioned upon a job arrival or departure is minimized. To better illustrate our policy, we present in Table 1 the various node allocation changes that occur in response to these events for an 8-node system with $M = 1$ (hence, $N = P = 8$).

Initial System State	State after arrival event	State after departure event
{ }	{8}	
{8}	{4,4}	{ }
{4,4}	{3,3,2}	{8}
{3,3,2}	{2,2,2,2}	{4,4}
{2,2,2,2}	{2,2,2,1,1}	{3,3,2}
{2,2,2,1,1}	{2,2,1,1,1,1}	{2,2,2,2}
{2,2,1,1,1,1}	{2,1,1,1,1,1,1}	{2,2,2,1,1}
{2,1,1,1,1,1,1}	{1,1,1,1,1,1,1,1}	{2,2,1,1,1,1}
{1,1,1,1,1,1,1,1}	{1,1,1,1,1,1,1,1}	{2,1,1,1,1,1,1}

Table 1. State transitions when applications enter and leave the system. The transitions are for an eight-node system.

2.2 Static (Adaptive) Partitioning

The system nodes are statically divided into K partitions each of size $S \equiv (N/K) M$, where we only consider values of K that evenly divide N; i.e., $K \in \{1, 2, \ldots, N/2, N\}$. A job arrival is allocated S nodes if one of the K partitions is available, otherwise the job waits in the FCFS system queue until a partition becomes free. Each parallel job is executed to completion without interruption and all S nodes are reserved by the application throughout this duration. Upon a job departure, the available partition is allocated to the job at the head of the system queue, if any. Since the node partitions cannot be modified, jobs do not incur any reconfiguration overhead. The only overhead incurred by each job is the cost to set up the job for execution on the S nodes allocated to it.

Our decision to consider equal-sized node partitions is motivated by the results of several studies (e.g., [30, 22]) showing that adaptive/static strategies in which the system is divided into equal-sized partitions outperform other adaptive/static policies when job service time requirements are not used in scheduling decisions. A number of research studies, under different workload assumptions, have also shown that adaptive partitioning yields steady-state performance comparable to that of the best static partitioning policy for a given system load [26, 27, 32]. Hence, when this relation holds, the mean job response time under adaptive partitioning is accurately approximated by the static policy that provides the lowest response time for a given load, and the results of Section 6 are also representative of a comparison between adaptive and dynamic partitioning policies.

3 Experimental System Platform and Applications

In this section we describe four aspects of our experimental platform: the hardware, the system software, the parallel applications and the workloads studied.

Our focus is on distributed-memory systems where there are a set of independent nodes that do not share memory. Each node runs independent operating system images that communicate through message passing. The operating system runs a special distributed scheduler (DS) that interacts with applications to perform distributed space-sharing.

3.1 System Hardware and Operating System Configurations

We experiment with two different distributed-memory environments, namely a network of workstations (NOW) and the IBM SP2 machine.

NOW. A group of workstations connected by a token ring that has a bandwidth of 16 megabits/sec. The workstations are Model 980F machines which use 62 MIPS PowerPC processors. These machines run AIX 3.2.5.

SP2. The IBM SP2 is a distributed-memory multicomputer that is connected by a high-speed switch. We use TCP/IP to communicate over the switch to make the port of the software easy. The nodes run 133 MIPS PowerPC processors. These machine run AIX 4.1. The applications do not use the fast user-level communications of the switch.

Distributed Scheduler Architecture. A parallel application is submitted by a *launcher*, such as a shell, to a distributed scheduler (DS). The DS allocates a partition for the application or places it in the FCFS system queue to wait for an available partition, as described in Section 2. Under dynamic partitioning, the nodes controlled by the DS are divided into multiple, dynamically-created and dynamically-changing non-overlapping partitions, whereas the node partitions are fixed under static partitioning. Each partition is comprised of a group of nodes, and each application runs in its own dedicated partition until it completes. The DS informs the application of node allocation changes at runtime. The application then reconfigures itself based on the new set of nodes available to it. The DS implements both DEP and SP policies, the performance characteristics of which are examined in this paper. We refer the interested reader to [14] for more details on the architecture of our distributed scheduler.

3.2 Parallel Application Structure

Many parallel applications are written such that the number of nodes allocated to them can only be set when they start. However, it is desirable for a parallel application (if it runs under a scheduler that supports dynamic partitioning) to be able to handle, at any time during its execution, fewer or more nodes than it was initially allocated. We refer to applications that are able to react to such changes as *reconfigurable*. There are a variety of ways to structure parallel applications to make them reconfigurable. We present one such approach.

We assume that each application can use all of the nodes allocated to it during its lifetime. We also assume that these applications can be decomposed into the structure depicted in Fig. 1. This structure has been variously called bag-of-tasks[1, 10], master-slave parallelism[25] and task-queue model [15, 5].

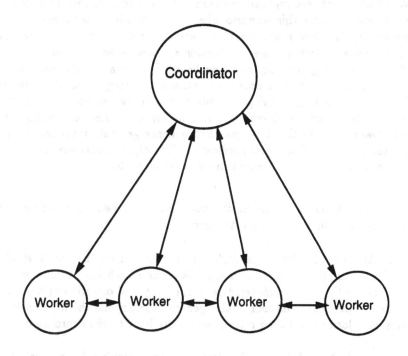

Fig. 1. Structure of an Adaptive Parallel Application

Each application consists of a coordinator process along with a set of worker processes as shown in Fig. 1. When an application starts it spawns a set of worker processes and the logically centralized coordinator. Each worker process is given a set of tasks to work on. When a worker is finished with its tasks it sends the results back to the coordinator, and waits for more tasks from it. The worker processes may also communicate with each other.

The coordinator is the point of contact between the system and the application. The DS notifies an application of node allocation changes via the coordinator. Under dynamic partitioning, each partition may shrink or grow with time, and a reconfigurable application must be able to handle such node allocation changes. For example, the scheduler may notify the coordinator of an application that it has lost a node. It does so by sending a reconfiguration message to the coordinator. The coordinator must then work with the worker processes to handle the lost node. This requires sending a reconfigure message to each of the worker processes. The worker processes checkpoint their data with the coordinator, and then wait for further instructions from it.[3] The worker that

---

[3] An alternative would be to throw away the current task set on the node which is being preempted. We will explore this alternative in our future work.

resides on the lost node is terminated. The other workers are sent more work and then they continue their normal processing. The applications we chose (see Section 3.2) are large-grained applications for which checkpointing at the coordinator is not a bottleneck.

We assume that reconfiguration does not involve process migration but only data migration. Under this scenario when an application loses a node, it must checkpoint its data and gracefully terminate the process running on that node. The system then starts the new application's processes on that node.

The parallel programming model we have chosen is a popular one, and it is easy to make adaptive. It is possible to structure a large class of applications in this manner, including Adaptive Quadrature [1] (a method for performing numerical integration), AtEarth [3] (a simulation of the flight of neutrinos from the sun towards the earth), DNA parallel sequence generation programs [3] and Computational Fluid Dynamics applications [26, 27]. Furthermore, many Linda programs are inherently structured in this manner [4, 3].

The Applications. We examine the performance of two applications in this paper: Adaptive Quadrature and AtEarth.

AtEarth. AtEarth simulates the flight of neutrinos from the sun toward the earth. The simulation consists of many trials where each trial simulates a neutrino's flight with given characteristics (e.g, energy and direction of flight). The trials are independent. The coordinator generates tasks, and the workers execute the trial simulations and then return the results back to the coordinator.

Adaptive quadrature. Adaptive Quadrature is an algorithm for numerical integration. It is an approximation algorithm where the area under the function to be calculated is approximated with a parallelogram. If the approximation is above a certain threshold the process is recursively refined. In the parallel version of the algorithm the region to be integrated is split into Z parts, where Z is the total number of regions in the problem. The running time is a function of the desired accuracy of the intergration, the interval over which the computation is being performed, and the function(s) to be computed.

Reconfiguration. When the scheduler changes the size of a partition, the corresponding application (i.e., its coordinator) is notified of its new partition size through a special reconfiguration message, which contains a list with the lost (if the partition is about to shrink) or new (if the application is about to expand) nodes.

The application worker processes checkpoint their work with the coordinator, which is now free to choose a totally new parallelization. The coordinator informs the scheduler that it has checkpointed. If a partition shrinks, the processes on the nodes being reassigned are gracefully terminated. If a partition expands, new worker processes are launched on the additional nodes. The coordinator must reset the communication links with all the worker processes, and set up the appropriate data structures so that it can communicate with the workers and the individual processes can communicate with each other.

3.3 Workloads

Current and expected workloads for large-scale parallel computing environments consist of a mixture of applications with very different resource requirements, often resulting in a highly variable workload [26, 27, 13, 18, 19]. We therefore use a simple probability distribution to control and vary different mixtures of instances of the two applications discussed in Section 3.2, where an instance is determined by both the application and its input data set. In other words, we model the system workload by probabilistically determining which instance we submit on each job arrival.

The results presented in Section 6 are based on three of the workloads considered in our study. These workloads were chosen because they are representative of the trends we have observed in our investigations of different parallel systems. These three instances can be characterized by their execution times: very small, small, medium and large. Table 2 summarizes the different probabilities used for these parallel workloads for each of the three workloads. As a specific example, we present in Fig. 2 the speedup curve of workload 2 in the NOW environment.

Job Size	Very Small	Small	Medium	Large
Workload 1	0.0	0.2339	0.274	0.491
Workload 2	0.0	0.66	0.34	0.0
Workload 3	1.0	0.0	0.0	0.0

Table 2. Three workloads used in the experiments.

4 Analytical System Models

In this section we summarize an analytic model of the distributed-memory, dynamic partitioning system described in Section 3, as well as an analytic model of the corresponding parallel system under static/adaptive partitioning. The technical details of our models and their solutions are beyond the scope of this paper. We refer the interested reader to [35] for derivations of an exact solution of each model, including expressions for performance measures of interest. Additional details on the models can be found in [35, 36].

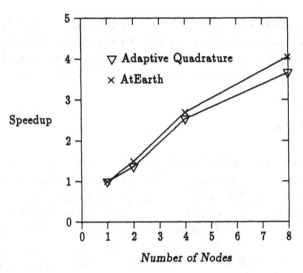

Fig. 2. Speedup of the Applications in Workload 2 on NOW-cluster.

4.1 Dynamic Partitioning

We model a parallel computer system consisting of P identical nodes that are scheduled according to the (basic) DEP policy defined in Section 2.1. Recall that the node allocations are reconfigured whenever a job arrives to a system with $0 \leq i < N$ jobs and whenever a job departs from a system with $1 \leq i \leq N$ jobs. The exact details of the node allocation decisions made by the scheduler in each case, as well as the overheads of making these decisions and of reconfiguring the applications involved, are reflected in the model parameter distributions and the analysis of the corresponding stochastic process [35]. In this manner we can model various types of dynamic partitioning strategies, although our focus in this paper is on DEP.

The interarrival times of jobs are modeled as independent and identically distributed (i.i.d.) random variables with a phase-type probability distribution $\mathcal{A}(\cdot)$ and mean interarrival time $1/\lambda$. When the system is executing i jobs, the service times of each of these jobs are modeled as i.i.d. random variables with a phase-type distribution $\mathcal{B}_i(\cdot)$ and mean execution time $1/\mu_i$, $1 \leq i \leq N$. The times required to repartition the nodes among the i jobs being executed (either due to a departure when the system contains $i + 1$ jobs or an arrival when the system contains $i - 1$ jobs) are i.i.d. random variables having a phase-type distribution $\mathcal{C}_i(\cdot)$ with mean repartitioning overhead $1/\gamma_i$, $1 \leq i \leq N$. The use of phase-type distributions [28] for our model parameters is motivated in part by their important mathematical properties, which can be exploited to obtain a tractable analytic model while capturing the fundamental aspects of dynamic partitioning. Just as important, however, is the fact that any real distribution can in principle be represented arbitrarily close by a phase-type distribution, and a number of algorithms have been developed for fitting phase-type distributions to empirical data [2, 12, 20]. As our measurements confirm, this results in an extremely accurate modeling analysis of dynamic partitioning in real parallel systems.

This DEP model is solved for relative system loads $\widehat{U}$ in the range 0.02 to 0.98 in increments of 0.02. The corresponding mean job response times, $\overline{T}_{\text{DP}}(\widehat{U})$, are then computed from these model solutions.

4.2 Static (Adaptive) Partitioning

We also model the above parallel system under the SP policy defined in Section 2.2. Recall that the nodes are statically divided into K partitions each of size $S \equiv (N/K)\,M$, where we only consider values of K that evenly divide N.

This static system model is solved for each value of $K \in \{1, 2, \ldots, N/2, N\}$ and the corresponding mean response times, $\overline{T}_{\text{SP}(K)}$, are computed. The mean job response time under the best SP policy, for a given relative load $\widehat{U}$, is then given by the minimum of these response times. That is,

$$\overline{T}_{\text{SP}^*}(\widehat{U}) = \min_{1 \leq K \leq N}\{\,\overline{T}_{\text{SP}(K)}(\widehat{U})\,\}.$$

As previously noted, the value of $\overline{T}_{\text{SP}^*}$ is representative of the mean response time under adaptive partitioning in many system environments.

5 Overheads Associated with Dynamic Equi-Partitioning

In this section we present some of the results from our experimental testbed on the overheads associated with implementing dynamic space-sharing strategies in the NOW and the SP2 environments described in Section 3. There are two types of overheads associated with the dynamic partitioning schemes: those that are experienced by the system and those that slow down the application. For the applications we have considered, reconfiguration overheads are independent of the size of the data sets. To ensure the accuracy of these measurements, each set of experiments were repeated 50 times and we present the average of these runs.

System Overhead. For each new application entering the system, the DS first makes sure that a new partition can be created as explained in Section 2.1. Once the DS determines that it can create a new partition for an application it goes through the following steps:

- Determine which of the nodes (we call them *moving nodes*) will be assigned to the new partition.
- Send a reconfiguration notification only to the applications (i.e., to the appropriate coordinators for each application) that may use the *moving nodes*. The reconfiguration message includes information on how many and which nodes are to be preempted.

- Wait until it receives from each coordinator an acknowledgement that reconfiguration has completed. At this point it issues a kill message which gracefully terminates all the application's processes that run on the *moving nodes*. (The processes do not exit after a checkpoint; this is discussed in more detail in the paragraph on application overhead). Now, all of these *moving nodes* are free and ready to be used.
- Update its data structures to reflect the changes (e.g., partition sizes, and which nodes belong to which partitions).
- Initialize the new data structures with the *moving nodes*.

At this point, the new partition is initialized and ready, so the DS launches the new application to run on it.

The DS follows similar steps upon the termination (normal or abnormal) of an application. The difference is that now the DS divides the available nodes among the remaining applications, instead of "squeezing" the applications to use fewer nodes. Here are the steps taken by the DS:

- Determine which of the remaining partitions (we call them expanding partitions) will be assigned the moving nodes.
- Send a reconfiguration notification to each application (i.e., to its coordinator) that runs on an expanding partition. The reconfiguration message includes information on how many and which nodes are added.
- Wait until it receives an acknowledgement from each coordinator that reconfiguration has completed.
- Update its data structures to reflect the changes (e.g., partition sizes, which nodes belong to which partitions).
- Deallocate the data structures associated with the partition that was eliminated.

At this point, for each expanding partition, the DS starts executing the application program on the newly available nodes.

Application Overhead. A component of the reconfiguration overhead actually occurs in the communication library linked with the application. The break down of these overheads are as follows:

- When an coordinator receives a reconfiguration notification (the message contains information on the new size and set of nodes) it sends a checkpoint message to all of its worker processes.
- Once the workers complete their current phase, they checkpoint and they send an acknowledgement to the coordinator that they are ready. Then they cut their old connection with the coordinator and they try to establish a new one and start from the beginning.
- Meanwhile, the coordinator waits to receive all of the acknowledgements. Once this happens, it sends an acknowledgement back to the DS that checkpointing has completed.

– Then it starts accepting connection requests but only from the workers of valid nodes (nodes that belong in the partition). A new node that has just joined the partition is obviously considered valid. If a worker of an invalid node (i.e., one that has been allocated to another partition) tries to reconnect, the coordinator refuses the connection.

When all connections are reestablished, the coordinator assigns work to its new set of workers and the application resumes.

5.1 Overheads for Dynamic Equi-Partitioning

We present both the overheads of the system and the total (system plus application) overheads associated with DEP. Partitions shrink in size when an application enters the system (if the current number of jobs is less than the maximum number of partitions) and expand when an application exits.

In the following we present the overheads of starting with a system with no application, and then measure the overheads as more and more application enter the system until the number of applications is equal to the maximum number of partitions. We call this the *shrinking phase* since the partitions keeps shrinking in size. We then reduce the number of applications one by one until there are none left, which we call the *expanding phase*.

The overheads of shrinking partitions as an increasing number of applications enter the system is given in Fig. 3 for eight nodes, and in Fig. 4 for four nodes. The transitions and the individual partition sizes for each of the points on the graph are shown in Table 1, which describes the overheads when $P = 8$ and $M = 1$. The overheads include those of the system and the application reconfiguration. The corresponding overheads for shrinking partitions in a 12-node NOW system are provided in Fig. 5.

The overheads of expanding partitions starting with 8 applications, each executing on a partition of 1 node, is shown in Fig. 6. Similarly, the overheads of starting with 4 applications and 4 nodes is given in Fig. 7. The corresponding overheads for expanding partitions in a 12-node NOW system are also provided in Fig. 5.

From these figures we observe several trends. First, an expanding event is more expensive than a comparable shrinking event. For example, the transition $\{1,1\} \rightarrow \{2\}$ is more expensive than the transition $\{2\} \rightarrow \{1,1\}$. The system overheads are the same in both cases, however, in the $\{1,1\} \rightarrow \{2\}$ case the application overheads for the new partition of $\{2\}$ are greater than the new partitions $\{1,1\}$ in the transition $\{2\} \rightarrow \{1,1\}$. This is due to the fact that in the former case (expanding) the coordinator reconnects with two workers, while in the later (shrinking) each worker reconnects with one (different) coordinator. This effect is more pronounced as the number of nodes is increased (there is more congestion in the network). Second, the SP2 overheads are lower due to the faster CPU and the fast SP2 interconnect, as expected. The total overheads on the SP2 are about 2 to 4 times lower than the comparable overheads on the

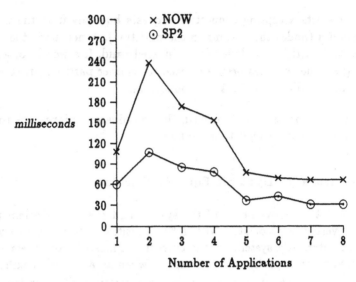

Fig. 3. Overheads associated with Shrinking a partition as number of applications is increased. The policy is DEP.

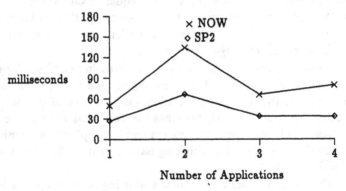

Fig. 4. Overheads associated with Shrinking a partition as number of applications is increased. The total number of nodes is 4. The policy is DEP.

NOW.[4]

The overheads are greater when few large applications (many nodes per application) are reconfigured. This is expected since creating a new partition while keeping the sizes balanced implicates applications, specially if they are large. When there are many jobs in the system, fewer applications are interrupted and the number of nodes per partition involved in a reconfiguration is small. As the number of applications approaches the maximum number allowed into the system, the reconfiguration cost becomes a fixed overhead as only one partition, of size 1 (the minimum partition size) in our example, is reconfigured.

---

[4] On the SP2, we believe many further optimizations are possible particularly from the perspective of communication.

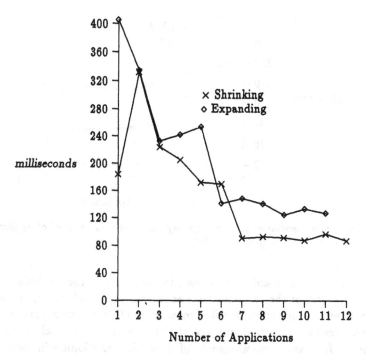

Fig. 5. Overheads associated with Shrinking and Expanding with 12 nodes. The policy is DEP.

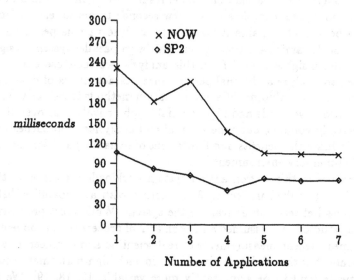

Fig. 6. Overheads associated with Expanding partitions as number of applications is decreased from 8 to 1.The policy is DEP.

6 System Performance

In this section we present some of the results of our detailed analysis of dynamic partitioning in the NOW and SP2 system environments. The measurement data

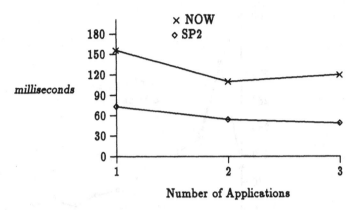

Fig. 7. Overheads associated with Expanding partitions as number of applications is decreased from 4 to 1. The policy is DEP.

presented in Sections 3 and 5 were used to parametrize the analytic models of Section 4. Several of the response time estimates predicted by our models were then compared against corresponding measurements from our experimental testbed. These results show that our analytic estimates are in excellent agreement with the performance measurements of dynamic partitioning in both parallel systems executing real scientific/engineering workloads, and thus validate our analytic models. We note that the model results are computed in an extremely efficient manner, requiring less than a few seconds to obtain each set of results presented below. This makes it possible to analyze various performance characteristics of dynamic partitioning across a large parallel system design space. Based on the insights gained from this analysis, we then use our experimental testbed to analyze additional performance characteristics of dynamic space-sharing strategies, including different allocation methods to reduce the impact of reconfiguration overheads and highly variable job arrivals. Our overall objective is to effectively combine our experimental and analytical approaches to quantitatively evaluate the benefits and limitations of dynamic partitioning in distinct distributed-memory environments.

The results in this section are for system workloads consisting of the application mixes described in Section 3.3, together with a probability distribution for the times between job arrivals to the system. While most previous parallel scheduling studies have assumed a Poisson arrival process (i.e., exponential interarrival times), recent measurements of real scientific and engineering workloads demonstrate that the job interarrival times in such high-performance computing environments tend to be significantly more variable [13, 18, 19]. We therefore consider hyperexponential interarrival times that statistically match the workload measurements presented in [13, 18, 19], and we compare these results with those obtained under the exponential interarrival assumptions of previous work.

The characteristics of the different scheduling policies, together with their corresponding overheads, cause each of the various parallel systems considered in our study to saturate (i.e., the response times become unbounded) at different job arrival rates. The best possible service rate, or *capacity*, for the DEP system under a particular workload is bounded above by the value of $N\mu_N$[5] for that workload, and saturation is guaranteed for all arrival rates $\lambda \geq N\mu_N$. Although this capacity $N\mu_N$ is not actually achievable due to the overheads incurred under DEP, we use this capacity value to define a relative measure of system utilization as the basis for all of our performance comparisons. The capacity values of the SP2 system are chosen for this purpose since this environment has lower service times and overheads (hence, higher capacities) than the NOW environment under each application workload considered. We therefore use *relative system load* to refer to the ratio $\widehat{U} \equiv \lambda/N\mu_{N,SP2}$. The results that follow for each system are all plotted as functions of the relative system load over the interval $(0, 1)$. We note that the corresponding curves for the NOW environment will span a smaller region of this $\widehat{U}$ interval due to its lower capacities.

Mean Response Times. Our first set of results considers the performance characteristics of DEP for each workload and system environment. In Fig. 8 we plot mean response times for application workload 1 (W1) in 8-node NOW and SP2 system environments under hyperexponential job interarrival times as a function of relative system load (labeled W1(Ahyp,Bcv)). For the purpose of comparison, Fig. 8 also includes response time results for W1 under Poisson arrival times (labeled W1(Aexp,Bcv)), as well as results for the case where the coefficient of variation[6] of the workload service times is doubled (labeled W1(Aexp,B2cv)). The corresponding curves for application workload 2 (W2) and workload 3 (W3) are presented in Figs. 9 and 10, respectively.

We observe that the response times under DEP are consistently worse in the NOW environment than those realized in the SP2 environment. This may be as expected due to the larger service times and reconfiguration overheads measured for the NOW environment (see Section 5). We also observe from these results that the more realistic hyperexponential interarrival times yield significantly higher response times under DEP than those obtained under Poisson arrivals in both system environments. This is due to the fact that, under the more variable hyperexponential distribution, a considerable amount of time is spent repartitioning applications only to be interrupted before completion by a subsequent arrival, thus causing a new repartitioning without making any progress on behalf of the jobs involved. This suggests that the mean response times under DEP in distributed-memory systems may be considerably larger than those predicted by previous studies, at least within the context of the systems and workloads considered in this paper. We further observe that the mean response times of DEP tend to also increase under more variable workload execution times, although to a considerably smaller degree than under more variable interarrival times at light to fairly heavy system loads.

Each of the above performance characteristics are similarly observed for the DEP system under W2 and W3, as illustrated in Figs. 9 and 10. We note, how-

---

[5] $1/\mu_N$ is the mean service time, excluding overhead, of a generic job when the system contains at least N jobs.

[6] The coefficient of variation is the ratio of the standard deviation to the mean.

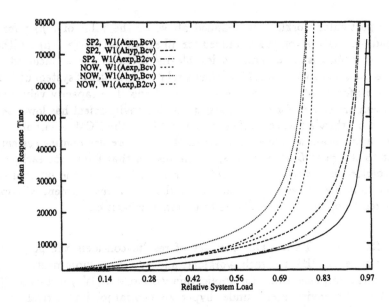

Fig. 8. Mean Response Times under DEP, for Workload 1 and $P = 8$

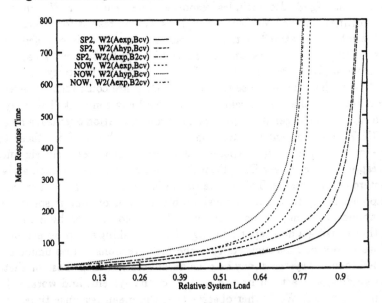

Fig. 9. Mean Response Times under DEP, for Workload 2 and $P = 8$

ever, that there is a reduction in the relative performance differences among the curves going from W1 to W2, which is reduced even further going from W2 to W3. This can be explained in part by observing that a larger fraction of the workload is comprised of jobs with smaller execution times upon moving from W1 to W2 to W3.

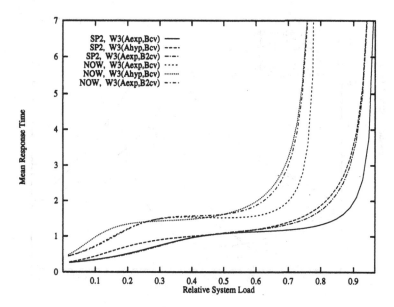

Fig. 10. Mean Response Times under DEP, for Workload 3 and $P = 8$

Relative Response Times. Our next set of results quantifies the performance benefits of DEP with respect to static/adaptive partitioning. Taking the ratio of the mean response time under the best static policy to that achieved by the dynamic policy, we obtain mean response time ratios as a function of $\widehat{U}$. The corresponding results for W1, W2 and W3 under both parallel system environments are plotted in Figs. 11, 12 and 13, respectively. While the mean response time trends observed above were quite similar, here we see very different performance characteristics in comparison to static/adaptive partitioning for the various workloads.

For the base W1 execution times, DEP provides poorer response times relative to those obtained under the static/adaptive policy at light to moderate loads, independent of the interarrival distribution. The larger performance degradations and the smallest performance improvements are observed for the NOW environment when compared against those for the SP2 system. The overheads of repartitioning the nodes and of the allocation decisions of the dynamic scheme tends to outweigh its benefits relative to the static/adaptive policy under W1 at these system utilizations. This is particularly true at light loads since the overheads for reconfiguration are greater at these utilizations (see Figs. 3 and 6). These reconfiguration overheads and the aggressive repartitioning decisions degrade the relative performance even though the long run percentage of reconfigurations is low (see Fig. 14). Moreover, larger relative performance degradations are observed for the system under Poisson arrivals than under the more variable hyperexponential interarrival times in both system environments. The relative performance degradations (and benefits) for the NOW environment appear at smaller system loads than those in the SP2 system, and within each of these

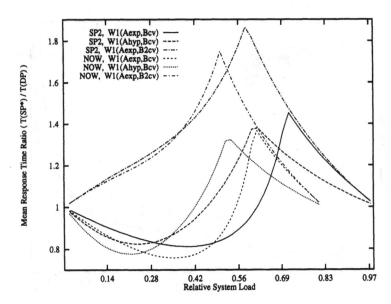

Fig. 11. Mean Response Time Ratios $(\overline{T}_{SP^*}/\overline{T}_{DP})$, for Workload 1 and $P = 8$

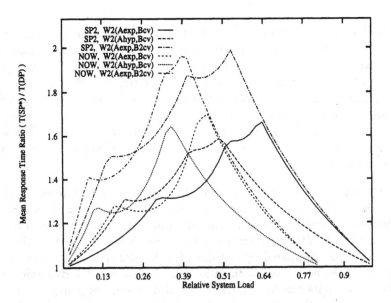

Fig. 12. Mean Response Time Ratios $(\overline{T}_{SP^*}/\overline{T}_{DP})$, for Workload 2 and $P = 8$

environments the relative performance degradations (and benefits) for hyperex-ponential interarrivals appear at lighter loads than those under Poisson arrivals.

Interestingly, DEP provides the largest performance benefits (and no degra-dation) relative to static/adaptive partitioning under the more variable W1 ex-ecution times. By adjusting scheduling decisions in response to changes in the

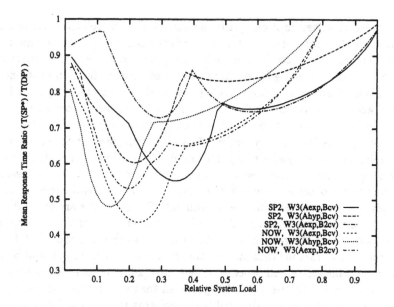

Fig. 13. Mean Response Time Ratios ($\overline{T}_{SP^*}/\overline{T}_{DP}$), for Workload 3 and $P = 8$

highly variable workload, the DEP policy provides more efficient utilization of the nodes when compared against the static/adaptive policy, which results in better response time ratios. These relative performance benefits tend to increase as $\widehat{U}$ rises from small to moderate values since workload changes are more frequent and DEP adjusts its node allocations accordingly to achieve superior steady-state performance.

As the system load increases, we observe considerable performance benefits under DEP relative to static/adaptive partitioning, with the largest response time ratios appearing in the SP2 system. We also note that the case of Poisson arrivals yields larger maximum (relative) performance benefits than the hyperexponential interarrival times in both system environments. Once again, by adjusting scheduling decisions in response to workload changes, the DEP policy provides a more efficient utilization of the nodes in comparison to static/adaptive partitioning for moderate to heavy loads under W1. These relative performance benefits tend to increase as $\widehat{U}$ rises, since workload changes are more frequent and DEP adjusts its node allocations accordingly to achieve superior steady-state performance. In the limit as the system approaches saturation, the probability that the system repartitions the nodes tends toward 0, i.e., the frequency of reconfigurations decreases to 0 as the system spends essentially all of its time with N or more jobs. It therefore follows that the DEP system converges toward the static policy with N partitions in the limit as the system approaches saturation.

Turning to W2, we observe that DEP provides the best space-sharing performance characteristics and that these relative benefits are even larger than those shown for W1. Here we see that the largest relative improvements in performance are generally obtained for the NOW environment. We again find that hyperexponential interarrival assumptions yield smaller maximum (relative) performance benefits than the corresponding Poisson arrival case. The response time ratios tend to increase as $\widehat{U}$ rises because scheduling decisions are being adjusted in response to workload changes, resulting in very efficient utilization of the nodes, and workload changes are more frequent with these increasing system loads. As noted above, the system under DEP eventually converges toward the static policy with N partitions in the limit as the system approaches saturation.

Conversely, the DEP policy under W3 yields significant performance degradations relative to static/adaptive partitioning across all system utilizations. We further observe that the response time ratios for the case of Poisson arrivals are worse than those obtained under hyperexponential interarrival times at all but light loads in both parallel system environments. These results are primarily due to the large repartitioning overheads relative to the job service times comprising the workload, where the ratio of execution time to overhead is roughly 6 to 1. It is for exactly these reasons that an adaptive partitioning strategy should be used for jobs with relatively small processing demands [26, 27]. Such information can be successfully given by users [18, 19] provided that countermeasures are taken by the system [8], it can be estimated with performance tools and run-time systems [11], and/or determined via standard methods such as multi-level feedback queues.

We should point out that the scalloped shape of the response time ratio curves for both workloads are the result of the response time behavior of the best static partitioning policy. Specifically, each of the points where the response time ratio reaches a local maxima (within a particular $\widehat{U}$ region) is due to a change in the number of partitions employed under the static/adaptive policy. This in turn causes the response time under DEP to be compared with a different static partitioning response time curve, which is further from saturation than the response time curve for the previous system load.

Reconfigurations. To better understand the system performance impact of the overheads of repartitioning, our next set of results considers the long run proportion of time that the system spends reconfiguring its node allocations, i.e., the steady-state probability p_r that the system is executing a reconfiguration. The corresponding results for W1, W2 and W3 are plotted as a function of $\widehat{U}$ in Figs. 14, 15 and 16, respectively. We observe a sharp initial increase in p_r as the relative load rises, and that this initial increase corresponds to the performance degradation under DEP for W1 and W3. Similarly, we observe that the shape of the p_r curves and the loads over which these characteristics are found, both correspond to the performance benefits exhibited in the response time ratio curves; e.g., compare Figs. 11 and 12 with Figs. 14 and 15. The NOW environment spends a larger percentage of its time repartitioning nodes than the corresponding SP2 system due to the larger reconfiguration overheads experienced in this environment (see Section 5). Moreover, the maximum values of p_r appear at smaller $\widehat{U}$ in the NOW system than in the SP2 environment. A Poisson arrival process tends to increase p_r over that observed under hyperexponential interarrivals, and this trend appears in both system environments.

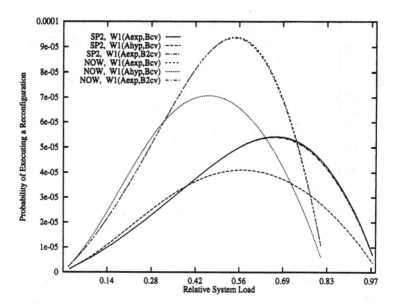

Fig. 14. Probability of Repartitioning the Nodes in Steady State, for Workload 1 and $P = 8$

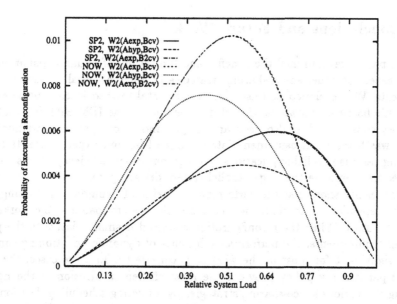

Fig. 15. Probability of Repartitioning the Nodes in Steady State, for Workload 2 and $P = 8$

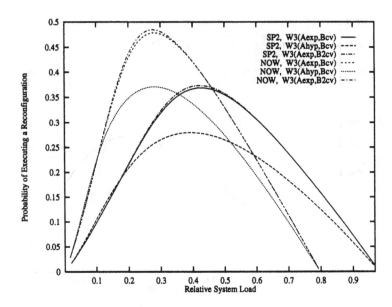

Fig. 16. Probability of Repartitioning the Nodes in Steady State, for Workload 3 and $P = 8$

7 Conclusions and Future Work

In this paper we examined the benefits and limitations of dynamic partitioning with respect to other space-sharing strategies in different parallel system environments. We developed and used an experimental testbed in computing environments based on networks of workstations and on the IBM SP2 distributed-memory computer. We also used an analytic model of dynamic partitioning, which was fitted to measurement data obtained from our experimental testbed running various parallel applications. The computational efficiency of this model allowed us to explore the large parallel system design space.

Our results show that the performance benefits of dynamic partitioning are heavily dependent upon its associated costs, the system load and the workload characteristics. When the reconfiguration overhead is small relative to the processing requirements, the performance benefits of dynamic partitioning can be quite significant for most of the workloads considered. In these cases, the dynamic partitioning policy provides the most efficient utilization of the nodes among the various space-sharing strategies by adjusting scheduling decisions in response to workload changes. These performance benefits tend to increase with rising traffic intensities, since workload changes are more frequent and dynamic partitioning adjusts its node allocations accordingly to achieve the best steady-state, space-sharing performance. When the reconfiguration costs are sufficiently large, however, this overhead tends to outweigh the benefits of dynamic partitioning, particularly at light to moderate system loads for the workloads studied.

Within the context of the parallel systems and application workloads considered in this paper, our results suggest that:

- Jobs with small resource requirements should not be dynamically reconfigured in distributed-memory environments. A workload consisting of a majority of such small jobs can suffer from a form of thrashing where the system spends a large percentage of its time reconfiguring node allocations.
- On the other hand, the measurements from our experimental testbed show that, in the majority of application instances expected for large-scale parallel computing, the repartitioning overheads tend to be small relative to the execution times of these application instances.
- Dynamic partitioning appears to be viable in a variety of different distributed-memory environments, provided that the applications are capable of executing on variable numbers of nodes and are capable of reconfiguring the number of nodes on which it executes. Our system approach provides the structure to extend this functionality to applications beyond those considered herein.

Furthermore, our results clearly demonstrate that the overheads of dynamic equi-partitioning in distributed-memory environments must be considered by the scheduling algorithms employed in practice, otherwise these reconfiguration costs can in general limit and/or eliminate the potential system performance benefits. We have been exploring several variants of dynamic partitioning to address these issues. One strategy for decreasing the overheads associated with dynamic equi-partitioning is to use the folding approach found in [24], which reduces the number reconfigurations performed under the greedy dynamic policy, at the expense of a less equitable allocation of the nodes among the competing jobs. Another approach consists of using the equi-partitioning method to equally divide the nodes among the jobs in the system whenever a repartition is performed, while placing a minimum period of time (which can be dynamically adjusted) between when the system can repartition its node allocations. In addition to reducing the number of reconfigurations, this approach tends to reduce the performance effects of job arrival variability by effectively smoothing the arrival process [6].

There is a fundamental tradeoff between these two dynamic partitioning approaches. Folding provides the advantage of immediately responding to workload changes, but it reduces the repartitioning overhead by interrupting fewer jobs to yield somewhat less equitable node allocations. Dynamic partitioning with smoothing, on the other hand, reduces the repartitioning overhead by reacting less quickly to workload changes, but it provides the advantage of dividing the system resources equally among the running jobs. The best solution to this performance tradeoff depends upon a number of factors, and it is particularly sensitive to the application workload characteristics and the job arrival process. For long running applications, it may be just as important or even more important to equitably allocate the nodes among the running jobs as it is to reduces the number reconfigurations performed.

Several preliminary experiments with these policies under workload 1 of Section 3.3 have consistently demonstrated that dynamic partitioning with smoothing exhibits lower mean response times, as well as a smaller variance in the execution times, than that observed for dynamic equi-partitioning and folding, with equi-partitioning consistently providing better response times than folding. The latter result is in contrast to those of Padhye and Dowdy [29] which show that folding generally outperforms equi-partitioning in a distributed-memory environment under a workload based on scientific matrix computation programs. The differences between the results of these two studies are primarily due to the differences in the respective workloads, where the workload used in our experiments consists of applications with larger execution times than those studied in [29]. This further highlights the fundamental tradeoff between the two above dynamic partitioning approaches for reducing the repartitioning overheads in distributed-memory environments. We are continuing to examine these and related scheduling issues in distributed-memory parallel systems.

References

1. G. R. Andrews. Paradigms for process interaction in distributed programs. *ACM Computing Surveys*, 23(1):49–90, Mar. 1991.

2. S. Asmussen, O. Nerman, and M. Olsson. Fitting phase type distributions via the EM algorithm. Technical Report 1994:23, Department of Mathematics, Chalmers University of Technology, May 1994.

3. Carriero, Freeman, Gelernter, and Kaminsky. Adaptive Parallelism in Piranha. *IEEE Computer*, 28(1):40–49, Jan. 1995.

4. N. Carriero and D. Gelernter. Linda in Context. *Communications of the ACM*, 32(4):444–458, Apr. 1989.

5. R. Chandra, A. Gupta, and J. Henessey. COOL: A Language for parallel programming. In *Proceedings of the Second Workshop on Programming Languages, and Compilers for Parallel Computing*, Aug. 1989.

6. C. S. Chang. Smoothing point processes as a means to increase throughput. Technical Report RC 16866, IBM Research Division, May 1991.

7. S.-H. Chiang, R. K. Mansharamani, and M. K. Vernon. Use of application characteristics and limited preemption for run-to-completion parallel processor scheduling policies. In *Proceedings of the ACM SIGMETRICS Conference on Measurement and Modeling of Computer Systems*, pages 33–44, May 1994.

8. E. G. Coffman, Jr. and L. Kleinrock. Computer scheduling methods and their countermeasures. In *Proceedings of the AFIPS Spring Joint Computer Conference*, volume 32, pages 11–21, April 1968.

9. K. Dussa, B. Carlson, L. Dowdy, and K.-H. Park. Dynamic partitioning in transputer environments. In *Proceedings of the ACM SIGMETRICS Conference on Measurement and Modeling of Computer Systems*, pages 203–213, 1990.

10. J. D. L. Eager and J. Zahorjan. Chores:Enhanced Run-Time support for shared-memory parallel computing. *ACM Transactions on Computer Systems*, 11(1):1–32, Feb. 1993.

11. K. Ekanadham, V. K. Naik, and M. S. Squillante. PET: A parallel performance estimation tool. In *Proceedings Seventh SIAM Conference on Parallel Processing for Scientific Computing*, February 1995.

12. M. J. Faddy. Fitting structured phase-type distributions. Technical report, Department of Mathematics, University of Queensland, Australia, April 1994. To appear, *Applied Stochastic Models and Data Analysis*.

13. D. G. Feitelson and B. Nitzberg. Job characteristics of a production parallel scientific workload on the NASA Ames iPSC/860. In *Job Scheduling Strategies for Parallel Processing*, D. G. Feitelson and L. Rudolph (eds.). Springer-Verlag, 1995. Lecture Notes in Computer Science Vol. 949.

14. L. L. Fong, A. S. Gopal, N. Islam, A. Prodromidis, and M. S. Squillante. Extensible resource management for cluster computing. Technical report, IBM Research Division, May 1996.

15. R. Gabriel. Queue based multiprocessing lisp. In *ACM Symposium on Lips and Functional Programming*, pages 25–43, 1984.

16. D. Ghosal, G. Serazzi, and S. K. Tripathi. The processor working set and its use in scheduling multiprocessor systems. *IEEE Transactions on Software Engineering*, 17:443–453, May 1991.

17. A. Gupta, A. Tucker, and S. Urushibara. The impact of operating system scheduling policies and synchronization methods on the performance of parallel applications. In *Proceedings of the ACM SIGMETRICS Conference on Measurement and Modeling of Computer Systems*, May 1991.

18. S. G. Hotovy. Workload evolution on the Cornell Theory Center IBM SP2. In *Job Scheduling Strategies for Parallel Processing*, D. G. Feitelson and L. Rudolph (eds.). Springer-Verlag, 1996. Lecture Notes in Computer Science, this volume.

19. S. G. Hotovy, D. J. Schneider, and T. O'Donnell. Analysis of the early workload on the Cornell Theory Center IBM SP2. In *Proceedings of the ACM SIGMETRICS Conference on Measurement and Modeling of Computer Systems*, May 1996.

20. A. Lang. Parameter estimation for phase-type distributions, part I: Fundamentals and existing methods. Technical Report 159, Department of Statistics, Oregon State University, 1994.

21. S. T. Leutenegger and M. K. Vernon. The performance of multiprogrammed multiprocessor scheduling policies. In *Proceedings of the ACM SIGMETRICS Conference on Measurement and Modeling of Computer Systems*, pages 226–236, May 1990.

22. R. K. Mansharamani and M. K. Vernon. Properties of the EQS parallel processor allocation policy. Technical Report 1192, Computer Sciences Department, University of Wisconsin–Madison, November 1993.

23. C. McCann, R. Vaswani, and J. Zahorjan. A dynamic processor allocation policy for multiprogrammed shared-memory multiprocessors. *ACM Transactions on Computer Systems*, 11(2):146–178, May 1993.

24. C. McCann and J. Zahorjan. Processor allocation policies for message-passing parallel computers. In *Proceedings of the ACM SIGMETRICS Conference on Measurement and Modeling of Computer Systems*, pages 19–32, May 1994.

25. J. Mohan. *Performance of Parallel Programs: Models and Analyses*. PhD thesis, Carnegie Mellon University, July 1984.

26. V. K. Naik, S. K. Setia, and M. S. Squillante. Performance analysis of job scheduling policies in parallel supercomputing environments. In *Proceedings of Supercomputing '93*, pages 824–833, November 1993.

27. V. K. Naik, S. K. Setia, and M. S. Squillante. Scheduling of large scientific applications on distributed memory multiprocessor systems. In *Proceedings Sixth SIAM Conference on Parallel Processing for Scientific Computing*, pages 913–922, March 1993.

28. M. F. Neuts. *Matrix-Geometric Solutions in Stochastic Models: An Algorithmic Approach.* The Johns Hopkins University Press, 1981.

29. J. D. Padhye and L. W. Dowdy. Preemptive versus non-preemptive processor allocation policies for message passing parallel computers: An empirical comparison. In *Job Scheduling Strategies for Parallel Processing,* D. G. Feitelson and L. Rudolph (eds.). Springer-Verlag, 1996. Lecture Notes in Computer Science, this volume.

30. E. Rosti, E. Smirni, L. W. Dowdy, G. Serazzi, and B. M. Carlson. Robust partitioning policies of multiprocessor systems. *Performance Evaluation,* 19:141–165, 1994.

31. S. K. Setia. *Scheduling on Multiprogrammed, Distributed Memory Parallel Computers.* PhD thesis, Department of Computer Science, University of Maryland, College Park, MD, August 1993.

32. S. K. Setia and S. K. Tripathi. A comparative analysis of static processor partitioning policies for parallel computers. In *Proceedings of MASCOTS '93,* January 1993.

33. K. C. Sevcik. Characterizations of parallelism in applications and their use in scheduling. In *Proceedings of the ACM SIGMETRICS Conference on Measurement and Modeling of Computer Systems,* pages 171–180, May 1989.

34. K. C. Sevcik. Application scheduling and processor allocation in multiprogrammed parallel processing systems. *Performance Evaluation,* 19:107–140, 1994.

35. M. S. Squillante. Analysis of dynamic partitioning in parallel systems. Technical Report RC 19950, IBM Research Division, February 1995.

36. M. S. Squillante. On the benefits and limitations of dynamic partitioning in parallel computer systems. In *Job Scheduling Strategies for Parallel Processing,* D. G. Feitelson and L. Rudolph (eds.). Springer-Verlag, 1995. Lecture Notes in Computer Science Vol. 949.

37. A. Tucker and A. Gupta. Process control and scheduling issues for multiprogrammed shared-memory multiprocessors. In *Proceedings of the Twelfth ACM Symposium on Operating Systems Principles,* pages 159–166, December 1989.

38. J. Zahorjan and C. McCann. Processor scheduling in shared memory multiprocessors. In *Proceedings of the ACM SIGMETRICS Conference on Measurement and Modeling of Computer Systems,* pages 214–225, May 1990.

Locality-Information-Based Scheduling in Shared-Memory Multiprocessors

Frank Bellosa

University of Erlangen-Nürnberg
Computer Science Department - Operating Systems - IMMD IV
Martensstraße. 1, 91058 Erlangen, Germany

Abstract. Lightweight threads have become a common abstraction in the field of programming languages and operating systems. This paper examines the performance implications of locality information usage in thread scheduling algorithms for scalable shared-memory multiprocessors. The elements of a distributed scheduler using all available locality information as well as experimental measurements are presented.

Most shared-memory multiprocessors use multiple stages of caches to hide latency. Data structures and policies of a scheduling architecture have to reflect the various levels of the memory hierarchy in order to achieve high data locality. Per-processor data structures avoid lock contention and help to reduce memory traffic. While CPU utilization of processes still determines scheduling decisions of contemporary schedulers, we propose novel scheduling policies based on cache miss rates and information about synchronization. All data gathered at runtime are transformed into affinity values inside a metric space, so that threads migrate near to their (sub)optimal operation points defined by location and timing of execution. The distribution of data structures and the usage of locality information characterizes the proposed memory-conscious scheduling architecture. A prototype implementation shows that a locality-conscious scheduler outperforms centralized and distributed approaches ignoring locality information.

1 Introduction

Cache-coherent multiprocessors with non uniform memory access (**NUMA** architectures) have become quite attractive as compute servers for parallel applications in the field of scientific computing. They combine scalability and the shared- memory programming model, relieving the application designer of data distribution and coherency maintenance. But cache locality, load balancing and scheduling are still of crucial importance.

Large caches used in scalable shared-memory architectures can avoid high memory access time only if data is referenced within the address scope of the cache. Consequently, locality is the key issue in multiprocessor performance. One goal of software development is a high degree of locality from the system up to the application level. Even if application designers develop code with high locality, the impact of caches is reduced when scheduling policies ignore locality information. Disregarding locality, the scheduler will initiate switches into uncached process contexts. The consequences are cache and TLB misses for the processor in question and cache line invalidations in caches of other processors.

NUMA architectures like KSR or Convex SPP already provide locality information gathered by special processor monitors or by the cache coherence hardware. The latest processor generations - e.g. HPPA 8000, MIPS R10000 or Ultra SPARC - include a monitoring unit. A processor monitor can count events like read/write cache misses and processor stall cycles due to load and store operations.

Locality information about each process/thread, such as the duration of the last active period, the cache miss rate, the processor stall time, and the processor of last execution, can be used to calculate an affinity value. Furthermore, cooperating threads can be identified by synchronization events and collocated at the same processor, whereas a trade-off between collocation and load balance has to be provided.

The parallelism expressed by "UNIX-like" heavy-weight processes and shared-memory segments is coarse-grained and too inefficient for general purpose parallel programming, because all operations on processes like creation, deletion and context switching invoke complex kernel activities and imply costs associated with cache and TLB misses due to address space changes.

Contemporary operating systems (like SUN's Solaris or MACH) offer middle-weight kernel-level threads decoupling address space and execution entities. Multiple kernel threads mapped to multiple processors can speed up a parallel application. But kernel threads only offer a middle-grained programming model, because thread management implies expensive protected system calls. The potential benefit of using locality information increases with the frequency of scheduling decisions, because the scheduler is the instance evaluating locality information. Consequently, the benefit of using locality information in the kernel will be limited by the low frequency of scheduling decisions.

By moving thread management and synchronization to the user level, the cost of thread management operations can be drastically reduced to one order of magnitude more than a procedure call [1]. Some advantages of user-level threads are:

- All scheduling operations belonging to a single application are handled inside the same address space. Cache and TLB misses are reduced to a minimum.
- The scheduling algorithm and its interface can be designed with respect to the needs of a specific application, thus offering the optimum in performance and functionality. For example, preemptive or priority-based scheduling of threads can be omitted to achieve low thread management overhead, if a lean scheduler is sufficient for an application.
- Data structures for processes and threads are deeply rooted in most kernels. Only the user level offers the necessary flexibility in adapting data structures to the degree of parallelism inherent in an application ranging from several to thousands of threads.

In general, light-weight user-level threads, managed by a runtime library, are executed by kernel threads, which again are mapped on the available physical processors by the kernel. Efficient user-level threads are predestined for fine-grained parallel applications. User-level schedulers make frequent context switches affordable and therefore draw most profit from the use of locality information if the lifetime of cachelines exceeds scheduling cycles.

Problems with this two-level scheduling arise from the interference of scheduling policies on different levels of control without any coordination or communication. A loss of parallelism and the occurrence of a deadlock situation is possible due to blocking system calls invoked by user-level threads. Solutions to these problems are discussed in [10].

In this paper we propose a non-preemptive user-level threads package with an application interface to trigger prefetch operations to hide memory latencies based on scheduling decisions of the runtime system. We outline several scheduling policies using locality information and present results from a prototype implementation on a Convex SPP 1000/XA. This machine can be characterized as a cache-coherent NUMA multiprocessor.

The rest of the paper is organized as follows. Section 2 describes the architecture of the Erlangen Lightweight Thread Environment (ELiTE), a scheduling architecture for cache-coherent NUMA multiprocessors developed and implemented at the University of Erlangen. Several affinity policies are evaluated in Section 3. Finally, we conclude in Section 4.

2 Erlangen Lightweight Thread Environment (ELiTE)

In NUMA architectures with their discrepancy between computing and communication performance, memory-conscious scheduling is essential to minimize the total completion time of an application by reducing inter-processor communication. Cache affinity scheduling for bus-based multiprocessors has been investigated [16][21] in detail because cache architectures become more and more dominant. The decisions within this type of scheduling base on CPU utilization and information about the processor where a specific thread was most recently executed. State timing information from each process is additionally be used e.g. in SGI's IRIX operating system [3]. Our approach to memory-conscious scheduling goes beyond the use of information about timing and execution location by using cache miss information for each level of the memory hierarchy.

Most thread schedulers attempt to optimize load balance while reducing the costs for thread management including queue locking. This strategy is reasonable for bus-based shared-memory architectures with uniform memory access. The most valuable resource of these architectures is the computing power of the processor and the bandwidth of the bus system. Thus, these scheduling policies focus on a high processor utilization while reducing bus contention [1].

The focus of thread scheduling has to move when we look at scalable shared-memory architectures with non-uniform memory access. Modern superscalar RISC-based processors are able to perform multiple operations per clock cycle while simultaneously performing a load/store operation to the processor cache. A multiprocessor system can only take advantage of this immense computing power if the processors can be supplied with data in time. The bandwidth of interconnection networks is no longer a bottleneck for today's scalable parallel processors (e.g. the Scalable Coherent Interface (SCI) of the Convex SPP has a bandwidth of 2.8 GBytes/s). But switches as well as affordable dynamic memory cause a latency of about a hundred nanoseconds, while processor cycles need only a few nanoseconds. The consequence of this discrepancy is that scheduling policies for NUMA architectures have to satisfy three essential design goals:

(1) **Distributed Scheduling:** Data structures of the scheduler (run queues, synchronization objects and pools for reusable memory regions) are distributed. There are no global structures with the potential risk of contention.

(2) **Locality Scheduling:** Threads are assigned to the processor which is close to the data accessed by the thread. This policy aims to reduce processor waiting time due to cache misses. Fairness among threads of the same application is not necessary, as each optimally used processor cycle within an application helps to increase throughput.

(3) **Latency Hiding:** Prefetch operations cause overlapping of computation and communication.

As contemporary threads packages, developed for use on shared-memory multiprocessors with a modest number of processors, have design goals which cannot be applied to scalable NUMA multiprocessors with a high number of processors, novel scheduling architectures have to be designed. After presenting the architecture of the Convex SPP, a cache-coherent NUMA multiprocessor, we describe the architecture and implementation details of the ELiTE runtime system.

2.1 Architecture of the CONVEX SPP

The Convex Exemplar Architecture [6] implemented in the Convex SPP multiprocessor is a representative of cache-coherent NUMA architectures. A symmetric multiprocessor called hypernode is the building block of the SPP architecture. Multiple hypernodes share a low-latency interconnect responsible for memory-address-based cache coherency. Each hypernode consists of two to eight HPPA 7100 processors, each having 1 MB direct mapped instruction and data cache with a cache line size of 32 bytes. The processors on a single hypernode can access up to two GBytes of main memory over a non-blocking crossbar switch. The memory in remote hypernodes can be accessed via the interconnect. To reduce network traffic, part of the memory is configured as a network cache with 64-byte cachelines. Load/store operations step through various stages depending on the locality of the referenced memory region (see Figure 1).

There are non-blocking prefetch operations to concurrently fetch data regions from a remote node into the local network cache. These operations can be used to overlap computation and network traffic in order to hide latency.

Performance-relevant events can be recorded by a performance monitor attached to each CPU. The performance and event monitor registers cache misses satisfied by the local or a remote hypernode and the time the processor waits for a cache miss to be served. For high resolution time stamps, several timers with various resolutions are available. There is also a system-wide clock with a precision of 1μs.

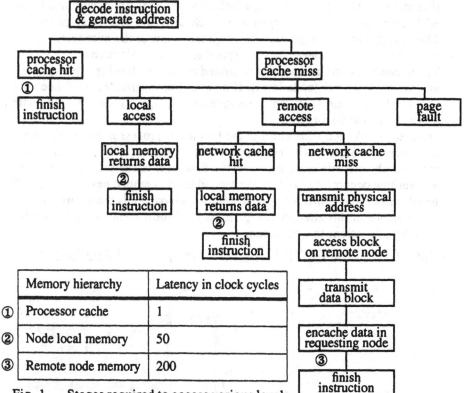

Fig. 1.   Stages required to access various levels
of the memory hierarchy

The operating system is a MACH 3.0 microkernel with a HP/UX-compatible Unix server on top. It provides the system call interface from Hewlett-Packard's Unix and an additional system interface to create and control kernel threads.

2.2 Scheduling Architecture of ELiTE

The overhead associated with lightweight processes goes beyond the cost of thread management, because of memory transfers between the various levels of the memory hierarchy. We present a scheduling architecture outlined in [5], refined and implemented in [17].

The following architectural features characterize the ELiTE runtime system:

– Division of thread control block (TCB) and stack allocation (see Figure 2): Each processor manages its own pool of free TCBs ① and stacks ③. If a new thread is created, the creating processor allocates and initializes a free TCB. After initialization the TCB is enqueued in a startqueue ②. A processor with an empty runqueue ④ fetches a TCB from a startqueue and can run the thread after allocating and initializing a stack. By separating TCB and stack allocation, memory objects of a thread, which have to be modified, will be allocated from memory pools managed and touched by the modifying processor. The consequence is a high cache reusage and a low cache miss rate.

- Pool and startqueue hierarchy correspond to memory hierarchy:
The number of startqueue entries is limited on the first level (processor level) and the second level (node level). If an overflow occurs, the TCB becomes enqueued in the next level. The consequence is a high degree of locality with an implicit load distribution.

When the stack- and TCB-pools of the first level (processor level) are empty, new memory objects will be enqueued from the second level. Likewise, memory objects will be moved from the first level to the second level when an overflow occurs. If a pool on the second level is empty, new memory will be allocated from global memory. Therefore, global pools are not useful. The consequence of this strategy is high reusage of local memory while keeping memory allocations to a minimum.

Architecture of the ELiTE Runtime System   SPP Architecture

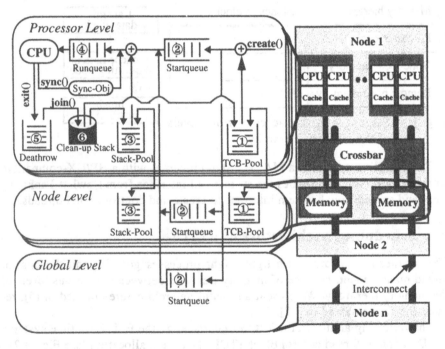

Fig. 2.   Scheduling Architecture ≈ Memory Architecture

- Local runqueues with load balancing:
Each processor manages its own priority runqueue (see Figure 2 ④). The priority of a thread depends on its affinity. The scheduler prefers threads with high affinity. A processor with an empty runqueue, finding no threads in the startqueues, scans the runqueues of the processors in the same node and fi-

nally the runqueues of all other processors for runable processes. The advantages of local runqueues are high cache reusage, low data cache invalidation and minimal contention for queue locks.

– Local deathrow with local clean-up stack:
When a thread exits, its context is stored in the deathrow (see Figure 2 ⑤) of the processor. The processor executing the join() reads the exit status of the joined thread and pushes an entry on the clean-up stack (see Figure 2 ⑥) of the processor, which executed the exit(). The processors periodically scan their local clean-up stacks and remove the contexts of joined threads from the deathrow and push memory objects (stacks and TCBs) into the local memory pools. Because processors executing a join never modify the deathrow and memory pools, cache invalidations can be avoided and the memory locality will be preserved. Cache misses are reduced to a minimum, because the push onto the clean-up stack concerns only a single cacheline.

We measured the number of threads a single thread can fork and join if n CPUs can start and run the created threads. We compared an approach with central pools and another with distributed pools (see Figure 3). The results show that the

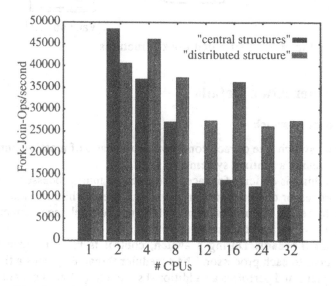

Fig. 3. Central vs. distributed hierarchical structures

fork-join-rate of the centralized approach drops when using 4-8 processors due to lock contention and dramatically drops when using more than 8 processors (more than one hypernode) due to allocation of stacks not cached on the local node. The distributed approach does not scale because of the limited fork rate of the single forking thread. But there is no severe performance degradation, because all stacks are allocated from local pools with encached memory. Furthermore, locking of central structures (pools and queues) and remote memory ac-

cess can be reduced to a minimum by the mechanisms of local deathrow and clean-up stack.
- Distributed synchronization objects with local wake-up stack:
  Unlike common UNIX sleep queues with hashed entries [12], the ELiTE runtime system binds blocked threads to synchronization objects (see Figure 4 ②). If a process becomes unblocked, a reference to its TCB will be pushed on the wake-up stack (see Figure 4 ③). Likewise the deathrow management, the processors scan their local wake-up stacks periodically and enqueue unblocked threads in the local runqueue (see Figure 4 ①).

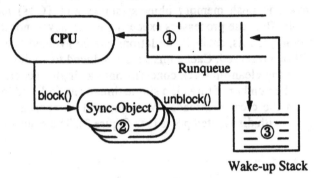

Fig. 4.   Distributed Lock Structures

2.3 Implementation Details

2.3.1 Fast context switch

A fast context switch free of race conditions is the basis of most synchronization mechanisms inside a runtime system.
Context switching is delicate for race conditions on multiprocessor systems, because one processor could resume an enqueued thread while its stack is not yet completely frozen by the processor of its last run. To implement context switching, we have investigated two models:
- **Scheduler Threads**: During a switch, control is returned to a scheduler thread local to each processor. The scheduler thread enqueues a thread from the run queue and performs an additional switch to it. Races cannot occur because the freezing of a thread is performed on the stack of the scheduler. However, this simple and secure switching model is very time consuming, as two context switches are necessary per thread switch.
- **Preswitch**: After saving the state of the old thread, the stack of the new thread is used to enqueue the TCB of the old thread without the danger of a race condition. This mechanism assumes that the next thread is known and existent before the switch occurs and that the next thread already owns a stack, which makes lazy stack allocation difficult.

  As switching efficiency is essential for a fast runtime system, preswitching is used in ELiTE. Based on the QuickThreads package of the University of Washington [8], which provides the preswitch model for various processor architectures, we have ported QuickThreads to the HPPA-RISC processor architecture. On a CONVEX SPP using this type of processor, the following times for a context switch can be reported:

Operation	Clock Cycles
Context switch between threads with all data in cache	153
Context switch between threads in the same node	1122
Context switch between threads in different nodes	1805

The proportion for a context switch with thread control blocks in the three levels of the memory hierarchy is 153/1122/1805 = 1/7/12. These are almost exactly the proportions expected to result from a memory latency of 1/50/200 cycles and 32/(64) Bytes (network-) cache lines. Most of the time is spent saving and restoring the callee-saves registers. The consequence is that switching can only be optimized by reducing the number of registers to be saved. These are the callee-saves registers, regulated by the calling conventions (e.g. by the HP PA-RISC calling conventions). As context saving and restoring for most contemporary RISC processors (an exception is the SUN SPARC processor with its register windows) is a sequence of machine instructions and not part of the instruction set, a change in the calling conventions could make context switching much more efficient by increasing the caller-saves registers and reducing the callee-saves registers.

2.3.2 Fast synchronization

Lim and Agarwal [13] have investigated waiting algorithms for synchronization in large-scale multiprocessors. With increasing CPU numbers, the type of synchronization has a significant influence on the performance of fine-grained parallel applications. As proposed we use two-phase locking with a fixed number of spin cycles in the ELiTE runtime system.

The proposed two-phase waiting algorithm combines the advantage of polling and signaling. A thread blocks after a default polling interval. The polling threshold depends on the overhead of blocking.

We count the number of clock cycles a lock is held and calculate the average duration (in clock cycles) of the last 8 times each specific lock was acquired. If the average of lock-holding cycles exceeds a proposed value (default is 50% of the cycles for a context switch), we block at once. Otherwise we spin the default number of cycles. To reduce memory accesses while spinning we use exponential backoff. For details refer to[17].

We have measured the peak performance for synchronization by starting 4096 micro-threads (8 kBytes stack and no workload) doing nothing but synchronizing. The total amount of memory is about 4096*8192 KBytes = 32 MBytes.

With central queues we see a severe performance loss due to lock contention and data cache corruption as a consequence of non local memory accesses (see Figure 5)

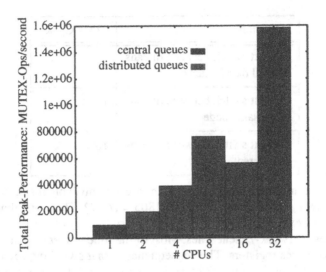

Fig. 5. Fast synchronization and context switch
with 4096 threads

Using a distributed approach, the time for a synchronization depends on the time to save/restore the stacks into the processor/network-caches and to access the synchronization objects. We reach the peak performance of about 100000 synchronizations/second per processor (1-8 processors in Figure 5), if all data can be held in the processor caches. If the stacks can be stored in the processor caches, but the synchronization objects have to be touched in part from multiple nodes, the synchronization performance deteriorates to about 50000 synchronizations/second per processor (32 processors in Figure 5). If the stacks do not fit into the processor-caches (16 processors), they are stored in the network caches (= local memory). This effect reduces the performance to about 40000 synchronizations/second per processor

The scheduling approach presented in this paper considers the locality behavior of individual threads at runtime. This approach is possible if the hardware provides information about cache misses. An additional optimization is possible, if we look at the interaction of threads on the same memory regions, by comparing their working set. In [15] TLB information is used to find cooperating processes on kernel level. For fast interaction a user-level readable TLB would be necessary, accessible as fast as the processor cache and with a fine resolution in the range of 1 kByte. This could be a feature of new processor generations. The knowledge of synchronization events is an alternative way to identify cooperating threads. This approach will be discussed in section 3.3.

2.3.3 Queue Structures

The decisions of a memory-conscious scheduler depend on the affinity of the threads to a specific memory region, e.g. cache or node local memory. Consequently, threads have to be enqueued according to their affinity. Several data structures for priority queues exist [9], where Fibonacci heaps and relaxed heaps [7] need only O(log #threads) operations for the time-critical 'find_and_remove_maximum'-operation, which is necessary to identify and extract the processes with maximum locality from the priority queue. But heap-structures are not suitable for runqueues, because heaps can not be partitioned fast enough in the case of load imbalance.

Priority queues implemented as binary trees make fast de- and enqueueing possible and can be divided very easily into partitions with entries of high or low locality.

2.3.4 Kernel Interface

User-level runtime systems use kernel threads as virtual processors, assuming an equivalence of physical and virtual processor. This assumption does not hold, because events like page faults, I/O and system calls block the virtual processors. The equivalence of physical and virtual processors can be achieved by notification of the user-level threads package, which can thus react adequately.

Scheduler Activations, proposed in [2], use kernel threads to upcall the runtime system. This strategy suffers from the fact that a free processor is needed to run the kernel thread upcalling the user level. But there is no free processor in the case of a request for suspension of a virtual processor. The consequence is an expensive context switch on kernel level causing TLB misses and data cache corruption.

In [11] and [21] communication mechanisms between the kernel and a user-level thread library are proposed to reduce the performance losses when threads block in the kernel or are preempted in critical sections. The kernel and the threads package communicate using shared memory whenever possible to avoid the need for synchronization interaction. Software interrupts signal to the thread package whenever a scheduling decision may be required. For example, polling of shared memory in a safe suspension point is used to instruct the runtime system to suspend a thread, while signalling is used to inform the runtime system that a thread can be resumed or a new kernel thread can be created. Signalling is used to prevent idling of a processor while information exchange over shared memory is used whenever quick response to events is not so important.

A strategy offering fast response to blocking events is proposed in [10] and is used in ELiTE. The runtime system parks spare kernel threads in the kernel. In the case of a blocking call, the kernel deblocks a parked thread to maintain a fixed number of running kernel threads. When the blocking request is resolved, the kernel informs the runtime system of the deblocking via a shared page or shared-memory segment. If this deblocked user-level thread is selected for execution, the corresponding kernel thread initiates a system call to park in kernel again and to release the blocked kernel thread. The system is in the same state as before the blocking call.

2.3.5 Application Interface

Contemporary NUMA architectures like Convex SPP or KSR1/2 have non-blocking prefetch operations in their instruction set to concurrently fetch data regions from a remote node into the local network cache, overlapping computation and network traffic and thus hiding latency. If thread-specific data can be stored in a single block, a pointer to this block and its length can be stored in the thread control block. If there is an interface to the scheduler, a currently running thread can ask the runtime system to prefetch the data of the thread which will run in the near future. This idea was motivated by implementations of adaptive numerical methods [4][14], where thousands of threads, each corresponding to a point of an adaptive grid, resume the threads representing the grid points in the neighborhood after calculating the local grid point before they suspend themselves. This numerical method, called *active threads strategy* can only run with high efficiency on NUMA architectures if all thread-specific data is resident in the cache before the context switch occurs.

3 Affinity Scheduling

The performance of a computer is considerably influenced by the fast supply of data to the available processing units. Only if the data essential for operation is cached in fast memory can the processor work without latency and contention. Affinity scheduling tries to prefer processes with a high amount of cached data in order to increase throughput.

Besides information about processor number and time behavior, we use information about data locality in our scheduling architecture. Locality information about each process/thread like the cache miss rate, the processor stall time, and the processor of last execution can be used to calculate an affinity value. A prerequisite is a computer architecture providing information about cache misses and CPU latencies due to memory access. Contemporary architectures like Convex SPP and KSR1/2 provide this information, future processor architectures like HPPA 8000, MIPS R10000 or Ultra SPARC will gather this information on chip. This information is usually only used for off-line profiling. But why should we ignore information for optimizing the behavior of multithreaded applications at runtime?

In the next subsections we describe several affinity strategies and the prospect of the proposed technique.

3.1 Scheduling Strategies

We have designed and implemented a user-level runtime system, offering the possibility to easily import new affinity strategies. The strategies examined are listed in the table below:

Scheduling strategy	Basis of decision	Policy
No Affinity	Processor location	LIFO
Virtual Time	Sequence numbers	Most recently run
Minimum Misses	Cache misses	Thread with minimal # of cache misses
Reload Transient	Cache misses	Minimal reload transient based on a Markov chain

- Using virtual time stamps, each thread is assigned a sequence number after its run. This strategy does not need cache miss information, and can be used on every type of hardware. Threads with the highest time stamp given by the same processor will be preferred. If a fast global time source with high resolution is included in the hardware, more precise timing strategies can be used [3].
- The *Minimum Misses* strategy compares the number of cache misses during the last run. The thread with the lowest number of cache misses is preferred. This strategy favors threads that block frequently, since they have shorter runs and few cache misses.
- The reload transient model [18] is more complex, but offers some potential. We refer to the working set of a thread that is present in the cache as its footprint in the cache. The reload transient is defined as the cost to establish the footprint of a thread after restarting it. We use a Markov model to calculate the footprint of each thread. In the state transition diagram in Figure 6. each node V represents a state with v valid cache lines of a thread residing in the cache. Our direct mapped cache consists of N cache lines.

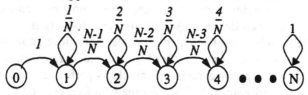

Fig. 6. Markov chain of valid cache lines

The probability to increment the number of valid cache lines as a consequence of a cache miss during the run of a thread is $(N - v)/N$. The probability that a cache miss hits a valid cache line is v/N. We can generate the transition probability matrix and calculate the M-step transition probability matrix for each node V, describing the probability for a thread to have a certain number of valid cache lines in the cache after M cache misses happened. Equivalently, we can calculate the transition probability matrix for a blocked thread. The number of resident cache lines is decremented with a certain probability for each cache miss caused by the intermediate run of an other thread.

Using these probabilities we calculate the expected footprint size F after each run. The size of the footprint depends on the number of cache lines v still valid at startup and the number of cache misses cm which occurred during this run $E[F|V = v, M = cm]$.

We can also compute the expected number of lines V still valid depending on the footprint f of a specific thread and the number of cache misses om caused by other threads $E[V|F = f, M = om]$.

Basis of our cache affinity calculation is the expected footprint size F of a thread in its last run and the expected number of valid cache lines V before its potential run. The reload transient is defined as the expected number of cache misses $E[M|F = f, V = v]$ when rebuilding the working set of a rescheduled thread. Our scheduling policy selects the thread with minimal reload transient. A characteristic of our approach is that the order among runable threads remains the same even if the scheduler enqueues new runable threads. Consequently the reload transient has only to be determined, when a thread is deblocked and enqueued. By pre-computing expected reload transients for a set of footprints and a set of different cache miss numbers the priority calculation of the scheduler can be reduced to a simple table lookup [20].

3.2 Interpretation of Measurements

We have implemented and tested the proposed strategies as part of the ELiTE architecture on a Convex SPP 1000/XA in a range from 1 to 32 processors. The test environment includes synthetic tests with artificial workloads as well as real-world numerical kernels like gauss elimination, LU-decomposition and adaptive solvers on irregular grids[14][4]. All measurements show that a fine-grained parallelization does not inherently imply low performance. On the contrary, a fine-grained numerical efficient algorithm outperforms most conventional methods, because fine-gained parallelism implies a high data locality in most cases. This locality can be used by a sophisticated scheduler to achieve good overall performance even if we register some overhead for complex strategies. But the impact of scheduling in a fine-grained environment affects performance much more than with a coarse-grained approach. The runtime of a fine-grained LU-decomposition can vary by a factor of ten, depending on the scheduling architecture.

With a synthetic workload of 1024 threads, each snooping through a working set of 64 kBytes between synchronizations, we can get a good impression of affinity strategies (see Figure 7). We measure how many synchronizations can be executed in one second with different numbers of processors. This example resembles parallel numerical applications with regular execution order like iterative solvers on block-structured grids.

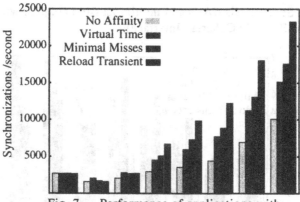

Fig. 7. Performance of applications with regular execution order

Applications with irregular execution order make high demands on the scheduling policy. We measure the number of smoothing operations per second on an unstructured grid executed by a full-adaptive iterative solver [14]. To demonstrate the influence of the scheduling strategy on the application performance, we compare the smoothing rate of the proposed affinity strategies with the *No Affinity* strategy. A relative smoothing performance of 2 means, that the adaptive solver executes twice the number of smoothing operation under the affinity scheduler compared to an execution under the *No Affinity* scheduler (see Figure 8)

- *No Affinity* will be outperformed in general by all strategies using locality information
- The simple *Minimal Misses* strategy performs quite well in cases with homogeneous execution behavior. As this strategy favors threads that block frequently, anomalous behavior is possible if some threads acquire locks during the polling interval whereas other threads block.
- The *Virtual time* approach only uses timing behavior and the processor number of the last run. It never shows anomalous behavior and performs very efficiently with moderate processor numbers (1-16 processors) because it offers the minimal overhead compared to the other strategies. It should be the policy of choice for UMA architectures not offering cache miss information (see [3])
- The *Reload Transient* strategy shows the best performance in multinode architectures with non-uniform memory access. The overhead of gathering cache miss information and computing the expected working sets is only justified when memory latency really strikes. This is the case on all contemporary and future scalable parallel processors like Convex SPP, KSR 1/2, SUN

Ultra MPP, Sequent NUMA-Q and multiprocessors coupled with SCI-Hardware (SCI = Scalable Coherent Interface).

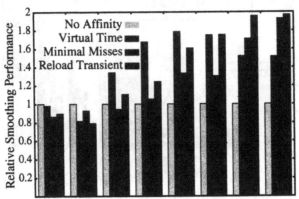

Fig. 8.   Performance of adaptive applications
with irregular execution order

The hardware of the Convex SPP 1000 used for our implementation cannot distinguish between processor- and network-cache misses, but these two types of cache miss differ by a factor of 4 in their penalty. Coming SPP generations offer information about both types of cache fault, which permits a much better calculation of the working set and will clearly outperform all other proposed affinity techniques.

3.3   Towards Optimal Affinity Scheduling

Scheduling policies should use all available information to calculate the best possible process mapping. For optimal process scheduling, knowledge about synchronizing threads is necessary. Cooperating threads can be identified by synchronization events and collocated at the same processor, whereas a compromise between collocation and load balance has to be made. To decide an ideal point defined by the location and timing of execution, we define gravitational and repulsive forces between threads by the frequency and extent of information sharing.

The forces influence affinity in a metric space, so that threads migrate near to their (sub)optimal operation point. This affinity model resembles the computational field model for migrating objects proposed in [19].

A thread A running on processor X with a great cache affinity exerts a gravitational force on thread B running on processor Y with just a small cache affinity. Thread A exerts the force by increasing the affinity of thread B to processor X each time A synchronizes with B. The value used for increasing the affinity depends on the size of the memory region shared by the two threads (see Figure 9). In the ELiTE runtime system we use the number of cache misses occurring during the modification of the shared-memory region as the basis of the affinity adjustment.

Cooperating threads with a high compute load and rare synchronization events exert repulsive forces on each other (see Figure 9). Threads showing this behavior can be recognized by a high number of cache misses and a long time-frame between blocking events. If these threads run on the same processor, they decrease the affinity of their synchronization partner. Threads with a low affinity can be caught by an idle processor.

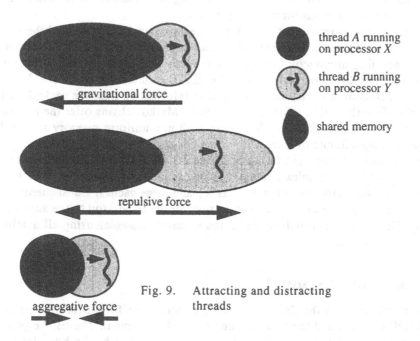

thread *A* running
on processor *X*

thread *B* running
on processor *Y*

shared memory

gravitational force

repulsive force

aggregative force

Fig. 9.   Attracting and distracting
          threads

Threads with low affinity sharing a memory region which is large relative to the private working set exert aggregative forces on each other (see Figure 9). Before unblocking, the affinity values of a synchronization partner will be modified such that the partner will run up on the same processor as the unblocking thread. The aggregative force is influenced by the number of cache misses on shared and thread-private memory regions.

The proposed strategy has the potential to come closer to the optimum operation point of all threads concerning location and timing of execution. By introducing gravitational and aggregative forces, the number of cache misses of cooperating threads can be reduced, while compute-intensive threads with low synchronization rate exerting repulsive forces can be distributed very easily.

The fact that the hardware of the Convex SPP 1000 cannot distinguish between processor- and network-cache misses, together with the high costs for reading the cache miss counters (costs of one read are equivalent to a user-level context switch), means that there are no publishable results of our implementation. Coming processor generations with fast readable on-chip miss counters will allow reasonable measurements using this promising scheduling strategy.

4 Summary and Conclusions

Algorithmic optimizations of the application and scheduling mechanisms for the management of parallelism determine the overall throughput. The applications designer cannot be relieved of algorithmic considerations concerning memory locality, but he can take advantage of a scheduling strategy which makes a fine-grained architecture-independent programming style possible thanks to its efficient memory-conscious thread management.

As maximum throughput is the goal of our efforts, we have presented the architecture of the Erlangen Lightweight Thread Environment (ELiTE). The focus of this scheduling architecture lies on the reduction of cache misses. Distributed data structures like those proposed in the ELiTE architecture are an absolute necessity. Scheduling strategies using locality information improve cache locality and therefore throughput. Strategies based on Markov chains offer the best process reordering in scalable architectures with non-uniform memory access despite their algorithmic overhead.

The trade-off between scheduling overhead and performance gain due to better locality will favor complex strategies using cache miss information particularly in architectures with high memory latency and large caches. Consequently, the proposed scheduling techniques can be used from the desktop to the supercomputer. Further research will be dedicated to novel strategies using all available locality information.

5 Acknowledgments

I would like to thank the Convex operating system group for providing their Convex SPP software and their background in OS development. The ELiTE project in cooperation with Convex Computer Corp. is supported by the Bavarian Consortium for High Performance Scientific Computing (FORTWIHR).

6 References

1. T. Anderson; E. Lazowska; H. Levy: The Performance Implication of Thread Management Alternatives for Shared-Memory Multiprocessors, *ACM Trans. on Computers*, 38(12), Dec. 1989, pp. 1631-1644

2. T. E. Anderson; et al.: Scheduler Activations: Effective Kernel Support for the User-Level Management of Parallelism. *ACM Transactions on Computer Systems*, 10(1), Feb. 1992, pp. 53-79

3. J. Barton, N. Bitar - SGI Corp., A Scalable Multi-Discipline, Multiple-Processor Scheduling Framework for IRIX", In *Proc. of IPPS'95 Workshop of Job Scheduling Strategies for Parallel Processing*, LNCS 949, Apr. 1995

4. F. Bellosa: Implementierung adaptiver Verfahren auf komplexen Geometrien mit leichtgewichtigen Prozessen, University Erlangen-Nürnberg, IMMD IV, TR-I4-94-07, Oct. 1994

5. F.Bellosa: Memory-Conscious Scheduling and Processor Allocation on NUMA Architectures, University Erlangen-Nürnberg, IMMD IV, TR-I4-95-06, May 1995

6. Convex: Exemplar SPP1000/1200 Architecture, Convex Press, May 1995

7. J. Driscoll; H. Gabow; R. Shrairman; R. Tarjan: Relaxed heaps: An alternative to Fibonacci heaps with applications to parallel computation, Communications of the ACM, 32:1343-1354, 1988

8. D. Keppel: Tools and Techniques for Building Fast Portable Threads Packages, University of Washington, TR UWCSE 93-05-06, May 1993

9. D. Knuth: The Art of Computer Programming, Vol. 3: Sorting and Searching, Addison-Wesley, Mass. , 1973

10. C. Koppe: Sleeping Threads: A Kernel Mechanism for Support of Efficient User-Level Threads, In *Proc. of International Conference of Parallel and Distributed Computing and Systems PDCS'95*, Washington D.C., Oct. 95

11. T. J. LeBlanc; et al.: First-Class User-Level Threads, Operating Systems Review, 25(5), Oct. 1991, pp. 110-121

12. S. Leffler: The Design and Implementation of the 4.3BSD UNIX Operating System, Addison-Wesley, 1990

13. B. Lim; A. Agarwal: Waiting Algorithms for Synchronizations in Large-Scale Multiprocessors., *ACM Transactions on Computer Systems*, 11(1), Aug. 1993, pp. 253-297

14. Ulrich Rüde: On the multilevel adaptive iterative method, *SIAM Journal on Scientific and Statistical Computing*, Vol. 15, 1994

15. P. Sabalvarro, W. Weihl: Demand-based Coscheduling of Parallel Jobs on Multiprogrammed Multiprocessors, In *Proc. of IPPS'95 Workshop of Job Scheduling Strategies for Parallel Processing*, LNCS 949, April 1995

16. S. Squillante; E. D. Lazowska: Using Processor Cache Affinity in Shared-Memory Multiprocessor, Scheduling. *IEEE Transactions on Parallel and Distributed Systems*, 4(2),Feb. 1993, pp.131-143

17. M. Steckermeier: Using Locality Information in User-Level Scheduling, University Erlangen-Nürnberg, IMMD IV, TR-I4-95-14, Dec. 1995

18. D. Thiebaut, H. Stone: Footprints in the Cache, *ACM Transactions on Computer Systems*, 5(4), Nov. 1987, pp. 305-329

19. M. Tokoro: Computational Field Model: Toward a New Computation Model/ Methodology for Open Distributed Environment, Sony Computer Science Laboratory Inc., SCSL-TR-90-006, June 1990

20. J. Torellas, A. Tucker, A. Gupta: Evaluating the Performance of Cache-Affinity Scheduling in Shared-Memory Multiprocessors, *Journal of Parallel and Distributed Computing*, Vol. 24, 1995, pp. 139-151

21. A. Tucker: Efficient Scheduling on Multiprogrammed Shared-Memory Multiprocessors, Phd Thesis, Department of Computer Science, Stanford University, CS-TN-94-4, Dec. 1993

Author Index

Springer
and the
environment

At Springer we firmly believe that an
international science publisher has a
special obligation to the environment,
and our corporate policies consistently
reflect this conviction.
We also expect our business partners –
paper mills, printers, packaging
manufacturers, etc. – to commit
themselves to using materials and
production processes that do not harm
the environment. The paper in this
book is made from low- or no-chlorine
pulp and is acid free, in conformance
with international standards for paper
permanency.

 Springer

Lecture Notes in Computer Science

For information about Vols. 1–1083

please contact your bookseller or Springer-Verlag